HOW THE HEBREW LANGUAGE GREW

HOW THE HEBREW LANGUAGE GREW

by

EDWARD HOROWITZ, M.A., D.R.E.

HEBREW DEPARTMENT
THOMAS JEFFERSON HIGH SCHOOL
BROOKLYN, NEW YORK

Illustrated by

PAUL SHARON

KTAV PUBLISHING HOUSE INC.

Library of Congress Cataloging-in-Publication Data

Horowitz, Edward, 1904-
How the Hebrew language grew / by Edward Horowitz. -- Rev. ed.
p. cm.
Includes bibliographical references (p.).
ISBN 0-88125-487-8
1. Hebrew language--History. 2. Hebrew language--Grammar. 3. Hebrew language--Grammar, Comparative--Semitic. 4. Semitic languages--Grammar, Comparative--Hebrew. I. Title.
PJ4545.H6 1993
492.4'09--dc20 93-35398
CIP

Manufactured in the United States of America

לְאָבִי מוֹרִי

שְׁמוּאֵל יִצְחָק בֶּן ר׳ יַעֲקֹב הַלֵּוִי אִישׁ הוֹרוֹוִיץ ז״ל

לְאִמִּי מוֹרָתִי

בְּרַיינְדֶל בַּת ר׳ מֵאִיר מִבֵּית עֶרֶענְפֶעלד ז״ל

וְזָכַרְתִּי לָהֶם חֶסֶד נְעוּרַי, אֶת הָאַהֲבָה שֶׁאָהֲבוּ

אוֹתָנוּ וְכָל רֹב הַטּוֹבָה שֶׁהִשְׁפִּיעוּ עָלֵינוּ

יְהֵא זֵכֶר צַדִּיקֵינוּ אֵלֶּה לִבְרָכַת עוֹלָם.

TO

SAMUEL ISAAC AND BERTHA EHRENFELD HOROWITZ

for the life they gave us and the love they lavished upon us; for the grace and charm of a way of life that left behind a thousand memories of pride and joy; and for the love, too, they bore the words of the Hebrew language that in the days of their youth had come back to life on the lips of men and women and little children.

Table of Contents

Why this book was written and for whom

What this book contains

Why this Book was written and for Whom

This book was written with several purposes in mind. The most important of these is the tracing of the growth of the Hebrew language from the very earliest days. Many thousands of years ago—how many we do not know—the most primitive ancestor of Hebrew probably consisted of no more than a small number of words. Many or most of these words had no more than one syllable. Since that time Hebrew has grown greatly and has become a modern language with a vast literature and a large vocabulary.

Every language has its machinery of prefixes, suffixes, and infixes by means of which a single word or root may become the center of a large number of related words. We will trace all these family relationships between Hebrew words. You will see clearly how this very highly limited number of roots (probably less than two hundred) has produced literally tens of thousands of words. It will be, or should be, an intellectual adventure to note the existence of relationships where none has been noted or suspected before. There is great practical value in this for the student. Words that are related and whose relationship is seen and understood are easier to master and retain.

One of the faults in Hebrew teaching is the failure of the Hebrew teacher to answer the question " Why " when teaching Hebrew vocabulary and grammar.

An even greater fault is the failure to stimulate the asking of the question why. For language is logical. Almost all of its phenomena have reasonable, logical explanations. Students love to know why the thing is so, why the word means what it does, why the rule has this or that exception. Hebrew, in particular, is remarkably logical in its general structure. In almost all cases of so called irregularity in Hebrew grammar, there is a sound, a sensible and an easily explainable reason for the departure from the normal. It is poor practice to drill the students in such matters as the missing "nun", the dropping of the weak letters "he, vav and yod" without making it absolutely clear what they are all about—just why it is that they vanish out of the word. One of the purposes of this book will be to present in a systematic way the rational explanations for Hebrew linguistic phenomena, insofar as they touch on word building.

Great scholars, men of intellect and vast learning, have spent lifetimes searching out the secrets and the mysteries of the Hebrew language. The quest for the primitive Hebrew roots is never-ending. They study intensively the sister languages of Hebrew, using them to throw light upon the development of Hebrew words.

They utilize the results of the great archaelogical explorations. However, their findings are usually written in a highly technical linguistic jargon, and are scattered over a vast array of learned publications and scholarly magazines —and incidentally, in many different languages. The results of their researches, fascinating once they are made intelligible, have rarely been set down in plain and simple English for the ordinary, average, intelligent student of Hebrew to read.

"How the Hebrew Language Grew" is meant for students whose mother tongue is English. There are an amazing number of similarities between word-building in English and in Hebrew. There is hardly a single process of word-building in English that cannot be duplicated in Hebrew. This book will point out all these parallels clearly. English language habits will thus be utilized in the study of Hebrew.

Above all, the book means to give to the reader a sense of the restless energy and the tremendous creative power of the modern Hebrew language in the Israel of today, and to show with what ease and facility Hebrew is meeting the linguistic demands of civilized life in this mid-twentieth century.

A WORD ABOUT ETYMOLOGY

This is important to bear in mind. Etymology tells us where specific words come from and something of their history. In the field of etymology there are wide differences of opinion among scholars, even among the very best of them. For example:

Professor Louis Ginzberg, the world's greatest scholar in the field of Jewish studies of the twentieth century, holds that אֲמַתְלָה, a pretext, is derived from the word אֱמֶת with the addition of the ל—a plausible suggestion. Others say no—that it is simply a borrowing from the Aramaic אֲמַתְלָה the Aramaic form of the Hebrew word, מָשָׁל an example.

Professor William F. Albright, America's ranking Semitist and archeologist, cleverly suggests that שָׁכַח, forget, is a metathesis of חשֶׁךְ, darkness. Forgetting is really equivalent to being in the dark about something. Others say that this is pure speculation and that it has no plausibility. Paul Haupt says that קַר cold, comes from מָקוֹר a well, the one continually cold spot found in warm lands. Others say that this is hardly likely, that more probably קַר is onomatopoeic—something like the English who say " brrrrr " when they are cold. And so we have these never ending differences between equally highly respected authorities.

Rest assured, gentle reader, that all explanations of words given in this work have, if not the agreement of all, at least the backing of many important scholars. Some of the etymologies offered here may appear strange, startling, or unusual. For example, it may surprise you to learn that לִקְרַאת has nothing to do with קָרָא called; that לְמַעַן comes from the root עָנָה and that it really means " in response to ". All the explanations represent, however, considered opinion of outstanding Hebrew scholars of our time.

A few words of thanks

A book of this sort, a popularization of the work of the great Hebrew linguists of all times, owes so much to so many that it is not possible to do more than to mention a few of the outstanding personal obligations.

I want first to express my warmest thanks to the faculties of the Teacher's Institute and the Rabbinical School of the Jewish Theological Seminary of America. These men were all certainly touched with greatness. I was in their intellectual and spiritual company for many years and they made life for me a far richer and more enjoyable experience than it could possibly have been otherwise. They were, in their respective fields of Jewish learning, among the world's greatest. In addition, they all loved and were masters of the Hebrew language.

Professor Morris David Levine זֵכֶר צַדִּיק לִבְרָכָה who taught Hebrew literature and grammar, discussed this book with me over a period of many years. וּלְהַבְדֵּל לְחַיִּים אֲרֻכִּים Professor Shalom Spiegel has read the manuscript with great care and has made many, many, valuable suggestions.

Professors William F. Albright, Naftali H. Tur Sinai and Alexander Sperber were kind enough as to answer a large number of questions which I addressed to them on some difficult etymological and grammatical points.

Many other scholars, colleagues, and friends have read

the manuscript and offered valuable suggestions and criticisms.

I want to express my warmest gratitude to a group of five readers of the United Synagogue—Professor Simon Greenberg, Dr. William Chomsky, Dr. Azriel Eisenberg, Dr. Abraham Ezra Milgram, and Dr. Louis Kaplan; to Daniel Persky, Mordecai H. Lewittes, George Horowitz, Rabbi Dr. Leon Katz, and my father-in-law, Sol Solomon. Yudel Mark, distinguished Yiddish philologist, discussed with me the section "How Hebrew Borrowed Words Back from Yiddish."

Mr. Simon Certner of the English Department of the Thomas Jefferson High School helped me edit the copy for the printer.

The Library of the Jewish Theological Seminary of America and the Jewish Room of the New York Public Library have been constant and ready sources of help.

There were many complicated technical problems involved in the printing of this book. For assistance and advice in these matters, I want to express my appreciation to my brother Jacob L. Horowitz.

Judah Lapson, Director of the Hebrew Culture Council of the Jewish Education Committee of New York has guided, encouraged and advised me. He has helped me see the book through from manuscript to printed page.

Paul Sharon, artist and Hebrew scholar, has enriched the book with illustrations that are beautiful and ingenious and in which the principles and structure of the Hebrew language have been put in visual form for the very first time.

Harvey Satenstein, President of Book Craftsmen Associates, Inc., New York, who is in his own way an artist of distinction, supervised the actual composition of the book, and his specialized company in the field of Hebraica saw the book carefully through the Press.

My Hebrew 7-8 class at Thomas Jefferson is generally a small seminar group. It was with these boys and girls that I worked out and tested the material in this book. Three of my students, Marta Berle Shapiro, Ettie Hagler Yanowski, and Miriam Balmuth helped me with the typing of the manuscript. My wife, Silvia, and my children Tamar Lynn, Carmi Yosef, Hadasa and Jonathan Samuel were all patient with me when I tested the material on them, and all generously helped with the reading of the proof.

EDWARD HOROWITZ

Chapter I

In the Beginning there were Words

How did language originate?

It is very important that you know. There happens to be a very simple answer. We do not know. Scholars do not know. It all happened so long ago, that it will be in all likelihood impossible for men ever to wrest this secret from the dim and shadowy past. Primitive men needed desperately to communicate one with the other, to warn each other of danger, to express all their common human wants and passions. Somehow or other each group got to agreeing on what to call certain things; how, we do not know.

Of course, scholars have speculated endlessly. Some of their speculations are clever, even brilliant—but it all comes down to this—we really do not know. That's something.

There is, however, one group of words the origin of which we do know. These are the onomatopoeic words, the words which imitate sounds—words such as banging, buzzing, bubbling, etc. It is very obvious and natural that man would try to imitate what he heard. They form a very charming and poetic group of words and later on we devote a whole chapter to telling you more about them. There are also the babble words picked up by adults from the baby's first prattling, " eema, abba, and dawd " which the elders identified as mama, papa and uncle. But at the present you must simply realize that these are the solitary exceptions to our insoluble mystery of how words began.

When the historical curtain rises we already possess several great language families, fully formed and highly developed.

English, in which these words are being written, belongs to one of them—the language group called the Indo-European.

Hebrew, the language we are struggling to master, belongs to another—the Semitic. These two are the most important of the language families. Almost everyone has brothers and sisters and parents, and so have languages.

Let us try to understand exactly what the families of language consist of, and what is the place of English and Hebrew among them. First, let us consider the Indo-European language family.

Most of the languages of Europe and of many countries of Asia belong to this family. Different though they may seem to be and differ as they actually do, yet languages as far apart as English, German, French, Russian, Persian, and the languages of India are all descended from the same primitive ancestor language. The common words in all these languages, such as the words for father, mother, sister, brother, star, light, et cetera are, allowing for certain regular phonetic changes, the same. If you are studying German or French you will notice, and the teacher will point out to you, what a really enormous number of words English has in common with them.

Hebrew, on the other hand, belongs to an entirely different family of languages, one which bears the name

Semitic. When you are studying Hebrew you will notice that no such striking similarities exist between Hebrew and English. The words for common things in Hebrew and English are utterly unlike. It is true that Hebrew and English do have a few hundred words in common, but they are not the common, everyday words and they constitute but a small fraction of their total respective vocabularies. The sister languages of Hebrew are languages such as Assyrian, Babylonian, Arabic, Syrian, Ethiopic, and also, as has been lately discovered, Egyptian. With these, its own sister languages, and not with the Indo-European group, Hebrew is intimately bound up. All the common Hebrew words are found with only slight changes in all the other Semitic languages. A good Hebraist knows literally hundreds of Arabic words without ever having studied Arabic, because Arabic and Hebrew have such a large number of words in common. Almost all the words borrowed by English from the other Semitic languages, namely, the Arabic, the Syrian, et cetera, can also be found in Hebrew. All the Semitic languages go back ultimately to an ancient parent Semitic language.

These two great families of languages have lived in close proximity one to the other for thousands of years, and have borrowed words one from the other rather freely. Usually we can tell who borrowed from whom. We know for example that Greek borrowed "Sabbath", "amen" from the Hebrew; and " sack " from another Semitic language—Phoenecian.

We know that Hebrew borrowed " פַּרְדֵּס – an orange grove or tree garden ", originally a Persian word, and הֶדְיוֹט meaning a simple fellow from the Greek.

Usually we can tell the source. But sometimes the bor-

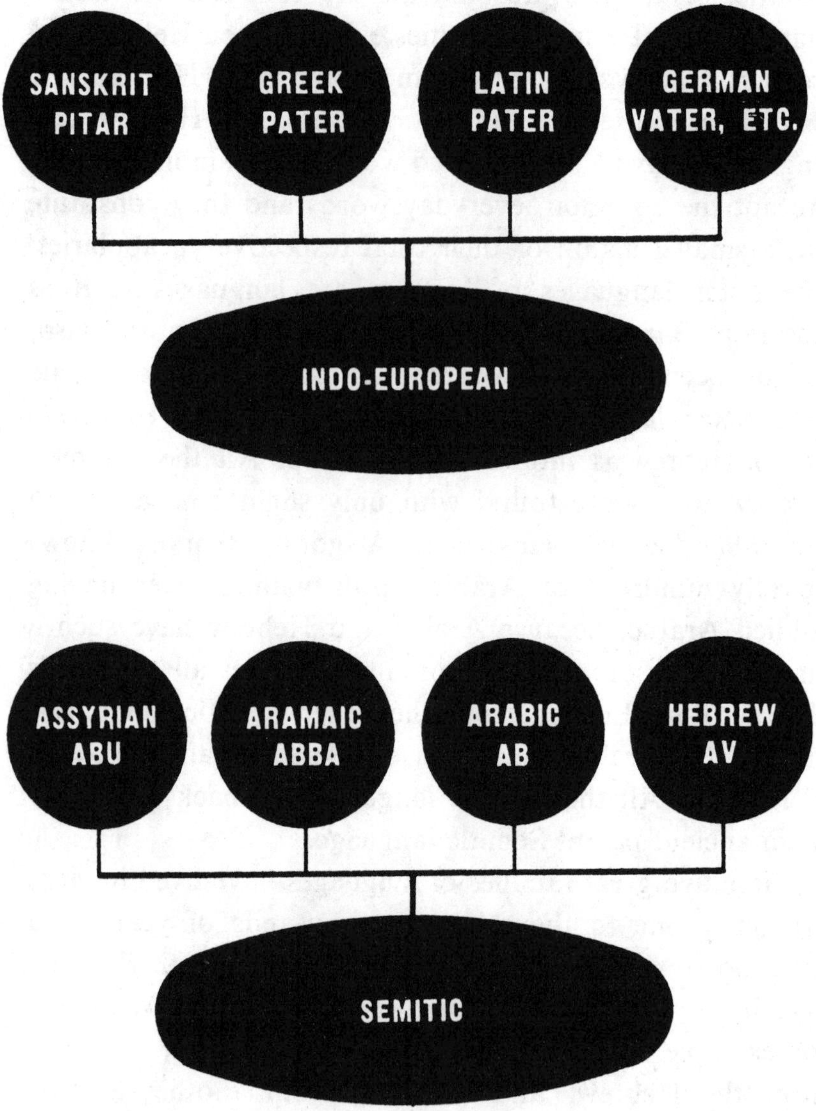

WORD FOR FATHER IN INDO-EUROPEAN AND SEMITIC

rowing is so ancient that scholars do not know which language did the borrowing and which was the original owner. A word like " קֶרֶן – horn " is already found in the most ancient Hebrew and Latin literature, as is the word " יַיִן – wine ". There is of course the possibility of accidental likeness. There is also the possibility of both having borrowed from a common source. This seems to be the case with the word " יַיִן – wine ". It has no clear etymology; that is no clear relation to other words, and it admits of no clear explanation in either Hebrew or Greek or Latin. It was probably borrowed by all these groups from some now lost and unknown language.

There are many puzzling similarities between the Indo-European and Semitic families and some scholars are led to think that in very ancient times these two families were originally one, and that only in the course of many thousands of years did they grow to be so completely different. The long separation resulted in the languages undergoing so many changes as to practically wipe out whatever common features they had. If this is true then the similarities are no longer puzzling but are seen as the natural remains of an original identity.

HEBREW ITSELF

Hebrew was the language of the children of Abraham who sojourned in Egypt, who were enslaved there, and who were led forth by Moses. They lived in Israel some 1700 years. In Israel was created the Hebrew Bible, incomparably the world's greatest single book. There existed many other literary works; these have practically all been lost.

Hebrew gradually ceased being a spoken language after 70 C.E., when the Jews were driven from the land of Israel by the Romans and were scattered throughout the world. Hebrew, of course, remained alive, and was used constantly in other ways. It was the language of prayer, study, reading the Torah, and correspondence. Above all it was used as the language of a tremendously rich literature of law, theology, philosophy, science, medicine, astronomy, poetry, grammar and other fields of human knowledge.

It was about eighty years ago that a young man was inspired with a vision that Hebrew could once again live as a spoken language. His name was Eliezer ben Yehudah. He went to work and write in Israel. At first he was thought an idle dreamer, but slowly and surely, something of the fire that burned within him spread to his friends and neighbors, and to wider and wider circles, until in a few years almost all Jews in Israel were speaking Hebrew. One of the greatest miracles of all modern times had come to pass. *This was the very first time in all human history that a language which ceased being spoken in ancient times, came back to life on the lips of men and women and little children.*

One of the greatest problems that Eliezer ben Yehudah faced was the lack of words in Hebrew that were needed to describe all the complex culture of modern life with its machinery and electricity, aeroplanes, radios, et cetera. He singlehanded wrote a great dictionary of the Hebrew language, recently brought to editorial completion, in seventeen volumes, a work generally undertaken by a large group of scholars. He also formed the Vaad-ha-Lashon now called הָאֲקַדֶמְיָה לַלָּשׁוֹן הָעִבְרִית – the Hebrew Academy, a group of the wisest and most learned men in the land, who have set for themselves the task of creating the thousands and tens of thousands of needed new words.

Not all, of course, had to be created. They ransacked the literary treasures of old, the Talmud and the Midrash, and the vast medieval literature which contained old and forgotten, but much-needed and useful words. There were many ancient Hebrew words whose meaning was doubtful or unclear or vague. To these words, the Vaad-ha-Lashon would assign a clear, sharp, specific meaning, restoring them to active and useful life. When they created new words, they fashioned them with great skill and cunning out of the old Hebrew three-lettered roots, and so skillful were they that we hardly feel the newness of these new words. They seem to have come from out of the heart and soul of the Hebrew language and to have been there all the time. There are a number of international words, that is, words used in the same form by almost all the languages of the world, such words as radio, telephone, telegraph. These words the Vaad-ha-Lashon would leave unchanged.

The Vaad-ha-Lashon has issued many special vocabulary books giving detailed lists of words used in different professions and activities. There is a special dictionary of about 3,000 words for athletics, a thousand word dictionary of kitchen terms; tremendously large dictionaries for such fields as medicine, electricity, plant and animal life, for use in printing, military science, and so on.

It is now possible to write in Hebrew clearly and exactly on any scientific or philosophic theme, however complex or abstruse.

QUESTIONS ON CHAPTER I

1. What do we know about how language originated?
2. Of what group of words do we know the origin?
3. Where do אַבָּא ,אִמָּא ,דּוֹד come from?
4. What are the names of the two great language families?
5. Why is the vocabulary of languages like German or French at least somewhat familiar to you? Why is this not true of Hebrew?
6. Why will a good Hebraist know hundreds of Arabic words, without especially studying Arabic?
7. What are some words that the Hebrews borrowed from the Indo-European languages? What are some that Indo-Europeans borrowed from Hebrew?
8. In what ways was Hebrew used even tho it had ceased being a spoken language?
9. What was the great and almost miraculous achievement of Eliezer ben Yehudah?
10. What did Hebrew need badly in order to become a twentieth century language? In what two ways did scholars fill this need?

Can you match these two columns?

1. Onomatopoeic words	1. Arabic, Assyrian, Syriac
2. Hebrew words in English	2. הֶדְיוֹט - פַּרְדֵּס
3. קֶרֶן - יַיִן	3. Jews lived in Israel
4. Hebrew no longer a spoken language	4. אִמָּא, אַבָּא, דּוֹד
5. Indo-European	5. Revival of Hebrew as a spoken language
6. Greek words in Hebrew	6. Found in ancient Latin and Hebrew
7. Ben Yehudah	7. Buzzing, banging
8. Prattle words	8. After 70 C.E.
9. 1700 years	9. Latin, Greek, and German
10. Semitic	10. Amen, Sabbath

Chapter II

From Pictures—Thousands of Them—to 22 Letters

It might strike you as rather odd, but the actual historical fact is that the Hebrew-Phoenecian alphabet is the mother of practically all the alphabets now being used in the world. The English alphabet we now use is directly descended from this Hebrew-Phoenecian alphabet. It follows largely the order of the Hebrew alphabet. The names of the English letters are actually fragments of old Hebrew words which were used as the names of the letters.

As students of Hebrew, we certainly ought to be interested in the creation of the alphabet and its march from far-off Israel across lands and seas to England and America.

Let us begin from the very beginning.

THE PICTURE STAGE

There are three steps in the history of writing. The first is the simplest of all. People drew pictures, and by means of these pictures indicated directly what they wished to say. The picture of a house burning, of a man raising his sword to strike, all convey a clear message. This first stage in the history of writing was attained in many widely scattered lands. We have excellent examples in early Egyptian writing. The picture writing of the American Indian is well known.

PICTURES BECOME SOUNDS

The second stage, first attained by the Egyptians, is an advance over the first.

In this stage the picture no longer indicates just the object itself which it originally set out to picture. It also indicates the presence of that sound in whatever other words it may occur. We'll use English examples, since you don't know Egyptian well enough, to make this clear.

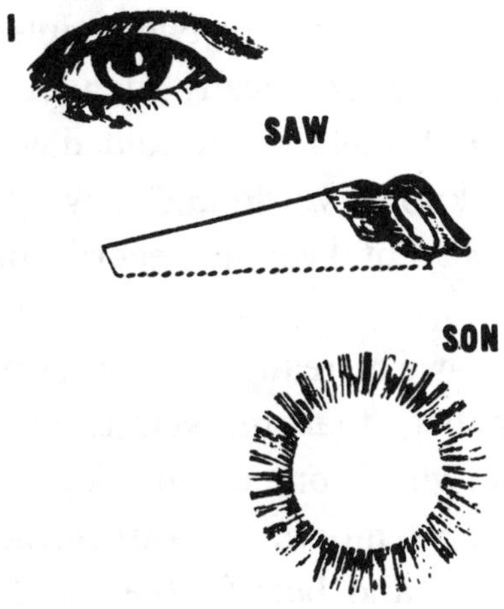

Here is the picture of a saw. Now this picture would then be used any time the syllable " saw " occurs or is needed; for example " I saw ", or " I sought ". The picture of a sun would also stand for the word " son " or for the first part of the word " sundae ". The picture of the eye would also stand for " I ".

This is a real advance, because it now becomes possible to express abstract ideas in writing. One can begin to write about goodness, truth, beauty, virtue, honesty, something that was totally impossible in the first or pure picture stage. Nevertheless, it is clumsy enough. In order to write, one would have to learn to make thousands of pictures. This was the stage which Egyptian writing had attained. It is also, incidentally, the stage at which Chinese writing is now. The poor Chinese school child has to learn something like two thousand pictures in order to read fluently.

Real writing and clear, ready expression of thought first becomes possible with the invention of the alphabet, the third and last stage in the history of writing. With it, writing was reduced from the enormously complicated problem of making an infinite number of pictures (the first stage); some two thousand pictures (the second stage), to only twenty two, the third or alphabetic stage.

THE THIRD OR ALPHABETIC STAGE

The Phoenicians lived just north of the Hebrews on a narrow strip of land hugging the coast, and the two peoples were cousins. Their languages were practically identical. The Phoenicians were the great traders of the old days, carrying their wares over all the known world and they felt keenly the need for a simple way of keeping records of their many transactions.

It was this people who seem—we're really not too sure —to have perfected the alphabet, that marvelous and precious instrument by means of which one could take the sounds that come from a person's mouth, or rather the thoughts that coursed and pulsed and beat in the minds of man, and put them down on papyrus, skin, stone, or wood. It was unquestionably one of the greatest inventions in the history of man, and one of the greatest triumphs of his intellect.

The discovery made by the unknown, unheralded genius, or possibly group of geniuses, who created the alphabet may seem to us childishly simple. Actually, it was a remarkable feat of analysis. He discovered that in spite of the hundreds and thousands of different words that men used when they spoke, there were altogether only a limited number and a quite highly limited number of actual sounds, amounting to some twenty-two. All the words that men used were simply varying combinations of this limited number of sounds.

Along with this discovery was born the great idea—an idea that was destined to change the course of world culture. *If there were approximately only twenty-two sounds, why not make a picture to represent each of these sounds*— and then learning to write would become a comparatively simple problem of learning to make twenty-two pictures.

In choosing his pictures our unknown inventor (he may have been a Hebrew; we call the alphabet Phoenecian because it was they who actually spread it throughout the world) showed his genius. He chose pictures that would at once suggest to the mind of the reader the sound it was to represent.

Thus if he wanted to indicate the sound " G " he drew a picture of the hump of a camel  . If the sound " B " he made an outline of a house. If the sound " M " he drew a wavy line to indicate  (water). This wavy line then stood for the sound " M ". Words, of course, are combinations of groups of sounds. To write words they simply combined these pictures which we now call letters of the alphabet.

Here are some of the letters which scholars say can definitely be traced back to specific Hebrew words. These are ancient Hebrew forms; they are not the ones we now use.

אָלֶף – the old Hebrew word for ox. Notice the two horns.
בֵּית – representing a house
גִּימֶל – camel
דָּלֶת – door
וָו – hook
יוֹד – hand
כָּף – palm of hand
מֶם – this letter represents the outline of the word water
עַיִן – once looked like an eye
פֵּה – mouth
רֵישׁ – once outline of a head
שֵׁן – represented a tooth

THE GREEKS LEARN TO USE THE ALPHABET

The first great nation the Phoenecians met as they travelled westward were the Greeks. They were impressed by the power, the beauty and the music of the Greek language. It did not take long for the Phoenecians to discover to their complete and utter amazement that this intelligent and gifted race could not read or write.

A group of Phoenecian traders were exchanging wares with some Greek merchants. The Phoenecians wanted the Greeks to write records of the transaction. The Greeks looked up in astonishment and said, " What do you mean—write? " The Phoenecian said, " You know, write down what we bought and sold." The Greeks said again, " What do you mean—write?" After this had gone on for a while it dawned on the Phonecians that this people did not know what writing was.

The Phoenecians then explained that writing meant

putting down on papyrus what had been said. The Greeks were now eager and willing to learn. " Show us how and we will write."

The Phoenecians then said, " Well, how do you say ' big ' in Greek? " " Mega." " Good," said the Phonecians. " For ' M ' we will make a picture of a wave. For ' G ' we will make a picture of a camel's hump. Thus we have  and whenever you see these signs it will mean ' big '."

" How do you say ' beautiful '? " " Kalon " was the answer. The Phonecians said, " We will make two signs, one for K and one for L."

" Oh, how wonderful," said the Greeks. " Show us more, teach us all the signs for all the sounds! "

The Phoenecians taught them all the twenty two letters of their alphabet. The Greeks went off by themselves and played this fascinating new game, the game of writing their beautiful Greek language with these strange-looking letters. After a while, they called over the Phoenecians and said, " Where are the letters for the vowel sounds? You know, a, e, i, o, u, etc.?" "Vowels?", said the Phonecians, " We never use vowels in writing, they don't count at all, you really don't need them."

The Greeks seemed puzzled at this answer. They were not at all satisfied. However, they again went off by themselves and tried to write Greek. Finally, in desperation, they begged the Phoenecians to come over.

" Something is wrong," they said, " perhaps you can write Phoenecian without vowels, but it is simply impossible to make sense out of Greek written without vowels

Now, what was the trouble? The Phoenecians soon found out.

THE GREEKS NEED PICTURES FOR THE VOWELS

In Greek as in other European languages, including, of course, English, the meaning of the word depended upon the vowels as well as the consonants. Different vowels when used with the very same consonants would create entirely different words having altogether different meanings.

Since you probably don't know Greek very well, I will illustrate this in English. Let us take the two consonants R——D.

Look what can happen:

R	a i	D	
	e a		
	e e		
	e a		y
	e		
	i		e
	i		
	o a		
	o		
	u		e

By changing the vowels of these two consonants we will get many, and for the most part entirely unrelated words. There is a world of difference between a " reed," " red " and " ride," and it would be altogether impossible or extremely difficult to read a writing made up only of consonants, and which omitted the vowel letters of those words. The Greeks simply had to have vowel letters.

However, just look at Hebrew. Take the word קדש. We can change the vowels of these consonants in many different ways, just as we changed the vowels of " R——D," and we will also get many words

However, all the words coming from קדש *namely*

קָדוֹשׁ – a holy person
קֹדֶשׁ, קְדוּשָּׁה – holiness
קַדִּישׁ – the mourner's prayer
קִדּוּשׁ – prayer declaring the Sabbath or festival night to be holy

have the same essential idea in them, namely " Holiness "

It is for this reason that it is quite possible, in fact, easy for a person with a fair knowledge of Hebrew to read Hebrew without vowel signs. Hebrew got along without any vowel signs for many centuries. It is quite impossible to do the same in Greek or English. The Hebrew vowel signs we now use were invented quite late and first came into use in the seventh century of the common era.

Actually, English does also use somewhat the principle of Hebrew, i.e., changing vowels to get different shades of the same idea. Several of the R———D group are actually connected: thus from " ride " arose " road " (where one rode). Raid was generally a particular kind of RIDE. *Ready* probably meant being prepared for the *road.*

THE GREEKS ADD VOWEL LETTERS

The Greeks were a clever people and solved this difficult problem very easily. They noticed that the Hebrew alphabet had several sounds that did not exist in Greek, so they took the letters which they did not need and used them to indicate vowels.

For example: The letter ע is a very deep guttural sound which the Greek could not use because he did not have that sound in his language. They took the ע

which in old Hebrew was written like an "O" and used it —you can easily guess—for the vowel sound "O"— which value it still has in English today. In this fashion, Hebrew א became A, the ה became "E", the ח an "AY" sound, and the י was used for the "EE" sound.

This adaptation by the Greeks of letters for the vowel sounds was a great and momentous forward step. With it the alphabet passes from the exclusive possession of the Semitic group and becomes an instrument useful for the writing of the Indo-European languages. In a certain sense the Greeks can be regarded as co-creators of the alphabet as used at present.

The old Hebrew alphabet is widely different from our present Hebrew writing. It was Ezra the Scribe, who about 440 B.C.E. adopted our present modern square Hebrew writing. It was the old Hebrew alphabet that the Greeks borrowed and passed on to Latin, and it is the old Hebrew alphabet that the Greek most closely resembles.

Greek used to be written as Hebrew is, from right to left. When the order was changed, that is when they began to write from left to right, they turned many letters around. If you turn around some of the old Hebrew letters you will see that they are almost identical with our present English letters.

𐤀—is old Hebrew א. Set it up straight; it is an "A".

𐤃—is old Hebrew ד. Turn it sideways and curve it slightly; it is a "D".

𐤄—is old Hebrew ה. Turn it around; it is "E". The Greeks used it for the vowel "E" since they had no need for it as a consonant.

𐤆—is old Hebrew ז. Turn it around; it is "Z".

𐤌—is old Hebrew מ. It resembles English "M".

O—is old Hebrew ע. The Greeks used it for the sound " O "; they had no ע sound.

ϙ—is old Hebrew ק. It resembles English " Q ". ק is a " K " sound made deep in the throat and in English it is used only in the combination " QU ".

X+—is old Hebrew ת, having almost exactly the same form as an English " T " has now.

W—is old Hebrew ש. Turn it sideways and curve the line; it will become an " S ".

QUESTIONS ON CHAPTER TWO

1. How are the Hebrew and English alphabets related?
2. What was the first stage in the history of writing? Why was it so inadequate?
3. How was the second stage, somewhat equivalent to the game of charades, a great improvement over the first?
4. What was the childishly simple and yet amazing discovery of the genius who invented the alphabet?
5. What sort of pictures did he choose to represent the separate sounds? Why was it easier for the Hebrew-speaking children of Israel to learn the alphabet than children anywhere else at any time?
6. Mention six letters and the specific Hebrew words from which they came.
7. Why did the Greeks have to add vowels to the alphabet they borrowed from the Phonecians? Try L———V or B———T and see how many words you can get.
8. Why did the Hebrews not need vowels in order to write intelligibly?
9. Name five Hebrew letters used by the Greeks as vowels.

PICTURE WRITING

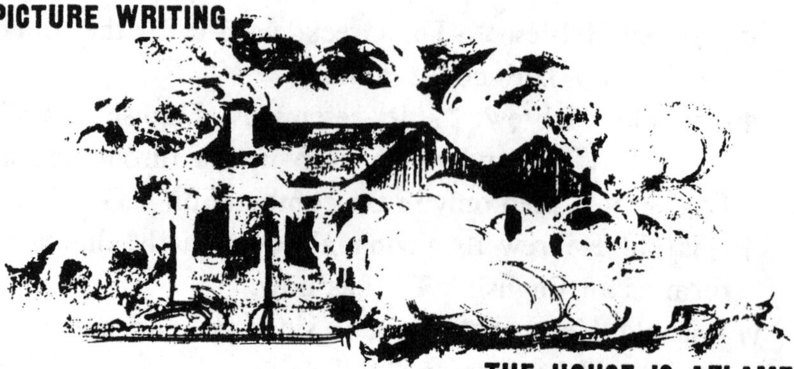

THE HOUSE IS AFLAME

CHARADE OR REBUS STAGE

2

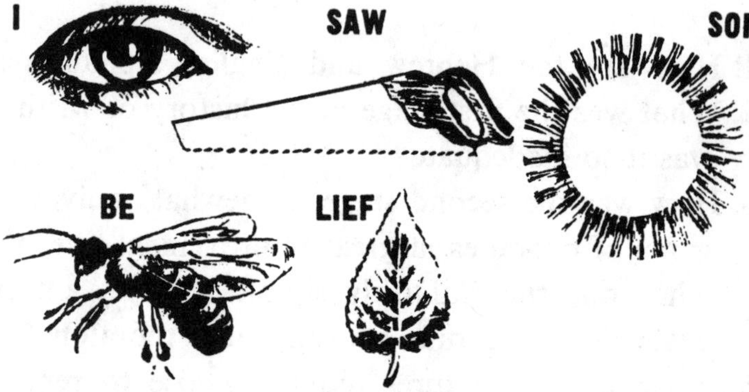

ALPHABET STAGE—ONLY 22 SOUNDS ONLY 22 PICTURES

3

ALEF-HORNS OF AN OX

MEM—WAVE OF WATER

SHIN— A TOOTH

SPOKEN WORDS BECAME WRITTEN THREE STAGES IN THE HISTORY OF WRITING

Can you match these two columns?

1. Added letters for the vowels	1. Our present square Hebrew writing
2. The realization that there were only 22 sounds	2. The very first stage in writing
3. Ezra	3. A wavy line intended to indicate a wave of water
4. The old Hebrew א	4. Greeks
5. Sound of מ	5. The second or charade stage in writing
6. Picture writing	6. Spread the alphabet
7. Did not need letters for the vowels	7. The picture of a tooth
8. Picture of sun equals son or picture of eye equals I	8. English letter " A "
9. Phoenecians	9. Invention of the alphabet
10. Sound of " sh "	10. Hebrews

Chapter III

The Hebrew Root has Three Consonants—usually

We now come to the central theme of all word building in Hebrew; it is the central rhythm of the whole, vast, far-flung structure of the Hebrew language.

This is it:

Practically all words in Hebrew go back to a root—and this root must have in it three consonants. You can do anything you want to the root: you can use it in any verb form or tense, you can turn it into any one of ten or twenty or more nouns. You can make it an adjective, adverb, preposition, or what you will...... *No matter what you do you will always see staring you in the face the three consonants of the root. You can never escape them.*

And equally important:

No matter what you do with the root, no matter into what word you turn it—that word must carry in it something of the meaning of the root. This is the irresistible logic of all word-building in Hebrew. It is by far the most important and most fundamental law of the Hebrew language.

Let us take a very simple root.

We have:

כָּתַב – he wrote
נִכְתַּב – was written
כִּתֵּב – he wrote busily
הִכְתִּיב – caused to write, dictated
הֻכְתַּב – was caused to write, was dictated
הִתְכַּתְּבוּ – they wrote to one another, corresponded

Or look what we can do with the root in the way of building nouns.

From it we derive:

כְּתִיבָה – writing
מִכְתָּב – a letter
כְּתָב – a document
כְּתָב יָד – a manuscript
כְּתֻבָּה – a marriage document
כְּתֹבֶת – address
מַכְתֵּבָה – desk
תִּכְתֹּבֶת – correspondence
כַּתָּב כַּתְּבָן – correspondent, writer
כְּתוּבִים – writings—the third section of the Bible
כְּתִיב – spelling

The first thing we note about this list is that every word on it has something to do with writing. Thus כְּתִיבָה is writing, מִכְתָּב a letter, something that is written; כְּתִיב spelling, i.e., the way we write; מַכְתֵּבָה a desk, i.e., the place where one writes; כְּתֻבָּה a marriage document, the most important piece of writing; כְּתֹבֶת address, the place to which one writes. All these are easily connectable with the concept " write ".

Then we note the rather interesting ways in which the root is twisted and turned to create needed new words.

There are prefixes such as appear in the word מִכְתָּב; there are suffixes such as in the word כַּתְבָן or מַכְתֵּבָה; there are infixes such as in the words כְּתִיב or כְּתִיבָה, or sometimes no consonants are added. The vowels of the root are simply changed, such as is done in the word כְּתָב.

Hebrew is enormously flexible. There are over a hundred ways in which the root can be changed about to create new words. Actually about fifteen are frequently used. These we will study later in detail.

In the root כָּתַב it is easy to see how every word from כתב is bound up with " write ". Often, though, the words derived from a root may have different meanings, which at first glance seem quite remote one from the other, and it is a real problem to work out what could be the root meaning that produced all these words.

Take the very common root חבר. Now look at the strange variety of words, apparently unrelated one to the other, which are derived from it:

חָבֵר – a friend
חִבּוּר – a composition
חֲבוּרָה, חֶבֶר – a group
חֶבְרָה – an association, congregation
מַחְבֶּרֶת – a copy book
מְחַבֵּר – an author

A friend seems to have little to do with a composition or a copy book, or an author with a group of people. And yet without too much intellectual exertion, it should be possible to work out the basic root meaning of חבר, a fundamental meaning which would lead easily and clearly to every word listed above.

חבר – means basically to be joined together

חָבֵר – a friend, is one who is joined or bound to you

חִבּוּר – a composition, means joining or putting words and thoughts together

חֶבְרָה — חֲבוּרָה — חֶבֶר – a group of people joined together

מַחְבֶּרֶת – a copy book—pages are joined together

מְחַבֵּר – author—like the word חִבּוּר, a composition wherein the writer joins together thoughts, stories, et cetera.

AMEN

AMEN is a root of unusual interest. Like חָבֵר it also shows how far and wide a word can travel.

The Hebrews loved the word " Amen ". In it they expressed their every hope that God would be merciful to them and grant them their heart's desire. From Hebrew the word spread to over a thousand languages. It now enjoys an unusual distinction. It has entered more languages and is used in more countries than any other word in human speech. The Hebrew Bible has been translated into over a thousand languages or more. All of them have retained and are using the Hebrew word Amen.

In Hebrew the root אמן which means " confirm or support " has had a very rich development. All of the many words coming from אמן grow out of or can be related to the idea of " support or confirmation ". To the basic meaning " confirm or support " is related the concept of true and faithful; it conveys the idea of being sure and certain in one's work, and possessed of strength.

Here are many but by no means all of the derived words.

אָמֵן – having the sense of " may this prayer come true ".

אוֹמֵן – foster father, as one who supports and nourishes.

אוֹמֶנֶת – foster mother

אִמֵּן – trained מְאַמֵּן – trainer הִתְאַמֵּן – was drilled

אִמּוּן – training

נֶאֱמָן – faithful אֱמוּנִים – faithful ones

הֶאֱמִין – believed

אֱמוּנָה, אֵמוּן, אֹמֶן – all mean faithfulness, fidelity

אָמְנָם – truly

אֱמֶת – faithfulness, truth, the " nun " has dropped out. (see page 32)

אִמֵּת – verified, הִתְאַמֵּת – was verified

אָמָן – master workman, as one who is firm and sure in his workmanship, used now in the sense of artist.

אָמָנוּת – art אָמָנוּתִי – artistic

אוּמָּן – also skilled workman, now used in the sense of artisan or craftsman

אוּמָּנוּת – craftsmanship

Another form of the root אמן is ימן. א frequently interchanges with י. We have for example אֶחָד and יַחַד or ארח and ירח.

From ימן we have

יָמִין – the right hand in the sense of the stronger hand

יְמָנִי – right (adj.)

הֵימִין – he went right (direction)

תֵּימָן – south, south wind, namely, what is on the right hand as one faces east.

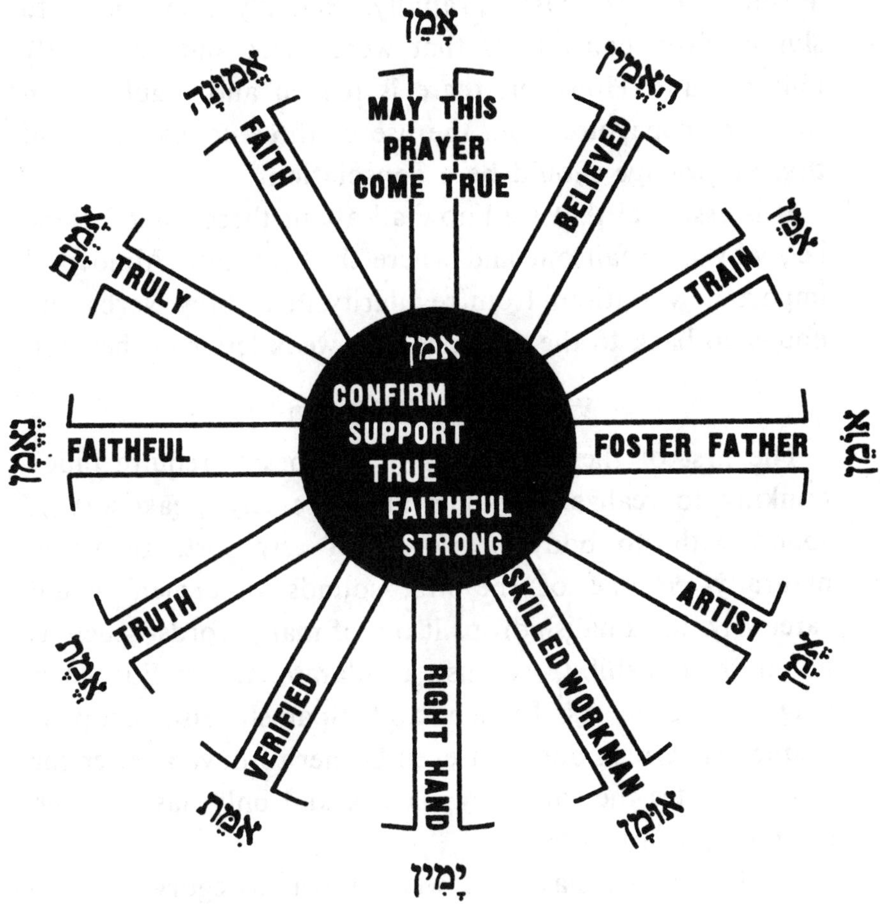
אמן
CONFIRM
SUPPORT
TRUE
FAITHFUL
STRONG
אָמֵן
MAY THIS PRAYER COME TRUE
הֶאֱמִין
BELIEVED
אִמֵּן
TRAIN
אוֹמֵן
FOSTER FATHER
אָמָּן
ARTIST
אוּמָּן
SKILLED WORKMAN
יָמִין
RIGHT HAND
אֻמַּת
VERIFIED
אֱמֶת
TRUTH
נֶאֱמָן
FAITHFUL
אָמְנָם
TRULY
אֱמוּנָה
FAITH

WEAK LETTERS

I am sorry to have to tell you something that mars and spoils all this three-consonantal regularity. The Hebrew alphabet has, unfortunately, three letters that cause a great deal of trouble. They are the three letters ה, ו and י. When men spoke hastily, rapidly, excitedly, they tended to slur or drop consonants that were weak and apparently unimportant. However, there is reason and regularity in this very departure from the use of three consonants and that knowledge should be a consolation.

It is essential that we know all about these three letters, i.e., why they fall out and where they fall out. Almost all important variations from regularity in Hebrew verbs and nouns go back to the presence of a weak letter in the root.

WEAK LETTER "ה"

The first of these letters is ה. It doesn't require much thinking to realize that ה is an extremely weak sort of sound with no body or power of any sort. It would naturally be one of the first sounds that men would carelessly slur. English drops it out of many words—such as honor, heir, exhibit, exhaust, exhilarate. Other European languages such as French and Spanish also drop it frequently. Greek does not even bother to have a letter for it; it indicates the sound by a mark and only has it at the beginning of a word.

In Hebrew we have the well known category of verb ל״ה—meaning that the last letter of the root is ה. The commonest verbs of this group are:

קָנָה	הָיָה	עָלָה
בָּנָה	חָיָה	עָנָה
רָאָה	פָּנָה	עָשָׂה

In the present tense plural קוֹנִים, קוֹנוֹת, the ה of the root disappears. It also drops out in the past tense forms such as:

קָנִיתִי
קָנִיתָ
קָנִינוּ
קְנִיתֶם
קָנוּ

And in the future tense forms such as:

תִּקְנִי
תִּקְנוּ
יִקְנוּ

The definite article ה is also swallowed up when it follows a consonant. We say לַבַּיִת to the house, it is usually not לְהַבַּיִת; בַּכַּדּוּר with the ball and not בְּהַכַּדּוּר.

Incidentally, the last letter ה of these verbs was originally י or ו—each of which is also a weak letter.

WEAK LETTER ו

That the second of the weak letters is ו may suprise you—for it doesn't sound weak at all—and actually ו is not a weak sound. The answer is that the sound of ו a long time ago wasn't " vav " at all but " w " and " w " is weak. It drops out of large numbers of English words—that is, in those words the " w " appears in the spelling but remains unpronounced, which usually means it was pronounced at one time but is now silent. Some of the words are " answer, sword, law, two, write " etc. " Vav " or rather " waw " used to be the sixth letter of the Greek alphabet (as it is of the Hebrew). It died completely out of the Greek language, leaving only one trace behind: in poetry there is an empty space where there once used to be a sound.

The Yemenite Jews of Arabia who retain an ancient, correct and pure pronunciation of Hebrew still pronounce the ו as " w "—as does Arabic, the close sister language of Hebrew. Incidentally, it is fascinating to listen to the Yemenite ceremonial reading of the Pentateuch. They not only pronounce ו as " waw " but distinguish between a ד with a dagesh and a ד without. The soft or undageshed ד equals a hard " th " in English, such as in the word " the " or " this ". They also differentiate between a dageshed and an undageshed ג. The former is equivalent to an English soft " g " as in the name " George ". Their undageshed or soft ת is equivalent to the English soft " th " as in the word sabbath. English words that derive from the Hebrew have this soft " th " for a ת without a dagesh.

The commonest verbs with the middle ו are:

מות	קום
בוֹא	שׁוּב
סוּר	רוּץ

נוּחַ

WEAK LETTER י

The third of the weak letters is י which is equivalent to the y sound in English. It is absorbed and is no longer heard in many English words such as " may, say, gay " etc. Often when it is swallowed up a long " ay " replaces it.

The י is weak in two positions in the Hebrew root—when it is the middle letter as in שִׁיר, רִיב, שִׂים, דִּין, and when it is the first letter in verbs like יָשַׁב, יָרַד, יָדַע, יָצָא. The future of יָשַׁב is אֵשֵׁב, there the " ay " vowel of the first letter is very long. You can almost hear the י which has been swallowed.

This is a group of nouns from which the weak י has been dropped.

שֵׁנָה – sleep is from יָשֵׁן sleep
דֵּעָה – knowledge is from יָדַע know
עֵצָה – advice is from יָעַץ advise
עֵדָה – group (called together by appointment) is from יָעַד appoint
שׁוּרָה – row is from יָשָׁר straight; as is also
שָׁרוֹן – the fertile maritime coastal plain
חֵמָה – anger is from יחם be hot
לֵדָה – birth is from יָלַד gave birth

It is rather important and not at all too difficult for you to understand that almost all the verbs whose first letter now is י were originally first letter ו verbs. ילד used to be ולד. We still have the word "וָלָד a child" in the Bible.

If you look at the first letter ו verbs in the verb patterns other than qal you will see this more clearly.

In נִפְעַל the verb יָדַע is נוֹדַע.
In הִפְעִיל the verb יָדַע is הוֹדִיעַ.
In הִתְפַּעֵל the verb יָדַע is הִתְוַדַּע.

NOUNS FROM פ״י VERBS

The nouns formed from these verbs would naturally retain the original ו when there is a prefix letter מ or ת. Here are a few examples with prefix letter מ.

From יָסַף add we have מוּסָף the additional prayers.
From יָלַד gave birth we have מוֹלֶדֶת native land.

From יָשַׁב dwell we have מוֹשָׁב, מוֹשָׁבָה settlement.
From יָסַד established we get מוֹסָד institution.
From יָעַד appoint we get מוֹעֵד an appointed time, holiday or appointed place, sanctuary.
From יָעַץ advise we get מוֹעָצָה council.
From יָרַד go down we get מוֹרָד slope, descent.

With prefix letter ת

From יָצַר produce we get תּוֹצֶרֶת product.
From יָשַׁב dwell we get תּוֹשָׁב inhabitant.
From יָצָא go out we get תּוֹצָאָה result.
From יָסַף add we get תּוֹסֶפְתָּא the Tosefta—the ancient authorative code of law—additional to the Mishna.

THE DISAPPEARING נ

There is a fourth letter the נ. It is not weak. It has the same strength and body as any other strong consonant —and yet it frequently vanishes from a word changing the original word almost beyond recognition.

What is wrong?

It seems that the letter " NUN " when it comes as the second letter of a syllable—not the first—is somewhat difficult to pronounce. It is therefore dropped right out of the word or is changed and it becomes the same as the following letter.

There are hundreds of words in English in which the " N " when it is the closing letter of a syllable falls out and the next letter is doubled. In English we say:

ILLEGAL—what we really mean is IN-LEGAL. However, it is a little difficult to pronounce the " N " when it is the second letter of the syllable and so the " N " is absorbed

ה FALLS OUT

IN ENGLISH—HONOR, HEIR, EXHAUST

IN HEBREW

מוֹרִים (ה) יִקְנוּ (ה)

לַבַּיִת (ה) קָנוּ (ה)

ו ORIGINALLY "W" FALLS OUT

IN ENGLISH—SWORD, ANSWER, TWO

IN HEBREW

בָּא (ו) רָץ (ו)

שָׁב (ו) קָם (ו)

י IS SWALLOWED UP

IN ENGLISH WORDS SAY, MAY, GAY

FALLS OUT IN HEBREW

אֵשֵׁב תֵּשֵׁב

שָׁר שָׂם

נ FALLS OUT

ILLEGAL (IN-LEGAL)

ILLUSTRATE (IN-LUSTRATE)

IN HEBREW

אֶפֹּל (נ) תִּפֹּל (נ)

מַשָּׂא (נ) מַתָּנָה (נ)

FOUR LETTERS FALL OUT

by and changes into the next letter "l". Similarly we say IR-RELIGIOUS and we mean IN-RELIGIOUS (just try and you'll see how much easier it is to say irreligious) and IM-MOVABLE for IN-MOVABLE.

Thousands of years ago in ancient Israel the Hebrews felt this same slight difficulty—and also cavalierly dropped the "NUN". The grammarians often put in a dagesh to indicate that the next letter was to be doubled.

Thus, the future of נָפַל is אֶפֹּל. There is a דָּגֵשׁ חָזָק in the פּ to indicate that it is to be pronounced twice: once for itself and once in memory of the missing נ. We say מִסֵּפֶר from a book instead of מִן סֵפֶר and again there is a דָּגֵשׁ חָזָק in the ס to indicate double pronunciation.

This is precisely what happens in English. The "n" is dropped and, so to speak, a דָּגֵשׁ חָזָק is put in the next letter, i.e., IN-religious becomes IR-religious. The similarity is almost startling in its completeness. For just as we don't actually pronounce the letter twice in English—no one says irreligious with two "r's" or immovable with two "m's"; so in Hebrew hardly anyone actually pronounces a dageshed letter twice. No one says אֶפְפֹּל or מִסְ־סֵפֶר. The poor "NUN" is just gone.

It is generally not too difficult to recognize verbal forms from which a "NUN" has fallen out because they follow regular patterns. Thus in qal:

נָפַל becomes אֶפֹּל
תִּפֹּל etc.
in נִפְעַל, נָשָׂא becomes נִשָּׂא
in הִפְעִיל, נָפַל becomes הִפִּיל

Of course, the "NUN" does not drop out in the הִתְפַּעֵל form, in words like הִתְנַפֵּל or הִתְנַשֵּׂא —for there is no difficulty in pronouncing an "n" after another consonant.

It is with nouns from which a " nun " has dropped that we have trouble. The roots of words with the dropped nun are difficult to recognize. For this reason it is helpful to make a list containing their roots and origins. There will be three columns; the word as it is now; what in all likelihood it was originally; and its root.

Word	*Originally*	*From root*
בַּת	בִּנְת The plural is regular namely בָּנוֹת. The Arabic word for girl is בִּנְת. Why doesn't the נ drop out in בָּנוֹת and in בָּנִים?	בן
מַצָּה not the famous, familiar and universally beloved matza that we eat. This word means a " quarrel ".	מ(נ)צה	The root is נצה. You're all familiar with the famous verse שְׁנֵי אֲנָשִׁים עִבְרִים נִצִּים " Two Hebrew men were quarreling one with the other. " Ex. 2:13
מַפָּה cloth, napkin, now also used for tablecloth, map.	מ(נ)פה	The root is נפה; like נוף, נפנף it means " to wave ". Because maps were painted on cloth, " mappa " in Latin came to mean " map ". In French the word be-

Word	*Originally*	*From root*
		came nappa; that gave rise to our word NAPKIN. " An apron ", meaning a cloth, used to be " a napron ". Thus the English word " apron " goes all the way back to the Hebrew word מַפָּה.
אֱמֶת	אמ(נ)ת	אמן In other words אֱמֶת and אֱמוּנָה are two forms of the same word.
אִשָּׁה	א(נ)שה This explains the plural form נָשִׁים.	אנש
מַקֶּבֶת hammer, excavation	מ(נ)קבת	נקב pierce
מַתֶּכֶת – metal	מַ(נְ)תֶּכֶת	נָתַךְ flow, be melted
חִטָּה – wheat	ח(נ)טה	חָנַט – grow
מַשָּׂא – burden	מ(נ)שא	נָשָׂא – carry
goal – מַטָּרָה	מ(נ)טרה	נָטַר – guard, watch.

Word	*Originally*	*From root*
		The goal is something that is watched intently and guarded.
הֹדּוּ – India	ה(נ)דו Like our English word Hindu.	
עֵת – time	ע(נ)ת This is similar to the other word in Hebrew for time עונה originally ...	ענת
מַפָּלָה – fall, defeat	מ(נ)פלה	נָפַל
מַשּׂוֹר – saw	מ(נ)שור	נסר – נשר נְסֹרֶת – sawdust
מַגָּע – touch, contact	מ(נ)גע	נָגַע – touch
מַתָּנָה – gift	מ(נ)תנה	נָתַן
מַתָּת – gift	מ(נ)תנת	נָתַן

A friend called to tell me his wife had given birth to a boy. I wished him מַזָּל טוֹב and asked the youngster's name. He said Matthew Jonathan.

I thought for a moment, "You can't do that. Those two names mean the same thing".

"You are talking nonsense, it's impossible. Those two names don't resemble each other in the slightest. For one thing Jonathan has two "n's" and Matthew has none."

So I explained to my friend that Matthew is a Greek form of the Hebrew name " מַתַּת־יָה " the gift of the Lord and that the word מַתָּת—gift originally did have two " n's " —but being locked up in the middle of the word, both dropped out. Jonathan is simply the English way of pronouncing יְהוֹ־נָתָן—the Lord has given.

THE כְּפוּלִים or ע״ע VERBS

I would like for the sake of completeness to say a word about a group whose last two letters are the same, a group called כְּפוּלִים, verbs such as חָגַג and מָדַד. In old Hebrew the last letter of these verbs dropped out in all tenses. The forms of this category are extremely complicated. There are as many as five completely different future tense forms in the qal.

Later, Mishnaic Hebrew very sensibly decided to drop the contracted conjugations, not, of course, in every case, and to treat almost all of these verbs as plain ordinary regular three consonantal verbs. Thus we have מוֹדֵד ,מָדַד, אֶמְדֹּד—this is conjugated just like שָׁמַר or כָּתַב. Only in intransitive verbs are the short forms regularly retained. Thus the

past	tense	of	קָלַל	be light is	קַל
"	"	"	חָמַם	be warm is	חַם
"	"	"	רָבַב	be many is	רַב
"	"	"	מָרַר	be bitter is	מַר
"	"	"	רָכַךְ	be tender is	רַךְ
"	"	"	דָּקַק	be thin is	דַּק
"	"	"	תָּמַם	be upright is	תַּם
"	"	"	צָרַר	be narrow is	צַר
"	"	"	תָּשַׁשׁ	be weak is	תַּשׁ

To sum up:

There are three factors that may account for your seeing a Hebrew root which has only two consonants.

1. The root in its present form may have in it one of the three weak letters י, ו, ה.
2. The root may have a נ as the first letter.
3. The root may be one of those in which the last two letters are the same.

QUESTIONS ON CHAPTER THREE

1. What is the great central principle of word building in Hebrew?
2. What do we know about the relations between a root and any word derived from it?
3. What are four different ways in which words could be built up from a root?
4. Why does the root חבר offer a certain difficulty?
5. What unusual distinction does the word אָמֵן enjoy?
6. Draw a tree with the roots labeled אמן and have each of the branches representing a word coming from אמן.
7. Give examples of the " h " sound dropping out of English words.
8. In which forms does the letter ה drop out of the present tense of בנה? the past? the future?
9. What was the original sound of the letter ו. Give several examples of English words from which that sound is dropped.
10. In what two positions in the verb can we find the weak letter י.
11. What are five nouns from which the י has dropped?
12. In what position does נ drop out of both English and Hebrew words?
13. Why does the נ not drop out in הִתְנַפֵּל?
14. Give five nouns from which the נ has dropped.
15. In which כְּפוּלִים verbs is the short form regularly retained? Give four examples.
16. What three factors can account for your seeing a Hebrew verb with only two consonants?

Can you match these two columns?

1. ה ו י	1. original sound of ו
2. " w "	2. shows that verbs with first letter י were originally first letter ו
3. the root of חִבּוּר and חָבֵר means	3. the Hebrew word קָנוּ also had a ה
4. אֱמוּנָה and אֱמֶת	4. noun suffix letters
5. honest	5. similar in Hebrew to a word like מַשָּׂא or אֶפֹּל
6. נ ה	6. the root has three consonants
7. illegal	7. to be joined, or to be put together
8. the central theme of Hebrew word building	8. similar in Hebrew to a word like אֵשֵׁב
9. הוֹדִיעַ and נוֹדַע	9. are words from the same root
10. gay	10. the three weak letters

Chapter IV

Some Interesting Hebrew Roots

We will now give a selection of some Hebrew roots that are interesting because of the large number of words derived from each, and also because of the wide range of meaning in these words. It will always be possible, though, to see the connecting links of the chain that binds the word to its root.

Before we start I would like to give an example of what happened to a simple root " עָזַב - left " and to show the way it was handled in the various sister languages (Semitic) of Hebrew. The root in the various sister languages has come to mean many different things—and yet it is not difficult at all to relate them to the root concept in עזב - to leave.

In Hebrew עזב gives rise to " עִזָּבוֹן - wares " *left* in the purchaser's hands.

In Assyrian the root עזב gives rise to a word meaning " a divorced person ".

In Arabic the root עזב gives rise to a word meaning " a bachelor ".

In Ethiopic the root עזב gives rise to a word meaning " a widowed person ".

נָשָׂא

The first Hebrew root we will study is נָשָׂא. It means

successively to take, to lift, to carry. After all, once you take something and move about with it you are already " carrying " it.

The following groups come from it.

TAKE

נָשָׂא – to take

נָשָׂא – is also a common Hebrew word for " to marry ".

Marrying a woman in days of old was very simply taking her.

לָקַח – to take, also means to marry

נִשּׂוּאִים – marriage

נוֹשֵׂא – a topic. Something that we take up for discussion.

מַשָּׂא וּמַתָּן – business, discussion.

Literally the phrase means taking and giving, which applies equally to business in the sense that we give merchandise and take money or the phrase applies to discussion where there is a give and take of ideas.

LIFT

נָשָׂא – lift

נָשִׂיא – prince, it is now commonly used for president.

נְשִׂיאוּת – presidency

נְשִׂיאַת כַּפַּיִם – the priests raise their hands in blessing the people.

מַשָּׂא נֶפֶשׁ – an ideal, that to which one lifts his soul.

מַשָּׂא פָּנִים – partiality. Literally it means lifting up a person's face.

CARRY

נָשָׂא - carry

נְשִׂיאִים - clouds, the clouds carry the rain

מַשָּׂא - burden

ARRANGE - סדר

It is easy to see how a root like " סדר - arrange " would branch out. There are so many things in this world that require arrangement or owe their existence to arrangement of some sort. Thus we have:

סִדּוּר - prayer book, the arrangement of prayers

סֵדֶר - Seder—the home festival on Passover night has been arranged in a set form

סִדְרָה - a section of the five books of Moses read weekly

שְׂדֵרָה - avenue

סָדִיר - regular

מַסְדֵּרָה - a linotype machine

מְסַדֵּר - type setter

הִסְתַּדְּרוּת - an organization—a group or institution that has arranged itself for efficient functioning

מִסְדְּרוֹן - porch, colonnade, corridor

כָּבֵד - HEAVY   קַל - LIGHT

כָּבֵד - means heavy, hanging down

כָּבֵד - is the liver, the heaviest of the internal organs

כָּבוֹד - honor. Literally " weightiness ". In English we speak of a " weighty matter " meaning a matter of great importance

מְכֻבָּד, נִכְבָּד, כָּבוּד – all these three adjectives simply mean " honored ".

כְּבוּדָּה – baggage

מַכְבֵּד – a broom made from heavy, low hanging branches probably gave rise to כַּבֵּד sweep.

לְדַבֵּר נִכְבָּדוֹת – to speak concerning an offer or proposition of marriage.

כִּבֵּד – to offer refreshment by way of doing honor to a guest.

The original meaning of יָקָר " precious " was weighty or heavy.

You would naturally expect the reverse to be true—that קַל which means light in weight would naturally come to mean " be lightly esteemed, to be looked upon with contempt." And so it is. There are many words from קלל or קלה, both originally mean " to be light " that have the sense of " ignominy, dishonor." We have:

נִקְלֶה – be dishonored

קָלוֹן – shame, dishonor

קַל בְּעֵינָיו – be lightly esteemed

קִלֵּל – to make contemptible, cause to be lightly esteemed, curse

קְלָלָה – curse

קִלְקֵל – destroy, spoil

קְלֹקֵל – worthless

הִקְלָה – esteemed lightly

מְקֻלְקָל – spoiled, damaged

שבר – BREAK

שָׁבַר – שִׁבֵּר – break

שֶׁבֶר – break, crash

Breaking is a concept around which many words would

naturally cluster. So many things in this world get broken. One of the commonest forms of purposeful breaking, in ancient times before coins were invented, was the breaking of bits of silver for making purchases. So

שָׁבַר – came to mean "to buy" and שֶׁבֶר the thing bought. Since the item most commonly bought was grain שֶׁבֶר came to mean grain.

הִשְׁבִּיר – sell—because you made someone break silver.

שֶׁבֶר – also came to mean the interpretation of a dream, i.e., breaking it down

מַשְׁבֵּר – crisis—the breakdown of the economic system.

מִשְׁבְּרֵי יָם – breakers of the sea.

שֶׁבֶר – a fracture

שָׁלֵם – BE WHOLE, COMPLETE

It probably never occurred to you and it may faintly amuse you to know that when someone says to you inquiringly "שָׁלוֹם לְךָ"—he is actually asking you whether you are whole, complete, in one piece. They want assurance that no part of you—fingers, toes, legs, arms, etc. is missing or broken. The root meaning of our familiar greeting word שָׁלוֹם is שָׁלֵם whole, complete. If you're whole, you're probably well and at peace.

הִשְׁתַּלֵּם – the reflexive, means to perfect oneself.

שִׁלֵּם – to pay for something, carries the meaning, to restore or make whole again. By paying a person for what you took from him you fill the gap you created in his possessions when you first took it.

שְׁלֵמוּת – entirety

תַּשְׁלוּם – payment; שַׁלְמוֹן – payment, may mean "bribe."

הִשְׁלִים – the hifil causative pattern could mean either "made peace" or "made whole", the word going back to either שָׁלוֹם or שָׁלֵם.

It is interesting to note that the English greeting " Hail ", has the same meaning as שָׁלוֹם, namely, " being whole ". When someone says " Hail " he is wishing that you are whole. " Hale " in the expression " hale and hearty " is from the same word as " hail." The Hebrew word שָׁלוֹם has given rise to a number of English words. There is Salem, a town in Massachussetts. " Salaam " is the cry of greeting spoken to a ruler or prince; it is usually accompanied by deep bows. Scholars say the English word of farewell " so-long " comes from " salaam."

BIND, PLEDGE – חבל

חָבַל – is to bind—also to bind a borrower legally by taking a pledge, a sort of collateral from him.

חֶבֶל – is a cord—something that binds. Since cords were used to measure land it came to mean one's portion of land, and hence in general one's portion in life. There are the famous and beautiful words of the psalmist חֲבָלִים נָפְלוּ לִי בַּנְּעִמִים " My lines have fallen in pleasant places."

חֶבֶל – also naturally came to mean a band of people —a group bound together for some purpose. Out of that meaning we have the phrase חֶבֶל נְבִיאִים—a company of prophets.

חוֹבֵל – a sailor, i.e. a rope puller

רַב חוֹבֵל – captain

תַּחְבּוּלָה – originally rope pulling (compare the English colloquial expression " knowing the ropes ", or " pulling wires "). The word now means " direction, counsel, device ".

עָבַר - TO CROSS OVER

עֶבְרָה - anger—crossing over the border of one's usual self control.

הִתְעַבֵּר - to become infuriated

עֲבֵרָה - sin—something like the English word transgress, going across.

עֲרָבָה, מַעְבָּרָה, מַעֲבָר - All mean a " place of crossing ".

עִבְרִי - Hebrew—probably goes back to the fact that the Hebrews were anciently nomads who passed over from place to place.

עָבוּר - produce, yield—what passes out of the earth.

בַּעֲבוּר - for the sake, because of

עֲרָבָה - The Jordan Valley is a great crack in the earth —cutting Israel in two from North to South. This rift is called the עֲרָבָה, the rift of the Jordan. It is probably a metathesis—that means the letters changed places—of עָבַר cross over. It means a place to be crossed.

עֵבֶר - side

מַעְבָּרָה - transient domicile. The most recent and most famous use of this word is to indicate the tent villages in which the immigrants to Israel were housed.

רֶוַח AND רוּחַ

רוּחַ - wind, breath. רוּחַ might possibly be onomatopoeic in imitation of the roaring of the wind.

The wind is not only one of the great primal forces on this earth but it is invisible as well. When a person died, one of the most striking things noted was that his breath left him; and so the Hebrews anciently used the word רוּחַ to mean spirit, that which combined power and invisibility.

The space between any two things is essentially the empty air that lies between them. So a slightly changed form of רוּחַ, namely רֶוַח, came to mean " space " and the verb רָוַח means " to be wide, spacious." When you have plenty of space, you are comfortable and relieved. So:

רָוַח לִי – means " I feel relieved ".

רֶוַח – also means profit in any enterprise. A profit is certainly a relief both material and spiritual for any business man.

הִרְוִיחַ – he profited

Coming from רוּחַ wind, is רֵיחַ odor, meaning a smell or a fragrance which is carried by the wind. From רֵיחַ we have הֵרִיחַ – he smelled, and מְרַחְרֵחַ he sniffed.

STRIKE פָּעַם

The meaning " a time " or " one time " for the word פַּעַם has so completely overshadowed its root meaning that most students hardly realize that the word " פָּעַם " meant " to strike, thrust, or impel ". The word " פַּעֲמוֹן – bell ", something that one strikes, is derived directly from the root.

The verb forms פָּעַם to impel; נִפְעַם to be disturbed, occur a number of times. פָּעַם strike, passes over to the sense of " one time " in the same way that in English the phrase " at one stroke " has come to mean at one time. Maybe you know the French phrase "tout à coup", at one stroke, all of a sudden, which also has come to mean at one time.

פַּעַם also means hoof beat—the striking of horse's hooves on the ground; it also means human " footsteps ". From this the word פַּעַם acquires the meaning " foot ", that which strikes the ground.

Similarly, the word רֶגֶל which means " a foot " also

means " time " as in the famous expression שָׁלֹשׁ רְגָלִים בַּשָּׁנָה " three times a year ". Another form of this verse is שָׁלֹשׁ פְּעָמִים בַּשָּׁנָה.

LOVE דוד

דוד is the most ancient Hebrew word for love. It is probably a primitive caressing syllable taken from the sound da-da that babies make. Babies' sounds are also the origin of words like אִמָּא – mamma, אַבָּא – papa. This accounts for words like these being found in so many different languages.

דוד – lover, has come to mean " uncle ". Next to the mother and father, the uncle was the lover and guardian.

דָּוִד – the name David simply means " beloved ".
יְדִיד – friend הִתְיַדְּדוּ – were friendly.
דּוֹדִים – means love-making, caressing.
דּוּדָאִים – mandrake flowers—called by this name in Hebrew because women believed these flowers stimulated their husbands' love for them. The mandrake flowers called דּוּדָאִים were thought to have the power of making men more affectionate.

ארח — ירח - WANDER

The root ארח — ירח means " to wander ".
The following easily relatable words come from it:

אוֹרֵחַ – a guest, one who wanders
אוֹרְחָה – caravan, the caravan wandered
אוֹרַח – a path or road that wanders along
יָרֵחַ – the moon—preeminently the wanderer of the sky. The moon is constantly moving about the heavens and hence its name.

יָרֵחַ – is a month. A month is simply the period of time it takes the moon to grow from a crescent, to attain fullness and then to wane. This takes approximately twenty-nine and a half days.

יַרְחוֹן – a monthly magazine

BE FIRM – כון

The verb is not used in the qal but in the nifal נכון means " be set up, established, fixed ". נָכוֹן is the commonly used word meaning correct, something that is established. In the hifil it is:

הֵכִין – to establish, set up, prepare. Also in the פּוֹעֵל it is:

כּוֹנֵן – to establish, set up

הִתְכּוֹנֵן – is to prepare oneself, to be established.

There is also a פִּעֵל form:

כִּוֵּן – means " to straighten, direct ", and finally and most commonly " to intend ". From it we have the noun " כַּוָּנָה – intention, meaning ".

כִּוּוּן – is direction

מְכֻוָּן – means intended

A few other words from כון are:

כֵּן – honest, right (the sense is being firm, upright)

מָכוֹן – foundation

מְכוֹנָה – in the Bible the word is used in the description of the building of Solomon's temple, to mean a base. The word, however, now is commonly used for machine. This use of the word is probably borrowed from the Greek.

כֵּן – a base, a pedestal—from כנן—a related root.

סָלַל – LIFT UP, CAST UP

Because the verb סלל is a member of the כְּפוּלִים group and the last letter frequently drops off, it is often difficult to recognize words coming from it. First we have the reflexive verb:

מִסְתּוֹלֵל – raise oneself up against
סוֹלְלָה – a mound—cast up to aid in case of a siege
מְסִלָּה – road
מַסְלוּל – road—usually at a slight elevation
סֻלָּם – ladder—the מ which is usually a prefix is here placed at the end of the word.

HEEL – עָקֵב

עָקֵב – heel, has developed a fairly wide range of meanings. We start off with the word עָקֵב – a heel. Then it comes to mean a mark made by the heel i.e. " a foot print ".

Then it becomes a verb: " to follow at the heel, to assail insidiously, circumvent, overreach." We then get the adjective עָקֹב insidious, deceitful, i.e. overreaching, and the noun עָקְבָה insidiousness.

" Following at the heels of " gives rise to the idea of " as a consequence of, because of "; hence the adverb: עֵקֶב – in consequence of.

" In consequence of " has the concept of " as a reward for " so עֵקֶב also means " a reward "—Note the famous verse בְּשָׁמְרָם עֵקֶב רָב " For the keeping thereof there is great reward ".

עָקִיב – consistent
עֲקִיבוּת – consistency

מָנָה – COUNT

The root מָנָה means to count, to count out on behalf of someone, to set aside for one, to assign to. From it we have the following words:

מָנָה – count נִמְנָה – was counted

מִנָּה – to assign, to appoint
נִתְמַנָּה – was appointed
מָנָה – part or portion—what is counted out and set aside. Also מְנָת means portion
מוֹנֶה – a counted number, a time.

We remember our father Jacob's bitter complaint against Laban וְהֶחֱלִיף אֶת מַשְׂכֻּרְתִּי עֲשֶׂרֶת מֹנִים "and he changed my reward ten times".

מָנֶה – minna—a weight of gold or silver, originally a specific measure.
מְנִיָּה – counting
מִנְיָן – the number ten required for congregational prayer.
מִשְׁלֹחַ מָנוֹת – the sending of portions, namely gifts on Purim.
עַל מְנָת – on condition that

עָלָה - GO UP

comes from the very simple word על on.

עָלֶה – leaf, foliage; also a leaf in a book.
עָלוֹן – leaflet, bulletin. עַלְעֵל – turn pages
עֶלְי – upper
עֲלִיָּה – attic, you have to climb up to get to it
עֲלִיָּה – the honor of being called to the reading of the Torah, i.e. of going up to the reader's desk
עֲלִיָּה – immigration—originally a trip to Jerusalem. Jerusalem is high up in the mountains.
עוֹלֶה – an immigrant
עֱלִי – pestle, the iron bar within the bronze mortar which pulverizes the spices. It is drawn up i.e. it rises each time before the downward blow is struck.

LEAF – עָלֶה

THE HONOR OF BEING CALLED UP TO THE TORAH – עֲלִיָּה

ELEVATOR – מַעֲלִית

TO THE HEIGHTS – אֶל עַל

GO UP – עָלָה

עוֹלָה – a burnt offering, that which goes up
עֶלְיוֹן – high, also the most high
מַעֲלֶה – an ascent
מַעֲלָה – a step, stair
מַעֲלָה – a virtue
מֵעַל – above, upwards
לְמַעְלָה – above
עִלּוּי – a young genius, infant prodigy
עַל – heights
מַעֲלִית – elevator

עֶצֶם – BONE, SELF, STRENGTH

עֶצֶם is the Hebrew word for bone. It has developed in two very interesting ways.

עֶצֶם has come to mean self—there isn't anything very much to a person without his bony structure. So בְּעַצְמִי means by myself; עַצְמָאִי means standing by one self or independent. יוֹם הָעַצְמָאוּת is Israel Independence Day. בְּעֶצֶם הַיּוֹם הַזֶּה means in this very day.

עֹצֶם has come to mean strength or power. There can hardly be any strength in the human body without the bones and the whole bony structure. עָצוּם means strong or powerful, מַעֲצָמָה means "power" in the sense of the great world powers. עָצוּם is commonly used for "terrific".

ערה – BARE, NAKED

What would you say to a word that begins with the meaning "skin", and ends up with the meaning "to contest, to protest against"?

עוֹר is skin. From it we have the word עָרֹם naked, which really means down to your skin.

We also have the verb ערה, which means "to be bare, naked". From it we have עֶרְוָה nakedness, immorality.

The verb ערה has developed in two different and interesting ways.

עָרָה is to pour out or to empty out a jar or receptacle. When you empty out a jar it is as though you are making it bare. When our mother Rebecca gave the camels drink the Bible describes it: וַתְּעַר כַּדָּהּ, " and she emptied her pitcher ".

עָרָה also means to break down the walls. When the walls are broken, it is as though the foundation or the area once covered by the structure is now laid bare. The Jews exiled in Babylon remembered their conquerers with the words:

זְכֹר ה׳ לִבְנֵי אֱדוֹם אֵת יוֹם יְרוּשָׁלָיִם
הָאוֹמְרִים עָרוּ עָרוּ עַד הַיְסוֹד בָּהּ.

" Remember O Lord against the sons of Edom the day of Jerusalem for they said, ' Destroy it, level it unto the foundations '."

From ערה we have the verb עַרְעֵר which means figuratively " to tear down, to undermine the foundations of, to protest against, to contest ".

פקד

Any one who has studied the Bible in Hebrew or who has even only a fair familiarity with it will remember coming across the word פָּקַד very often. It actually occurs several hundreds of times and in many seemingly unrelated senses. It would be worthwhile to tie them all together.

The root פָּקַד has the large general sense of " to give one's attention to ". From this large general meaning there have developed many specialized senses. These simply specify in detail various ways of giving one's attention.

Thus פָּקַד means:

1. to attend to

2. to observe
3. to remember
4. to seek, and sometimes to seek in vain, i.e. to need, to miss
5. to visit, and sometimes to visit in an evil sense. i.e. to punish, usually divine punishment
6. to number
7. to put someone in charge, to appoint

The nifal picks up three of these senses, and means: 1. was appointed, 2. was visited upon, 3. was sought vainly, i.e. missed. The hifil has the meaning to appoint and to entrust or deposit. The hitpael means, was numbered.

There are a number of nouns that come from this formidable list:

פְּקֻדָּה – visitation, numbering
פָּקִיד – overseer, officer
פִּקּוּד – a precept, because it means something appointed to be done, a charge
פִּקָּדוֹן – something entrusted, a deposit
מִפְקָד – numbering or mustering, appointment
תַּפְקִיד – function

A modern language cannot possibly use just one single word in these many important different senses and yet remain sharp, clear, and exact. It is just because of this very rich development that פָּקַד is today a beggar word; hardly anyone uses it in ordinary conversation. This word reveals the truth of the rabbinic dictum תָּפַסְתָּ מְרֻבֶּה לֹא תָּפַסְתָּ "If you seek to grasp too much, you grasp nothing".

The hifil הִפְקִיד though, is frequently used in the sense of to entrust. פְּקֻדָּה – command, פָּקִיד – officer, and פִּקָּדוֹן a deposit – are also in active use.

OLD WORDS DIE — NEW WORDS ARE BORN

Why do old words die?

One reason is very simply that the things they represent have become obsolete and unused, and so the names by which they were called died out. Other times we just don't know why a particular word dies and no better word takes its place.

Why are new words created?

Generally for the simple reason that a new thing is born and has to be named. This last century, particularly, has seen tremendous advances in all fields of human endeavor. New inventions are numbered by the thousands. This has created a need for an enormous number of new words.

Now what shall we call the new thing? How do we go about making a new name?

The first consideration may be: What does it look like? When the electric light bulb was first invented it looked like a swelling thing, something like an onion; hence the name—bulb. A potato looked like an apple that grew in the earth, so the French called it "pomme de terre" which in turn gave rise to the Hebrew תַּפּוּחַ אֲדָמָה. An orange looked like an apple of gold and hence תַּפּוּחַ זָהָב. Flowers have nothing very much to do except look pretty and so they will frequently have names that are descriptive. A gladiolus which looks like a sword is called סֵיפָן (like a סַיִף – sword). The chrysanthemum, is golden in color and so the Hebrew for it is חַרְצִית. חַרְצִית comes from the word חָרוּץ, which is an old poetic word for gold. (Incidentally the Greek word "chrys"—which means gold and forms the first half of many such English words as chrysanthemum, chrysolite, etc., itself come from the

Semitic word חָרוּץ gold). חַמָּנִיָּה is a sun flower and derives from the word חַמָּה – sun.

The second consideration in naming a new thing is a much more logical one. In it the word is made to answer the question: What does this thing do?

מַגְדֶּלֶת – is a microscope—it makes big, enlarges
מַקְרֶבֶת – is a telescope—it brings near
מַרְדִּים – is an anesthetic—it puts to sleep
מַגְבֵּר – amplifier—it makes the voice powerful
מַרְסֵס – a sprayer—it makes drops.

These, then, are the two considerations in name-making. The second of these, the logical one, the one which answers the question, What does this thing do? is the more important by far. We find that ninety percent of the new words created by the Vaad ha Lashon tell what the *function* of the new thing is.

It is amusing to note that occasionally when we have two names for the same thing they go back to these two different ways of naming: one word tells what the thing looks like, and the second what it does.

Thus we have:

Two words for " moon "

לְבָנָה – because it looks white
יָרֵחַ – because it wanders over the skies

Two words for " eyelid "

שְׁמֻרָה – because of its function—it guards the eye.
עַפְעַף – because of what it looks like—it flutters back and forth

Two words for " cloud "

עָב – thick—because it looks like a dense mass
עֲרָפֶל – also עָרִיף from the root עָרַף to drip—because from it drips water.

Two words for " pestle "
עֱלִי – its appearance—it goes up and down
מְדוֹךְ – its function—the crusher from the root דוּךְ.

WHAT THESE WORDS TELL US?

The words of a language reflect both directly and indirectly in a thousand subtle ways the life of the people who created it and spoke it.

I remember that when I was a boy of eleven I began to collect all the words for " ship " I came across in my reading. Within a few months I had gathered one hundred and seventy-five. Many years have passed since then and I have constantly come across additional words telling of different kinds of ships. I'm sure there must be over six hundred. It is a simple deduction that the life of the people who spoke this language must have been intimately bound up with ships, sailing them to all the seas, trading in them, and building them. All of this, of course, is altogether true of the English people.

The Arab language has five hundred words for camel—camels of all kinds, sizes, ages, breeds, degrees of swiftness, etc. and without any doubt the whole life of the people, economic and social, who spoke this language must be intimately bound up with the camel.

A study of the individual words in a language and of the ways their meanings develop lights up the past of the people, the conditions under which they lived, and reflects its morality and ethical life. What a revealing thing it is to observe that the same word in Hebrew צְדָקָה which means " charity " should also mean justice. We are left with the attendant thought that to the Hebrew mind the giving of charity was no more than a simple act of justice.

Or take the Hebrew word for stranger גֵּר. A stranger in Greek was " barbarian ", a person outside the pale. The Latin word for stranger was " hostis " which was associated with the idea of hostility and dislike. But think of the Hebrew word גֵּר a stranger. The word is filled with overtones of friendship and good-will. It tells of one whose rights were scrupulously respected.

" You shall love the stranger " – וַאֲהַבְתֶּם אֶת הַגֵּר· מִשְׁפָּט אֶחָד יִהְיֶה לָכֶם וְלַגֵּר הַגָּר אִתְּכֶם. " For there shall be but one law for you and for the stranger who dwells with you ".

On a less dramatic and more prosaic level the words below will tell us something of the life of the ancient Hebrews.

One of the commonest forms of wealth among the Hebrews must have been cattle, because the same words serve for two concepts: i.e., for cattle and for wealth or property in general.

מִקְנֶה – cattle; property—any possession that one acquires. (The root is קָנָה acquired.)

סְגֻלָּה – property or treasure in Hebrew is an old Assyrian word for cattle.

רְכוּשׁ – property, from רֶכֶשׁ – steed. This word is found in the Book of Esther.

נֶכֶס more commonly נְכָסִים property—is a Hebrew-Aramaic word that means " cattle for slaughter ".

The important role of dancing as a way of celebrating festivals is seen by the fact that the word חג originally meant a festival dance. It is the same root ultimately as " חוג to go around in a circle ". All holidays were celebrated by festival dancing, so the word חַג came to mean holiday. The Chasidim who do so much religious festival dancing are in the true ancient Hebrew tradition.

What do the following Hebrew words and place names tell us about the geography of Palestine:

the word יָם meaning west.

the word נֶגֶב meaning south.

the river named יַרְדֵּן. Think of the great hydro-electric plant.

the mountain named לְבָנוֹן?

the mountain named כַּרְמֶל

the name of the lake מֵי מָרוֹם

In Jerusalem you will see signs urging that animals not be driven too hard. These were put up by the Association for the Prevention of Cruelty to Animals.

The Hebrew name for this society is very unusual and interesting. It is from an old and very beautiful phrase, " צַעַר בַּעֲלֵי חַיִּים – The Pain of Living Things." Even thousands of years ago the Jews had laws that carefully protected animals against ill-treatment by their masters—and all these laws centered around this phrase צַעַר בַּעֲלֵי חַיִּים.

This happened in the fifth century C.E. Jerome, who later became St. Jerome, was not satisfied with the existing Latin versions of the Bible. They were not made directly from the Hebrew and contained a great many inaccuracies.

He lived in Palestine where there were many good teachers of Hebrew available. He set himself—a grown man—to the task of mastering Hebrew and then after achieving sufficient mastery he translated the Bible into beautiful, flowing Latin. This work which is called "The Vulgate", is still used in churches all over the world and is a great literary masterpiece. He made an error in one verse, an error that was immortalized in one of the world's most beautiful works of art. The Bible says that when Moses came down from Mt. Sinai קָרַן עוֹר פָּנָיו —" the skin of his face shone."

The word קֶרֶן originally meant " horn ". Because the rays of light coming off the sun in the hours of sunset look for all the world like gigantic horns, the word קֶרֶן also came to mean a " ray of light " and from " קֶרֶן ray of light " we have the verb " קָרַן - shone ".

St. Jerome understood קֶרֶן in its primitive sense of " horn " and he mistranslated the verse for the Vulgate in this way " Horns formed on his face ". A thousand years later drawing upon the Vulgate mistranslation Michelangelo created his immortal sculpture of Moses, a heroic and beautiful figure of the lawgiver, and from Moses' forehead there extended two horns!

Since קֶרֶן, the horn, was used to store oil it gradually came to mean a receptacle in general, or a place where things are stored. From this usage developed the meaning " a fund ". A fund is simply a place where dollars are stored. We are all familiar with the blue and white box of the קֶרֶן קַיֶּמֶת the Jewish National Fund. קֶרֶן also means the " capital funds " of a business enterprise.

The horns of an animal seem to symbolize his power and strength and so קֶרֶן came to stand figuratively for " might and dignity ".

From the horn of the ram was fashioned the shofar, so קֶרֶן also means a " shofar ".

The altar of the temples in Jerusalem had horn-like projections at each of the four corners. They were called קַרְנוֹת הַמִּזְבֵּחַ and from them or possibly from its curved shape קֶרֶן also got to mean " corner "

קַרְנַיִם·
HORNS

קַרְנֵי הַשֶּׁמֶשׁ
RAYS OF SUN

קֶרֶן קַיֶּמֶת
JEWISH NATIONAL FUND

קֶרֶן
CORNER

QUESTIONS ON CHAPTER FOUR

1. Give the various meanings of עָזַב in the Semitic languages and show their relation to the root meaning of עָזַב.
2. What are the three essential meanings of נָשָׂא. To which of these three meanings is נִשּׂוּאִים related? מַשָּׂא? נָשִׂיא?
3. What are three common words deriving from סָדַר?
4. What have the words " heavy " and " light " in Hebrew come respectively to mean? Give examples of each.
5. Trace שֶׁבֶר which means both the interpretation of a dream, and also grain, back to the root meaning.
6. Can you trace שִׁלֵּם repay, and שָׁלוֹם peace, back to their original root meaning?
7. חֶבֶל means a " group of people " and also a " portion of land ". Relate them to their root meaning.
8. Can you relate these two rather similar words, עֶבְרָה anger, and עֲבֵרָה transgression, to their common root?
9. How does רֶוַח come to mean relief?
10. Can you connect אוֹרֵחַ guest, אוֹרְחָה caravan, and יָרֵחַ moon?
11. Why should עֵקֶב mean both in " consequence of " and also a " reward?"
12. מָנָה has the two general senses of " to count," and " to set aside for one, or assign ". To which of these two meanings can מִנְיָן be related?
13. What are the three different meanings of the word עֲלִיָּה?

14. What are the chief considerations in naming a thing? Give two examples of each type of naming?
15. Why should the English language have so many words for " ship "; the Arab language for " camel "?
16. What are three words that mean both cattle or animals, and property in general?
17. Why should קֶרֶן mean a horn, a ray of light, as well as a fund?

Can you fill in the missing word or words?

1. The thought common to " being divorced ", a " bachelor " and " widower " is that each is ——.
2. נָשָׂא developed its three-fold meaning from a typical action-pattern: when you take something you are —— it, if you move one step with it you already —— it.
3. The Hebrew words for prayer book, for the celebration on the first night of Passover, and for a typesetter are joined by the common concept of ——.
4. In English a weighty matter, namely an important matter, finds its parallel in the two Hebrew words —— and ——.
5. הִשְׁלִים could mean either " made peace " or " made whole " because the word can be traced back either to —— or to ——.
6. רֵיחַ mean fragrance, odor, because odors are borne by the ——.
7. פַּעֲמוֹן means a bell and פַּעַם means foot steps or hoof beats because the root has the meaning ——.
8. David, דוֹד and יְדִיד are all from one common root meaning ——.
9. עִלּוּי means a young genius; such an unusual young man is so much —— all others.
10. עָרָה – " to pour out " and " to break down the walls " are both related to the concept of ——.

Chapter V

How Bright Are You?

Now we have for you a series of exercises in Hebrew word building that will test your intelligence as well as whatever knowledge of Hebrew you have. You are already well equipped with the essential principles and have had abundant examples showing the way these principles work. Let's see what you can now do on your own.

The important point to bear in mind when trying to work out the meanings of Hebrew words is this: All Hebrew words fall into one of two groups. One is made up of a tiny group numbering no more than a few hundred, which for want of a better name we shall call the primitives. A Hebrew word is a primitive when we can't go beyond it, when it doesn't come from any word that we now know. רֶגֶל is a foot, and that is about all there is to it. We don't know why it means a foot. It doesn't come from any more primitive root. שִׁבְעָה is seven and that is all there is to that. So is יַעַר forest and יָד a hand. These are typical primitives.

The second group, however, makes up the overwhelmingly greater part of the Hebrew language, in fact it includes all of the vast Hebrew vocabulary except for the few hundred primitives. *All of these words can be and must be forced to answer the question—why?* שָׁבוּעַ is a week, Why? מִגְדֶּלֶת is a telescope, Why? מִזְרָח is east, Why?

You must never pass over any Hebrew word that is not a primitive without compelling it to yield up to you the secret of its being, namely, why it means what it does.

Always remember the possibility that a weak letter might be present in the root—which will mean that a word coming from that root may have only two root letters. Also if a root is כְּפוּלִים, that is if the last two letters are the same, one may have dropped out. Finally if the first letter of a verb is נ it may drop in forms where the נ is the second letter of the syllable.

By far the most frequently used prefix letter is מ; ת occurs a number of times as a prefix; א and י quite rarely. In the way of suffixes ָה the feminine ending is most common; וֹן frequently occurs; ו and י are the two infix letters.

The exercises that follow are divided into three groups. The first group presents easy problems, the second group questions of intermediate difficulty and the last group problems that will really give you trouble.

Of course, the answers are printed at the end of the chapter—but please play fair and don't look until you have done your very best yourself. Forty right in each group means that you are excellent. If you get them all right you either approach genius, you are one or you have looked at the answers.

These are the easy questions:

1. Why does the word שָׁבוּעַ mean a week?
2. Why does the word מִזְרָח mean east?
3. Why does the word מַעֲרָב mean west?
4. Why is סְבִיבוֹן a Chanukah dreidel?

5. דָם is blood. אָדֹם is red. Which word in your opinion came first; the word for blood or the word for red?
6. The same for these words יֶרֶק grass and יָרֹק green; again, which word comes first?
7. The Hebrew word תַּחְתִּית strangely enough means both a " subway " and a " saucer ". Why?
8. The word תְּבוּאָה means produce of the field. Why?
9. What would be the connection between חֹדֶשׁ month and חָדָשׁ which means new?
10. Why does שָׁלִיחַ mean a messenger?
11. The word הוֹכִיחַ has two meanings "to prove, and to scold or rebuke ". Can you connect these meanings?
12. Why is עֲפִיפוֹן a kite?
13. Why does the word מִצְוָה mean " a commandment " and also a " good deed?"
14. Why does the word חַיָּה mean an animal?
15. Why is קָרוֹב a relative?
16. Why does מַעֲשֶׂה which means a " deed " also means a " story?"
17. Why is מְרַגֵּל a spy?
18. What is the connection between בֵּית הַכְּנֶסֶת synagog and כְּנֶסֶת the Israeli Parliament?
19. Why was the יַרְדֵּן so named?
20. What would be the connection between זָקָן beard and זָקֵן meaning old or grandfather.
21. What is the underlying idea of the two closely similar words חַמָּה " sun " and חֵמָה anger?
22. Why should מוֹצָא mean a " way out, an expedient?"
23. On Passover night the child asks the four קֻשְׁיוֹת. Why does the word mean questions?
24. The word לָשׁוֹן means a tongue. It also means a language. Why?

25. Another form of the root אֶחָד is יַחַד Why does יַחַד mean together and מְיֻחָד mean " special or particular ".
26. אַלּוּף means " leader " and is today used in the sense of " champion ". Exactly how many people were led by an אַלּוּף, a leader, in days of old?
27. Why is תַּהֲלוּכָה a parade?
28. Why is תִּזְמֹרֶת an orchestra?
29. Why should חָשׁוּב mean important?
30. How does the word חֲתוּנָה meaning wedding, show that man was regarded as being more important than woman? In ancient days at least. How does the word כְּלוּלוֹת partly correct this inequity?
31. Why should the two words אֶקְדָּח revolver and מַקְדֵּחַ drill come from the same root?
32. Can you connect עֶרֶב evening with עוֹרֵב raven?
33. Why were the לְבָנוֹן mountains so called?
34. Why should the Hebrew word לְוָיָה which really means an escort, also mean a funeral?
35. Why should דָּלַק which means " to burn " also mean " to run rapidly after "?
36. Why should שָׁעוֹן mean a watch?
37. Why should מֶלְקָחַיִם mean tongs?
38. Why should עַמּוּד mean a pillar or a column?
39. לֶקֶט was one of the three forms of free grain available to the poor in Biblical days. The poor people had the right to pick up or collect what the farmer dropped by chance as he harvested. Can you connect לֶקֶט with יַלְקוּט a wallet or receptacle?
40. What in all likelihood is the connection between כּוֹס a glass and כִּיס a pocket?
41. What is the relation between בָּלַל to mingle or mix and הִתְבּוֹלֵל to assimilate?

42. Why should מָנוֹחַ mean “deceased”?
43. Why should the word צַוָּאָה mean “last will and testament”?
44. Can you connect the two meanings of תְּשׁוּבָה. It means repentance and also means an answer?
45. Can you connect רְאִי a mirror and רְאָיָה proof?
46. Why should שׁוֹט whip give rise to שַׁיִט rowing?
47. רֹב majority can easily be related to רְבָבָה ten thousand. However, can you connect it with רַב master, teacher?
48. Can you connect דֶּבֶק glue with the דִּבּוּק a spirit that is sometimes supposed to enter a human being?
49. Can you connect מַחֲנֶה a camp with תַּחֲנָה a station?
50. כָּזַב means “to lie or to be a liar”. Why should “נִכְזָב disappointed” and “אַכְזָבָה disappointment”, come from this root?
51. Why should the word מַדְרִיךְ mean a “guide or a counsellor”?
52. Why are “בָּשֵׁל ripe” and “בִּשֵּׁל cook” from the same root?
53. Why should כְּדַאי mean “worthwhile”?
54. Why should פְּנַאי mean “leisure”?
55. Why should חָרַשׁ plow also mean to cut into, engrave, to work in metals or wood? Why should בֵּית חֲרֹשֶׁת mean factory?
56. Why should מְתֵי מִסְפָּר mean few in number?
57. נֶגֶד against really means what is conspicuous or else that which is in front of you. Why should נָגִיד mean leader?
58. בָּרַח which is used mostly in the sense, to flee, means to go through, to pass through. Why should בְּרִיחַ mean a bolt?

59. Why should the root צמד which means " to bind or to join " give rise to a) צֶמֶד, a couple, a pair, frequently used to indicate a span of oxen? b) צָמִיד a bracelet.
60. גַן a garden, מָגֵן shield and הֲגָנָה protection, defense are all from the same root גנן to protect or enclose. Why?
61. Why should כִּמְעַט mean almost? Detach the prefix letter. It will help you.
62. Why should שָׁקַל which meant originally to weigh, give rise to שֶׁקֶל – the coin shekel?
63. Why should פָּרַשׁ, which means to explain, to make clear or to make distinct, more commonly used in the piel לְפָרֵשׁ also mean "to separate oneself", as in the famous phrase, אַל תִּפְרֹשׁ מִן הַצִּבּוּר. " Separate thyself not from the community "?
64. Why should בָּלָה, which means to become worn out give rise to בְּלִי without?
65. Why should נָכָה mean reduce—that is, reduction in price?
66. What is the relation between אֻכָּף saddle and the extremely common expression מָה אִכְפַּת לִי? How does this concern me?
67. Why should צָרַף which means to melt or to refine metals come to mean to add or join to?
68. Why should פָּסַל basically to cut, to carve, to sculpture, give rise to פָּסוּל invalid, valueless, useless?
69. How does אָחוּז which really means taken, seized, come to mean per cent?
70. How does תְּנַאי which is the Aramaic way of pronouncing the Hebrew word שֵׁנִי second, (see the next chapter, where many examples are given of ש in Hebrew becoming ת in Aramaic) come to mean a condition?

These questions are harder

This set of questions is of intermediate difficulty and the procedure will be somewhat different. The questions come in groups of twelve or thirteen. At the top of the page will be found a number of roots together with their meanings. They will give you a clue to the solutions of these rather more difficult problems.

INTERMEDIATE GROUP I

כָּבַשׁ – to subdue, press down, conquer; נֹכַח – opposite, over against; נָהַג – drive, lead; נָעַל – close, lock; נָפַח – blow; חִלֵּק – divide; קָצַץ – cut; שָׁלֹשׁ – three; עָשָׂה – make; פָּסַק – be cut; קִבֵּץ – gather; שָׁנָה – repeat, do again. This comes from the word שֵׁנִי – second.

---

1. Can you connect the words מַחְלֹקֶת a quarrel, and מַחְלָקָה a class?
2. Why should the word קֵץ mean end?
3. Why should תַּעֲשִׂיָּה be industry?
4. Why should נוֹכֵחַ mean " one who is present "?
5. Why is פָּסוּק a sentence?
6. Why should שִׁלְשׁוֹם mean the " day before yesterday "?
7. Why should the word כְּבִישׁ mean a " road "?
8. Can you connect קַבְּצָן a beggar, and קְבוּצָה a group?
9. Why should the last prayer on Yom Kippur be called נְעִילָה? Why should the word נַעַל mean a shoe?
10. Why should שָׁנָה mean to learn? Compare the word מִשְׁנָה Mishna, the book that is " to be studied ".
11. Why should הֲלָכָה mean " law "?
12. Why should מִנְהָג mean a custom? Can you connect it with נֶהָג chauffeur?
13. Why should נַפָּח be a blacksmith? (You don't see many blacksmiths nowadays so this may be a hard question.)

INTERMEDIATE GROUP 2

שָׂפָה – lip; שֵׂעָר – hair; נוּחַ – rest; נָקַב – pierce, cut through; בְּעִיר – cattle; אָלַם – bind up a sheaf; נָשַׁךְ – bite; נָטָה – stretch; טָבַע – sink down; עוּד – testify; קָצַר – cut, reap; בָּחַר – chose.

---

14. Why should אִלֵּם mean dumb; that is, mute, not able to speak?
15. What sort of young man must a בָּחוּר have been?
16. Why is שָׂפָם mustache?
17. Why should נָקַב mean " to designate "?
18. Why is שָׂעִיר a goat? Why is שְׂעוֹרָה barley?
19. Why does the word בַּעַר mean stupid?
20. Why should the word מִטָּה mean " bed "? (The נ dropped out.)
21. Why should קָצָר mean short?
22. Why should תְּעוּדָה mean a document, certificate?
23. Why should נֶשֶׁךְ mean interest—at least from the point of view of the borrower? Why should רִבִּית be the word for interest from the point of view of the lender?
24. Can you relate נוֹחַ comfortable, and נַחַת pleasure or joy, to the root נוּחַ rest?
25. טַבַּעַת is ring. What were rings used for in days of old? Also, why should מַטְבֵּעַ mean a coin?

INTERMEDIATE GROUP 3

עוג – circle; פָּשַׁט – spread out; נָטַר – watch; עָרַךְ – arrange; סָרַט, שָׂרַט – scratch; הִזְהִיר – give light, enlighten; נִצָּב – stand; עָמֹק – deep; פָּתָה – be open; הָמָה – hum; יָנַק – suckle; חִלֵּל – desecrate.

---

26. Why should מַצָּב mean " condition " and מַצֵּבָה a monument?
27. Why should פָּשׁוּט simple and " פָּשַׁט undress " come from the same root?
28. Why should סַרְטָן mean a " crab"? Why should שִׂרְטֵט mean " sketch, draw a picture"?
29. Why should עֻגָּה mean a " cake"?
30. Why should מַטָּרָה (a נ has dropped out in this word) be a " target?"
31. Why should הָמוֹן be a " crowd"?
32. Why should עֵמֶק mean a "valley"?
33. Why should פֶּתִי mean a " fool"?
34. Why should תִּינוֹק mean an " infant"?
35. Why should עֵרֶךְ mean an " estimate, evaluation?"
36. Why should הִזְהִיר mean " warn?"
37. חֹל מוֹעֵד. The word מוֹעֵד means holiday and חֹל means the " intermediate days of the holiday week, when most occupations and activities can be carried on, i.e.; business, riding, writing, etc. Why is the word חֹל used to designate these days?

INTERMEDIATE GROUP 4

עֵת - time; חָלָק - smooth; לָמַד - learn; דִּין - judgment; חֶמְאָה - butter; חַסֵּל - finish off; חוּג - circle; סָפַן - cover; סָרַח - overrun, exceed; חָזָה - see, look over; עָטַר - surround; חקה - engrave; אָחַז - grasp.

---

38. Why should חֲלַקְלַקּוֹת mean flattery?
39. What sort of a boat must a סְפִינָה have been?
40. Why should עַתָּה mean now?
41. Why should מַלְמֵד mean oxgoad?
42. Why should מַחֲמָאוֹת mean compliments?
43. Why should מְחוּגָה mean compass?
44. Why should אֲחוּזָה mean property, inheritance?
45. Why should a locust be חָסִיל? Remember the words at the end of the Passover service חֲסַל סֵדֶר פֶּסַח כְּהִלְכָתוֹ?
46. Why should עֲטָרָה mean a crown?
47. In days of old what must have been the function of the חַזָּן at services?
48. Why does מָדוֹן mean strife, contention?
49. Why should סָרַח mean sin?
50. Why should the word חִקָּה mean imitate?

This is the most difficult group. These will really make you think hard.

1. Why should לַמְרוֹת mean in spite of?
2. How do we know from the Hebrew word for orange תַּפּוּחַ זָהָב that the orange is not native to Palestine?
3. The primitive meaning of בקר is to split. With this as a clue can you connect the following unrelated words בָּקָר cattle and בֹּקֶר morning?
4. How do we know that the ancient Hebrews drank at their banquets?
5. מְנוֹרָה is a candlelabrum, תַּנּוּר is a stove, נֵר is a candle. What would you guess is the meaning of the root of these three words?
6. שׁוֹטֵר in modern Hebrew as now used means a policeman. But, a שְׁטָר is a document. Can you guess what kind of officer a שׁוֹטֵר must originally have been?
7. The very common word בֶּגֶד as you know means a garment, but בּוֹגֵד means a traitor. That's very odd. Look at this combination: מְעִיל is a coat, מָעַל means to transgress. Are you clever enough to get the connection?
8. Why should סַר mean " resentful, sullen, stubborn?"
9. Why should the idiom בְּקֹצֶר רוּחַ mean impatiently?
10. A nice new word that has recently come from Israel is זְרִיקָה and it means " an injection ". Why?
11. What's faintly amusing about the words הִיא הִתְחַתְּנָה she was married?
12. פָּלִיט is a refugee, פֶּלֶט means the juice coming out of meat. Can you connect them?
13. Why should the word אַחֲרַאי mean responsible?
14. Can you connect פְּשָׁרָה compromise with פוֹשְׁרִים lukewarm, and with אֶפְשָׁר perhaps?

15. Can you connect אָפִיק a channel for conveying water with הִתְאַפֵּק which means " to restrain one self?"
16. What specific area is represented by the word מְדִינָה?
17. Why should אַרָעִי or אַרְעִי mean " by chance, not fixed, temporary?"
18. Why should קוֹמָה mean stature?
19. Why should הִתְעָרֵב which comes from the root עָרַב pledge, develop the sense of " making a wager?"
20. Can you connect עִתּוֹן newspaper and עַתָּה now? What is their common root?
21. Why should the פַּתַח vowel be so called?
22. Can you connect חֶרֶב sword and חָרוּב the fruit of the carob tree, generally known as St. John's bread?
23. בִּעֵר is an important and commonly used word meaning both to burn or kindle and destroy or wipe out. Can you connect these meanings?
24. The English word " before " which means " in front of one " also means " having already taken place ", something in the past. So in Hebrew לִפְנֵי literally " to the face of " means " before " and also something that has already happened. Similarly the word קֶדֶם " in front of one " means also " in the past ". With these as a clue can you work on the origin of the word תְּמוֹל yesterday? The ת is a prefix letter.
25. Why should the word מִגְרָשׁ mean pasture land?
26. Can you connect the concepts of עוֹלָם world, לְעוֹלָם forever and נֶעְלַם be hidden? They are all from the same root.
27. Why should the word הוֹדָה which means " give thanks " (the noun is תּוֹדָה) also mean " confess " (the noun is וִדּוּי confession)?

28. Why should מַדּוּעַ mean why? Can you break it up into two words?
29. Hebrew direction words are interesting. Above we asked for the origins of מִזְרָח and מַעֲרָב. Try these, they are somewhat more difficult. Always remember that the ancient Hebrews faced the rising sun when they gave names to directions.
Why should תֵּימָן which means south come from יָמִין the word for right hand. The Yemenite Jews were the ones who lived in the south, that is, south of Israel. The word Yemenite came from יָמִין.
30. Why should קֶדֶם mean east?
31. Why should טַעַם mean both taste and reason?
32. Can you connect the two meanings of מַקֶּבֶת – a hammer —(which may be the origin of מַכַּבִּי) and also an excavation or hole?
33. Why should כְּרִיכָה mean " the binding of a book " and כָּרִיךְ a sandwich? Why are burial shrouds called תַּכְרִיכִים?
34. עוֹד means " again ". Why should עֵד mean " witness?"
35. Why should חַף mean " innocent?" זַכַּאי mean innocent?
36. Can you connect בָּרֹד " spotted " and בָּרָד " hail "?
37. Why should מַדָּע mean " science "?
38. Can you connect צֹהַר a " window " with צָהֳרַיִם " noon "?
39. Can you connect מַטֶּה " a branch or rod " with מַטֶּה " a tribe "?
40. Why should חַס וְשָׁלוֹם mean " God forbid "? The word חָס means " may He (God) have pity ".
41. Can you connect קָרוֹב relative and קְרָב battle?

42. Can you connect בֶּצַע now meaning " profit, gain " with its first meaning בָּצַע cut?
43. Why should לִקְרַאת mean " toward "? It is not from the verb קָרָא call, that might come immediately to mind.
44. You're familiar with the expression חָלִילָה לִי. Can you connect it with its root חַלֵל desecrate?
45. טְלַאי is a patch. טָלוּא is spotted. Can you connect them?
46. How do we know that angels weren't supposed to be idle people?
47. A famous Jewish scholar was preparing for publication a radical book. An editorial assistant warned him, " Look out, Professor, for these views the religious will put you in חֵרֶם. The scholar, his eyes twinkling, answered, " I would like it much better if they would put me in a harem ". The English word " harem " comes from the Arabic-Hebrew root חֵרֶם ban. Can you connect them?
48. גִּמַטְרִיָּה is the Hebrew word to indicate the system by which letters stand for numbers, or are equivalent to numbers: the system by which א is 1, ב is 2, ג is 3. Gamma is the Greek way of pronouncing גימל. With this as a clue are you able to guess the origin of this common Hebrew word גִּמַטְרִיָּה? (This word sounds like " geometry " but has absolutely nothing to do at all with that word.)
49. Can you guess from what very simple word the verb בִּין, understand, has come?
50. Both הִזְעִיק and הִצְעִיק mean to call together, to assemble; they both come from the roots זָעַק and צָעַק which mean to cry out. With this as a clue, are you able to guess what is the origin of the word " קָהָל an assembly "?

51. Are you able to connect the two words רֶגֶל foot and רָגִיל customary. The imagery involved is somewhat similar to that of מִנְהָג custom and נָהַג lead.
52. Most of the Mohammedan religious terms come from words also commonly found in Hebrew. Can you guess what these words are? Remember that Hebrew שׁ is equivalent to Arabic שׂ.
    a) Koran—the Mohammedan Bible
    b) The names Moslem and Mohammedan (H = ח)
    c) The Caliph חָלִיף successor of Mohammed
    d) Allah
    e) The word Mosque written מִסְגָּד in Arabic
    f) Sultan
    g) Sura-Chapters or divisions of the Koran.
53. Why should the Hebrew word for a mariner's compass be מַצְפֵּן?
54. Can you connect the word חָרֵף to reproach, to say sharp things against (this gives the noun חֶרְפָּה shame) with the word חָרִיף which means a keen minded, highly intelligent person.
55. From what word does "אֻמָּה tribe, people", come?
56. The vowel name קָמַץ comes from the word קָמַץ to draw together. How does this vowel name קָמַץ prove conclusively that the men who created our present niqud or vowel system pronounced Hebrew with the Ashkenazic accent?
57. The word רֶגֶל also means a set time, as in the verse שָׁלֹשׁ רְגָלִים בַּשָּׁנָה. The Jews were commanded to visit Jerusalem three times a year. How then did the word רֶגֶל come to have its present meaning of holiday?
58. גָּרַע is to take away, remove. Why should גָּרוּעַ mean bad?

59. How did the word סַבָּא grandfather arise?
60. Why should כֹּה לֶחָי mean "many happy returns"?
61. The Hebrew word אַף which simply imitates the breath coming in and out of the nostrils very naturally came to mean nostril or nose. How does it come to have the meaning "anger"?
62. There are two general theories as to the origin of the words אֵל אֱלוֹהַּ GOD. One is that it comes from אֵל meaning "power, might" as in the famous phrase יֵשׁ לְאֵל יָדִי. GOD then is thought of as the Almighty, the All powerful, the Omnipotent One.
Another theory is that it comes from the root which gives rise to the word "אֶל to". This root means to stretch out, to reach after. GOD is thought of as one whom men strive to reach. Which explanation do you think is better?
63. Why should the first heavy rains in Israel that come in late October, or November be called יוֹרֶה?
64. Why does לְמַעַן mean "on account of"?
65. There are five Hebrew words meaning produce of the field. They all come from verbs of motion as if to indicate that the produce comes forth or is driven forth from the earth. One of these five words תְּבוּאָה is from the root "בּוֹא come". Can you guess the other four? This is the most difficult single question in the book.

Do you know the answers to these?

We don't know everything that went on in the minds of the ancient Hebrews. We don't know everything about their lives and their habits, and so, as a result, there are many words that we know very little about. These are mysteries that, for the present scholars are unable to solve. Perhaps you can suggest some good solutions.

1. There is the problem of the familiar words לֶחֶם – bread לָחַם – fought. One scholar has plausibly suggested that the obtaining of bread or rather food (לֶחֶם – means food in general) was always attended with struggle. The same scholar points out the following connections:
   טָרַף – to tear, seize as prey טֶרֶף – food
   צוּד – hunt צֵידָה – provisions
2. סִיר – pot סִיר – thorn
3. חֵלֶק – portion, חָלָק – smooth. The ח s are the same.
4. The word מָשַׁל means " to rule " as in the word " מוֹשֵׁל ruler " and מָשַׁל means " to be like ".
5. זִמֵּר is to sing or to play an instrument; זָמַר is to prune, to cut off twigs and branches.
6. חָמוּשׁ – battle array חָמֵשׁ – is five.
7. חֲנֹךְ – train חֲנִיכַיִם – gums.
8. שָׁחוֹר – black, and שַׁחַר – dawn.
9. נָשַׁק – kiss, נֶשֶׁק is weapon. Possibly נָשַׁק kiss is onomatopoeic.
10. כפר is the root of words which mean atone, village, lion, frost, deny, bowl and henna, which is a low tree with fragrant white flowers that grow in clusters.

Answers to easy questions.

1. It comes from the word שִׁבְעָה which means " seven ".
2. It comes from the root זָרַח which meant originally " rise ". The east was the place where the sun rose first. The word זָרַח now means " shine ".
3. The word comes from the root עָרַב which means " setting of the sun ". The west was the place where the sun set and then the evening would come.

4. It comes from " סָבַב go round and round ".
5. The thing came first; that is, first there was blood and then came the word אָדֹם for its characteristic color.
6. The same goes for grass and green; obviously it was grass that came first and then later came the word describing its color.
7. The root of this word תַּחַת means " under ". A subway is underground and a saucer is under the cup.
8. The word בּוֹא means come. תְּבוּאָה means what comes out of the field, namely the produce.
9. A Hebrew month means the beginning of the new moon. Look up in the sky the evening that a new Hebrew month is beginning, and you will see a thin, light, shiny crescent moon. We have another pair: " יָרֵחַ moon " gives rise to " יֶרַח month ".
10. The root שָׁלַח means " sent ".
11. Well, if you're scolding somebody you're trying very hard to prove something to him. As a matter of fact the English word, reprove, which means to prove over and over again also means to scold.
12. It is from " עוּף to fly ".
13. If the Bible commands us to do something, it must obviously be a good deed. So מִצְוָה commandment has come to mean good deed.
14. The root חיה means live; חַיָּה the word for animal in Hebrew really means living thing.
15. The root קָרוֹב means near. Relatives are persons who are near to you. In days of old the clan which included relatives all lived together in a large tribal unit.
16. A story tells you about deeds, otherwise it wouldn't be a story.
17. Spies in days of old went around on foot.

18. They both come from the root כָּנַס which means "gather or assemble".
19. ירד means "go down". The Jordan River drops sharply in the course of its wandering. As a matter of fact near the sea of Galilee the Jordan drops several hundred feet in the course of a few miles. There is a great hydro-electric plant there. The power of the down-running waters have been turned into electricity.
20. זָקָן is a "beard". A full beard was a sign of age. זָקֵן came to mean "one who had a beard", i.e. an old man.
21. They both come from the root חַם which means hot. The sun is hot and an angry person generates heat.
22. It comes from the root יָצָא "go out".
23. The root of this word is קָשֶׁה which means difficult. A קֻשְׁיָה really means a difficulty.
24. For one thing you can't speak very well without a tongue. This explains the word "language". In English the word tongue also means a language. A nationality is a group that possesses a common language. This is an essential characteristic of a national group.
25. Together means as one. "Particular" means that special, particular one.
26. It comes from the word "אֶלֶף a thousand".
27. הָלַךְ is to go or walk. תַּהֲלוּכָה is a group walking together, namely, a procession or parade.
28. זַמֵּר means to make music—instrumental or vocal. We use it more commonly now for singing. תִּזְמֹרֶת is a whole group playing instruments together, i.e. an orchestra.
29. חָשַׁב means to think, also to esteem. חָשׁוּב means "is esteemed".
30. חֲתוּנָּה obviously comes from the root חָתָן groom, although we now generally think of the bride as the

more important or as being the greater center of attention at the wedding. כְּלוּלוֹת is another word for wedding. It comes from the word כַּלָּה a bride. However, it is a poetic word, and used only rarely.

31. The root קָדַח means " to bore, to drill, and to make a hole ". This covers both a drill and a revolver.
32. " עוֹרֵב a raven " is a dark bird. " עֶרֶב evening" heralds the coming of darkness.
33. The root of לְבָנוֹן is לָבָן white. The Lebanon Mountains are perpetually covered with snow. I'll never forget how in Tiberias one hot summer day, I looked up and saw in the distance the snow covered Mt. Hermon, the highest of the Lebanon range.
34. A funeral לְוָיָה really is an escort, an accompanying of the dead to their last resting place.
35. When one runs rapidly, one burns up a great amount of physical energy. The body then becomes very hot—thus the word דָּלַק which really means to be burning.
36. שָׁעָה is an hour. The שָׁעוֹן watch tells what hour it is.
37. The root of מֶלְקָחַיִם tongs is לָקַח take.
38. The root of עַמּוּד column is עָמַד stand.
39. A יַלְקוּט, a receptacle, is a sort of collector.
40. כּוֹס a glass and כִּיס a pocket are both containers of a sort, quite different, but nevertheless having a certain similarity of function.
41. Mingling or mixing with the dominant cultural group would lead to assimilation of some sort.
42. מָנוֹחַ means one who is at rest.
43. The root צִוָּה means commanded. A person's will contains his commands about what should be done with his property.

44. Repentance is a return to the path of righteousness; an answer is a sort of return that one makes to a question.
45. Proof makes people see (רוֹאֶה) the truth of something; in a mirror you can see yourself.
46. The oars sort of whip or lash the water.
47. רַב means a great deal of something. רַב is one who has a great deal of wisdom or knowledge.
48. The root דָּבַק is to cling. Glue makes things stick. The דִּבוּק clings to one's body.
49. In a certain sense you camp or stay a while at a station.
50. When you're disappointed it is as though your hopes and expectations have turned out to be a lie or delusion.
51. He shows the דֶּרֶךְ, the road or path on which one should go.
52. They both indicate a stage of readiness to be eaten—one because of the warmth of the sun, and the other because of the heat of the fire that cooks.
53. דַּי means enough. כְּדַאי has the sense, " this is just about enough ", that is, the return or reward is sufficient.
54. It comes from פָּנָה to turn to. The sense is, I have time to turn toward or to give to this thing.
55. Plowing is really cutting into the earth. It is easy to go from there to cutting into metals or wood. חֲרֹשֶׁת means skillful working. בֵּית חֲרֹשֶׁת simply means the place where this skilled work, this cutting into metals or wood, was done.
56. מְתִים is a very ancient, hardly recognized word for men. מְתֵי מִסְפָּר simply means men of number, i.e. so few that they can easily be counted. There is another expression בִּמְתֵי מְעָט also having the meaning " consisting of a few men ".

57. נָגִיד really means the one who is in front, namely the one who leads, the ruler or the prince.
58. The bolt בָּרִיחַ passes through the iron ring, thus effectively locking the door.
59. When you speak of a couple or a pair it is more or less understood that they are bound or joined. This is particularly true of a pair of animals yoked together. צָמִיד bracelet is something which binds the hand.
60. A גַּן garden means an area enclosed and protected against casual marauders or animals. A מָגֵן shield protects or defends.
61. מְעַט in Hebrew means few or little. If you say, " I have כִּמְעַט - almost enough ", you are really saying that you have too few or too little.
62. This word goes way, way back to the days before there were coins. The merchants in those days simply weighed bits of gold or silver and used them for making payments. These later developed into a series of uniform coins. The monetary unit of the English, the pound, comes from the Latin word " penser " to weigh. The English word to " ponder " really means to " weigh ". The Spanish coin the peso is also from this Latin word penser—to weigh.
63. The central idea is making a distinction. When you separate yourself you are making yourself distinct from, apart from the community. Explaining something means making it distinct.
64. If something is בלה worn out, used up, it's rather obvious that you no longer have it, you are בְּלִי without it.
65. The root of הִכָּה strike, beat, is נכה. To reduce a price is to " knock off " part of it. This is similar to the English colloquial expression.

66. The basic thought here is " resting upon ". The saddle rests upon the horse. מַה אִיכְפַּת לִי really means how does this rest upon me, and figuratively, of course, how does this concern me.

67. To melt led naturally to to melt together, to weld (the only way of combining metals) to combine, to join. Metals were refined by melting or smelting so צָרֵף today has the two completely different meanings to refine and to join or combine.

68. The point of contact seems to be that in carving or sculpturing there is always a great deal of waste material, chips and valueless pieces. This was called פְּסֹלֶת. פָּסוּל invalid or worthless comes naturally from פְּסֹלֶת.

69. The missing word which fills out the thought is " part ". Five per cent means five parts taken out of a hundred.

70. This is an extremely interesting word and very, very few have worked out its extremely simple origin. תְּנַאי originally meant alternative which really means the second choice. It also developed the meaning of condition which again is the second part or second step. In the classic formulation of the תְּנַאי it is always the second part of an agreement.

A typical תְּנַאי

First part of agreement

I will marry your daughter

IF

Second part—the תְּנַאי — the שֵׁנִי

You give a marriage portion of 5000 dinarim.

Answers to questions of intermediate difficulty.

1. Both מַחְלֹקֶת quarrel and מַחְלָקָה a class imply clearly a division. מַחְלֹקֶת is a division of opinion. מַחְלָקָה is a division of the students into classes according to knowledge or ability.
2. קֵץ end is from the root קָצַץ cut. The end means that whatever process has been going on, has now been cut off.
3. The root of תַּעֲשִׂיָּה industry is עָשָׂה to do or make.
4. If someone is right in front of you he is very definitely present.
5. The end of a sentence פָּסוּק is simply the point at which the thought has come to an end.
6. The day before yesterday is like three days ago, counting today as one. It's a combination of שְׁלֹשָׁה and יוֹם.
7. A כְּבִישׁ road is made by stamping, pressing down gravel and earth together to make a hard surface.
8. A קַבְּצָן beggar makes his living by gathering or collecting alms. A קְבוּצָה group is a gathering of people.
9. נְעִילָה the last Yom Kippur prayer marks the closing of the services. נַעַל is a shoe, because it " encloses " the foot.
10. שָׁנָה, which means to repeat, also means to learn, because repetition is quite of the essence of the learning process.
11. הֲלָכָה law, means simply the path or way in which people go.
12. נֶהָג chauffeur, is the one who drives the automobile. מִנְהָג custom means the way in which people conduct themselves. The two ideas are closely related.
13. נַפָּח is a blacksmith because the blacksmith is continually

blowing on the bellows מַפּוּחַ to keep his fire at white heat. נַפָּחִיָּה is a blacksmith's shop.

14. When you're dumb it is as though your lips were bound.
15. בָּחוּר a young man obviously comes from the root, " בָּחַר choose ". The בָּחוּר was a young man chosen as fit for military service.
16. שָׂפָם mustache, is on the שָׂפָה lip.
17. The thought would seem to be to cut off for someone, to set aside for. There is an English use of the word " cut " that means " a share ".
18. שָׂעִיר goat, is so called because the goat gives the impression of hairiness. שְׂעוֹרָה barley also has a hair-like appearance.
19. בַּעַר stupid comes from בְּעִיר cattle; it means acting like cattle.
20. מִטָּה is something stretched out, or spread out on which a person slept.
21. קָצַר means cut. A short thing gives the impression of something that has been cut off.
22. A document testifies to or is a witness to the truth of some statement.
23. נֶשֶׁךְ interest comes from נָשַׁךְ bite. It means literally a piece of your money has been bitten off. From the point of view, though, of the lender the word for interest is רִבִּית because as far as he is concerned interest is an increase of his money.
24. Being comfortable and feeling pleasure means that you are at rest, at ease, not troubled by discomfort or sorrow.
25. טַבַּעַת a ring comes from טָבַע to sink down. Rings anciently were used to impress a signature on clay or wax. The signet rings of the king are familiar. מַטְבֵּעַ

coin is from the same root sink down. A coin was made by stamping a design on a round piece of metal.

26. Condition מַצָּב is the way things stand; a מַצֵּבָה monument stands permanently on one spot.
27. פָּשׁוּט simple really means something which is spread out before you. פָּשַׁט to undress, meant taking off and spreading out the one chief garment commonly worn, which was an outer cloak.
28. סַרְטָן crab. A crab scratches. שִׂרְטֵט to sketch means essentially to scratch out a design.
29. עֻגָּה a cake comes from the root עוג round. Cakes were generally round in shape.
30. The root of מַטָּרָה a target is נָטַר watch, regard. A target is something that is intently regarded.
31. הָמוֹן a crowd comes from הָמָה hum. The word is onomatopoeic and attempts to imitate the noise one hears when a crowd of people talk.
32. An עֵמֶק valley is really a deep עָמֹק place.
33. A man who is easily led by what anybody says to him is not very bright. " פֶּתִי a fool " means one whose mind is open in the sense of being easily influenced by anyone's words.
34. תִּינוֹק infant comes from the root יָנַק suckle. This is a very appropriate name. If the infant did not have the powerful instinct to suck it would starve.
35. Any sort of valuation requires as its first step an orderly arrangement and classification.
36. When you give warning it is as though you show someone the light, you enlighten him as to what you think is the right thing for him to do.
37. חֹל comes from חִלֵּל desecrate. חֹל הַמּוֹעֵד the inter-

mediate days of the holiday are the days which are not holy days.

38. חֲלַקְלַקּוֹת flattery comes from חָלָק smooth. Flattery is smooth words.
39. A סְפִינָה boat was a type of boat on which there must have been a cover, a deck, because סָפַן means to cover. From it we also get סִפּוּן a ceiling.
40. עַתָּה now, comes from עֵת time. It simply means at this time.
41. מַלְמֵד an ox-goad comes from לָמֵד teach. The goad teaches or tells the ox the direction.
42. The root of מַחֲמָאוֹת compliments is חֶמְאָה butter. Soft and smooth words butter up the listener, something like the word חֲלַקְלַקּוֹת flattery from the word חָלָק smooth.
43. The root of מְחוּגָה compass is חוג a circle.
44. When you grasp or take hold of something you are in effect taking possession of it.
45. The locust חָסִיל makes an end of, finishes off whatever produce there is in the fields.
46. The root of עֲטָרָה crown is עָטַר surround. The crown sort of surrounds or goes around the head.
47. The root of חַזָּן is חָזָה to see or look over. The חַזָּן in days of old was the overseer at the services. Since he frequently read the prayers, the word came to have the meaning of cantor.
48. It comes from דִּין judgement. אִישׁ מָדוֹן is a man always involved in law suits and legal strife.
49. Going beyond or exceeding the norm or the normal carries generally the idea of transgressing or sinning. Similarly, עֲבֵרָה sin comes from עָבַר.
50. When you carve something you are making a representation of it or in another sense an imitation of it.

Answers to hard questions

1. It comes from לְהַמְרוֹת to rebel against. The ה is a weak letter and, as so frequently occurs in Hebrew, fell out.
2. תַּפּוּחַ זָהָב " orange " is not so much a word as it is a complete description. It means literally " an apple of gold ". Had oranges been a native fruit in Palestine there undoubtedly would have been a single word for it.
3. Cattle in ancient days were chiefly used to draw the plow. This is equivalent to splitting the earth. The " בֹּקֶר morning" splits the darkness.
4. The root of " מִשְׁתֶּה banquet " is " שָׁתָה to drink ". It may be an abbreviation of מַאֲכָל וּמִשְׁתֶּה meaning eating and drinking.
5. נוּר flame or light.
6. A שׁוֹטֵר in Hebrew meant a scribe. He would write the שְׁטָרוֹת documents.
7. A " בֶּגֶד garment " was something that covered you. A בּוֹגֵד was a traitor who worked under cover. The same connection probably exists between מְעִיל a coat and מָעַל to transgress.
8. It comes from סָרַר meaning " to be stubborn, rebellious ".
9. " בְּקֹצֶר רוּחַ, impatiently ", literally means " with shortness of breath ". If a person is impatient, his breath comes short and rapidly.
10. The word זְרִיקָה means injection because its root זָרַק means to throw. An injection is essentially something thrown into the body.

11. The sentence הִיא הִתְחַתְּנָה literally means " she made herself into or became a חָתָן groom ". That's faintly amusing.
12. פָּלִיט is a refugee, one who has escaped from a land of danger or oppression. פֶּלֶט means the juice that has escaped or come out of the meat.
13. When someone stands behind something or backs it up we would say that he is the responsible agent. Appropriately enough the root of " אַחְרָיוּת responsibility " is אַחֲרֵי in back of or behind.
14. All three of these words, פְּשָׁרָה compromise, פּוֹשְׁרִים lukewarm and אֶפְשָׁר perhaps, have the general sense of " this or the other ". Lukewarm water means neither cold nor hot. פְּשָׁרָה means that neither side has the victory and אֶפְשָׁר means this may be so or that may be so.
15. The channel אָפִיק restrains the water.
16. The root of מְדִינָה is דִין law. A דַּיָּן is a judge. מְדִינָה seems originally to have been equivalent to the English word " jurisdiction ", the area over which a judge has jurisdiction.
17. It comes from the verb אֵרַע which means happened, occurred by chance.
18. קוּם means to rise. קוֹמָה means stature. It describes the way a man looks when he has risen.
19. The idea is that of exchanging pledges. הִתְעָרֵב is a reciprocal or mutual reflexive. I pledge to do something for you if you pledge to do something. The thought became that of striking a bargain, and that in turn developed into the meaning of making a wager.
20. The root of עִתּוֹן newspaper is עֵת time. The newspaper tells us about the events of our time.

21. When one makes the פַּתַּח vowel, one has to open the mouth wide.
22. The carob חָרוּב fruit was so called because it was shaped like a sword.
23. Fairly obviously, burning up something results in destroying or wiping it out.
24. The word תְּמוֹל, or אֶתְמוֹל yesterday, comes from the word מוּל before or opposite.
25. The root of מִגְרָשׁ is גֵּרֵשׁ drive. Pasture-land means the place or area to which the cattle are driven.
26. The connection may be that the end of the world is hidden. Or that the world itself is a mystery. לְעוֹלָם forever really means, as long as the world endures.
27. When one gives thanks to someone, it is a sort of confession of indebtedness, so it is not strange that הוֹדָה, which means to give thanks should also mean confess.
28. מַדּוּעַ why, is a quick way of saying, מַה יָּדוּעַ what is known.
29. The south תֵּימָן was at a person's right hand when he looked to the east.
30. קֶדֶם means what is before one. Hence, of course, the east, as one faced the rising sun.
31. טַעַם is both to taste and to perceive. One's reason is more or less one's perception of a matter.
32. A מַקֶּבֶת hammer is used to help dig a מַקֶּבֶת excavation.
33. All three unrelated things—book binding, sandwich, burial shrouds—are tied up with the idea of wrapping.
34. A witness simply tells again, repeats or reiterates what he saw or heard.
35. It comes from חָפַף to rub, to cleanse—used now mostly in the sense of shampooing hair. חַף means clean,

innocent in the same way that נָקִי which means " clean " also means " innocent ". זַכַּאי innocent is from זַךְ clean, pure.

36. There's a primitive sort of resemblance between hailstones and spots. Something that is spotted in a general sort of way would seem to have hail stones upon it.
37. It's a combination word—it comes from " מַה what " and the root יָדַע and really means " what is known ".
38. צֹהַר a window, is what lets in light. צָהֳרַיִם noon is the time of day when the sun is directly overhead and the light is most bright.
39. מַטֶּה is a branch: It has come to mean a rod or a stick. מַטֶּה tribe, is a branch of a nation. Incidentally שֵׁבֶט is also both staff and tribe.
40. The thought is, " May God have pity and not let this thing come to pass—and grant peace ".
41. They both go back to the concept of nearness: in קָרוֹב relative the nearness of the love and friendship of a family circle; in קְרָב battle the nearness of bloodshed, hatred and violence. In days of old almost all fighting was hand-to-hand combat, carried on at close quarters.
42. A colloquial expression in English for profit is a cut; בָּצַע means to " cut ". The idea seems to be the part that has been cut out for you.
43. קָרָה to meet or happen can also be spelled with an א. לִקְרַאת means simply " to meet ".
44. חִלֵּל is desecrate. חָלִילָה לִי means " It would be a desecration for me ". It has come to mean, " Far be it from me ".
45. Patches טְלָאִים gives the impression that the garment is טָלוּא spotted.
46. Well, for one thing the word מַלְאָךְ which means an

angel also means a messenger. Secondly the word מְלָאכָה work comes from מַלְאָךְ angel.

47. The harem is a forbidden area to all men—except the husband. All are forbidden to have anything to do with a person in " חֵרֶם—under ban ".

48. גְּמַטְרִיָּה really means the way of reckoning in which gamma גִּימֶל equals tria, three.

49. To understand בִּין is to discern, to get at the distinction between things. בֵּין is the common Hebrew word for between.

50. קְהִלָּה – assembly is an extended form of the word קוֹל voice or sound. It means a company assembled by means of the voice קוֹל – just as הִצְעִיק assemble comes from צָעַק cry out. This extension of ו to ה happens a number of times in Hebrew. Some other examples are מָהַל circumcise from מוּל, נְהָרָה light from נוּר.

51. רָגִיל tells of the way one customarily goes, the path on which one's foot רֶגֶל generally treads.

52. a) Koran—from קָרָא, that which is read.

    b) Moslem—from the root שָׁלוֹם which means one who is at peace with or rather one who has surrendered to Allah. Mohammed is from the root חָמַד desire and means " desirable ".

    c) Caliph—חָלִיף means one who is in place of another, a successor.

    d) Allah is equivalent to אֱלוֹהַּ.

    e) Mosque—מִסְגָּד is from סָגַד bow down.

    f) The root of Sultan is שָׁלַט rule.

    g) Sura is probably שׁוּרָה, row, orderly arrangement of verses.

53. The compass מַצְפֵּן points north צָפוֹן.

54. The mind of an intelligent man cuts through problems and difficulties. To reproach is to say sharp, cutting things about someone.
55. אֻמָּה tribe, people, is from אֵם mother.
56. The verb קָמַץ means to draw together. The Ashkenazim pronounce the קָמַץ with lips drawn together. That's how the vowel got its name. If the men who wrote our present niqud pronounced the קָמַץ as do the Sephardim, " ah ", they would certainly never have called it קָמַץ.
57. Because the times רְגָלִים at which they visited Jerusalem were the three holidays Pesach, Shavuot, Succot.
58. It really means that something has been taken away and is therefore missing. The thing, then, is defective.
59. It is a word created by the little children in Israel, following closely the word " abba ". The children were told to call this relative סָב but it was simply much easier for them to link both these older loving male adults with these two similar sounding names, אַבָּא and סַבָּא.
60. חַי is a very ancient, hardly remembered word for " a year ". The expression means " May it be this way the coming year ". When the angel promises Abraham his son he says כָּעֵת חַיָּה which means " At this time a year from now ".
61. Whenever you're really angry you breathe rapidly and furiously.
62. Most likely the Hebrew word for God comes from the word אֵל power.
63. You really have to be caught in one to appreciate the question. The word יָרָה means to shoot and these rains shoot down smashing open the ground.

64. It is a short way of saying לְמַעֲנֵה meaning in answer to, in response to, therefore, on account of. The word יַעַן on account of is also from עָנָה answer.

65. The other four are:

עָבוּר occurs in the phrase עֲבוּר הָאָרֶץ

יְבוּל from the word הוֹבִיל

גֶּרֶשׁ from the word גֵּרֵשׁ. The produce is represented as being driven forth from the earth.

צֶאֱצָאִים from יָצָא. You're more familiar with this in the sense of offspring. However it occurs twice in Isaiah in the sense of " produce of the earth ".

Chapter VI

The Hebrew Alphabet has four Twins and a Triplet

Exactly how many letters are there in the Hebrew alphabet? That would seem to be an easy question. Yet it is one of the trickiest questions that can be asked anyone.

One of my former teachers likes to tell of this adventure that befell him. He received a call from a friend, the rabbi of a local temple, asking him to take the beginners' Hebrew class for that day. My teacher, who was the chairman of the Temple's School Board, could not very well refuse. This, incidentally, was the first time the class was meeting. He did not know very much Hebrew but he began bravely enough by teaching the alphabet. A student raised his hand and asked, " How many letters are there in the Hebrew alphabet?"

The teacher was taken aback. He just did not know exactly how many there were. However, quick-wittedly, he went on to say, " Well, you see, children, it all depends on how you count them. Now look at the dots and dashes underneath the letters. They represent the vowels ". He went on to explain how the Hebrew vowels were written. By that time the students had forgotten entirely about the original question.

The Hebrew alphabet is not quite as simple as it looks.

It has twenty two consonant letters. Since however the שׂ and שׁ are really quite separate letters, this would make twenty-three.

The letters בּ, כּ and פּ are pronounced in two different ways among most groups of Jews, one a hard sound, and the other a soft one. This makes 26. The Ashkenazic Jews differentiate between תּ and ת (the real pronunciation of the ת is the soft English " th " as in the word " thin " (Bethlehem, Sabbath).

The Yemenite Jews still maintain the old distinction between a גּ with a dagesh in it, which is a soft " g " and a ג without a dagesh which is a throaty "r". They also distinguish between dageshed דּ which is " d " and un-dageshed ד, which is hard " th " as in the word " there ". We now have 29 consonant sounds.

However, all this is child's play compared to what is to come. The Hebrew alphabet has in it four twin letters and one triplet letter—that is four letters which represent the coalescence or coming together of two different sounds, and it has one representing the coalescence of three different sounds.

Let's take them up one by one.

AYIN IS A TWIN LETTER

The first is the letter ע.

Ancient Hebrew had two different ע sounds. These sounds were represented in our alphabet by the letter ע. One was a harsh, heavy ע. This is now lost, and no longer used in Hebrew. The other was a soft, mild ע. When the Greek Jews translated the Bible into Greek, they had to transliterate Hebrew names having the harsh ע in it. They used the Greek letter gamma for it—so you can just imagine how hard a sound it must have been.

This " ע gayin " has even come all the way down to English. The Hebrew place names עֲמֹרָה and עַזָּה both of which have this strong ע were transliterated into Greek as Gommora and Gaza. Didn't the odd forms of these place names in English ever puzzle you? In medieval times there was exported from Gaza a thin fabric which was naturally named " gauze " after the city of its origin.

Incidentally, Arabic a close sister language of Hebrew, still pronounces these two ע's differently, and what's more writes them differently.

This simple piece of knowledge about the existence of two different ע's, should clear up a great many puzzling different meanings that you will often find in a root that has an ע in it. Here are just a few examples: the words עֶרֶב evening and עָרֵב pleasant, look alike. In reality though, they are two different roots. The same goes for the following:

עֶלֶם – youth	עוֹלָם – world לְעוֹלָם forever
עָצֵב – sad	עֲצֵב – fashion, shape. From it we have the word עֲצַבִּים idols
עֹפֶר – a young deer	עָפָר – dust
עֹמֶר – sheaf	עמר – the root of הִתְעַמֵּר he dealt harshly with
צֶבַע – color	אֶצְבַּע – finger
עֹרֶף – back of neck	עָרַף – drip
עָלָה – go up	עָלָה – to be valued at, as in the well-known phrase בְּכַמָּה זֶה עוֹלֶה
עָצַם – strong	עָצַם – close
עור – be naked	עור – be awake

ח IS A TWIN LETTER

The second twin letter in the Hebrew alphabet is ח. Ancient Hebrew had a hard ח and a soft ח. Arabic still distinguishes between them, pronouncing and writing them differently. Again, we have a fairly large group of roots having ח in them that have meanings utterly unrelated and unconnectable. The simple solution to the whole problem is that we have here in each case two entirely different roots, tho both are written in Hebrew with the same letter ח. Originally different, they are now pronounced alike in Hebrew.

We have:

חַלֵל – pierce, which gave rise to

חָלָל – a mortally wounded person

חָלִיל – a flute

חַלוֹן – a window, which was originally only a hole in the wall.

AND

חַלֵל – desecrate, dishonor, which gives rise to the expression " to desecrate the Sabbath ", and so on.

ALSO

חָפַר – dig	חָפַר – be ashamed
פָּתַח – open	פִּתַּח – engrave
חָלָב – milk	חֵלֶב – fat
חִוֵּר – pale	חוֹר – hole
חָבַל – act corruptly	חֶבֶל – rope, bind
נַחֲלָה – inheritance	נַחַל – valley
חָצִיר – grass	חָצֵר – courtyard
חוּשׁ – hurry	חוּשׁ – feel
חֵרֶם – ban	חֵרֶם – fisherman's net

חֵרוּת – freedom	חָרוּת – engraved
מִתְחַטֵּא – purify oneself from the root חָטָא sin	מִתְחַטֵּא – importune, ask that favor and mercy be shown

SHIN IS A TWIN LETTER

The third twin letter is שׁ. Two different sounds are represented by the Hebrew letter שׁ. One is originally and really שׁ; the other is a " th " sound that coalesced into שׁ in Hebrew. Scholars write this second sound ת. Here, if you have studied a little Talmud you will be familiar with many Hebrew words that have שׁ in them but which in Aramaic are written with a ת.

Thus Hebrew שׁוֹר is תּוֹר in Aramaic. This word was borrowed by Latin; " taurus " is a bull. English has " toreador " and also (s)teer.

Hebrew פֵּשֶׁר explanation, interpretation. In Aramaic the word is פְּתַר explain, interpret. Hebrew borrowed the word back from the Aramaic. It is used a great deal when we speak of interpreting riddles or dreams.

The Hebrew word " שְׁנַיִם two "; שָׁנָה to repeat, to say twice, to learn, in the Aramaic has a ת; thus תנין is two. You are familiar with the word תַּנָּאִים the teachers of the Mishna. But Hebrew שִׁנָּה to change is שַׁנֵּה in Aramaic. The שׁ stays שׁ.

So, therefore, don't try to connect the following roots that have שׁ in them. In one word the שׁ is originally and anciently שׁ; in the other the שׁ was originally " th ".

שָׁמֵן – fat

שְׁמוֹנָה – eight. The שׁ here was originally a " th ". In Aramaic the word eight is תמני.

שָׁעַר – reckon. From this word we have שַׁעַר price

שַׁעַר – gate תַּרְעָא in Aramaic

נֶשֶׁר – eagle

נָשַׁר – drop or fall off. The שׁ here is a ת. Many have thought that the eagle נֶשֶׁר was so called because his hair fell out. This is not true. They're just different roots

שְׁאָר – remainder, what's left; the root of נִשְׁאַר was left, remained

שְׁאֵר – kin. The שׁ is ת

חָרַשׁ – plow

חָרַשׁ – be silent

עָשִׁיר – rich. The Aramaic form of this word עַתִּיר rich and עֲתֶרֶת wealth, abundance, are also used in Hebrew.

Generations of scholars have tried to find some connection between יָשֵׁן sleep and יָשָׁן old and have worked out the most ingenious solutions. Along came the discovery of the Ugaritic tablets at Ras Shamra and behold on these tablets the שׁ of " יָשָׁן old " is written with a ת proving that it is from an altogether different root and therefore cannot be connected with " יָשֵׁן sleep ". Also שֻׁלְחָן table is written a ת in Ugaritic showing that it has no connection with " שָׁלַח send ".

WOMAN IS NOT FROM MAN

The most utterly fantastic and incredible example of confusion over this שׁ which originally was a ת is found in the word אִשָּׁה. Strange and unbelievable as it seems the word אִשָּׁה has absolutely nothing whatsoever to do with the word אִישׁ.

In אִשָּׁה in the first place a נ has fallen out; the word is really אִנְשָׁה. The plural נָשִׁים gives some hint of that. The really important fact, though, is that the שׁ of אִשָּׁה is really a ת. In Aramaic the word for woman is either אִתָּא or more commonly אִתְּתָא. The root of אִשָּׁה, namely אָנַשׁ seems to mean " to be weak or to be delicate ".

The word אִישׁ is from another root which most scholars agree means " strong ".

All this is, of course quite contrary in some ways to modern medical opinion. Woman are considered in some ways to be the hardier sex.

ZAYIN IS A TWIN LETTER

The fourth twin letter is ז.

Hebrew has two ז s, one really and anciently a ז sound and the other a hard " th " sound which coalesced with the Hebrew ז. We have some common words in which these different ז's occur

זָרַע – sow
זְרוֹעַ – arm
אֹזֶן – ear
אזן – the root of " מֹאזְנַיִם – scales ". " אִזֵּן – weigh, test "
חָזָה – see, behold. From it חוֹזֶה a seer – מַחֲזֶה – a play.
חָזֶה – breast. From it חֲזִיָּה – vest, חָזִית – front of building, battle front.

TSADE IS THE TRIPLET LETTER

The triplet letter, the worst of the lot is צ. There are three entirely different צ's in Hebrew. Thus we have this trio:

צוּר – bind
צוּר – to treat as an enemy. There is the famous verse

" וְצַרְתִּי אֶת צוֹרְרֶיךָ. And I shall be an enemy to thy enemies ".

צוֹר – rock

All have different צ's. Again, a little knowledge of Talmud and the Aramaic found in it will be helpful in understanding it, because Aramaic still differentiates between these three צ's.

One of them originally a צ is just plain צ in Aramaic; the second appears as a ט and the third is an ע.

Thus צָרַח – shout is צָרַח in Aramaic
נָצַר – watch is נָטַר in Aramaic
אֶרֶץ – earth is אַרְעָא in Aramaic

There are two cities in Phoenecia צוֹר and צִידוֹן. In English צִידוֹן is Sidon, but צוֹר is Tyre. This is because the צ of צוֹר, Tyre, was really a form of ט and was still so pronounced when the Bible was translated into Greek.

Here, then, are some Hebrew roots having צ as one of their letters. Tho seeming to be the same these are in reality two or three separate roots, because the צ in some of them were originally quite different letters.

Similar to the צוֹר trio we have:

צָרַר – bind. We have the word צְרוֹר a bundle
צָרַר – to be an enemy
צָרַר – root of צֹר rock, a sharp edge

We also have these pairs:

נֵצֶר – a sprout, a shoot
נָצַר – watch; in Aramaic נָטַר

HEBREW HAS TWO ע'S

LOOK AT

עֶרֶב עָרֵב

PLEASANT **EVENING**

HEBREW HAS TWO ח'S

LOOK AT

חַלֵּל חַלֵּל

DESECRATE **PIERCE**

HEBREW HAS TWO ש'S

LOOK AT

שַׁעַר שׁעֵר

RECKON, ESTIMATE, GATE

HEBREW HAS THREE צ'S

LOOK AT

צוּר צוּר צוּר

BIND, BE AN ENEMY, ROCK

THE TWIN, TRIPLET LETTERS

Hebrew backborrowed it and נָטַר is now a common Hebrew word, which also means " to watch, or to keep ".

צְבִי – delight, ornament

צְבִי – gazelle

For centuries scholars, believing that there was only one root here, connected the two meanings by saying that the gazelle was a thing of beauty, a delight. But actually these two words are from different roots; the צ's are different.

חָצֵר – settlement, village   חָצֵר – courtyard

צוֹלֵעַ – lame   צֶלַע – rib

A strange and interesting thing happened with many of these Hebrew words which have צ as one of their letters. Aramaic also has these words, with the more original ט or ע. Hebrew often borrowed these words in their Aramaic form. As a result we now have doublets. The same word occurs twice in Hebrew, once in the Hebrew form with a צ and once in the form borrowed from Aramaic with a ט or an ע.

Here are some of these doublets.

A group צ more originally ט.

Hebrew נָצַר – watch   נָטַר – watch from Aramaic

קוּץ – loathe   קוּט – feel loathing

רוּץ – run   רַהַט – trough for running water, from the Aramaic

קַיִץ – summer   קַיְטָנָה – summer resort, is a modern Hebrew word, created from the Aramaic word קיט summer.

צלל – cover, gave rise to   צֵל – shadow

טלל – from Aramaic, gave rise to טַלִּית – a prayer shawl.

A group צ more originally ע.

Hebrew רָצַץ – crush　　רָעוּעַ – rickety, broken down from Aramaic

רָבַץ – lie down　　רָבַע – lie down

צָר – enemy　　עָר – enemy

Hebrew נָתַץ – uproot　　נָתַע – from Aramaic

צוּקָה – trouble-distress-pressure. The familiar Aramaic idiom is " דָא עָקָא – this is the trouble ".

Hebrew מָחַץ – strike: equivalent to מָחָא borrowed from Aramaic. In Aramaic it was originally מְחָע.

Now can you answer the question we started with?

How many letters are there in the Hebrew alphabet?

QUESTIONS ON CHAPTER SIX

1. How do the names Gaza and Gomorrah and the name Eli coming from עֵלִי show the existence of two " ayins " in Hebrew?
2. Give three examples of pairs of roots with " ayin " that are unconnectable because they come from entirely different letters " ayin ".
3. Why can you not connect the word מְחַלֵּל in the two different expressions, מְחַלֵּל שַׁבָּת and מְחַלֵּל בְּחָלִיל?
4. Give three other examples of pairs of roots with two different ח's.
5. How can the Latin " taurus ", bull, and the word " toreador " be related back to Hebrew שׁוֹר?
6. Give three examples of pairs of words with שׁ, that are unconnectable because in one case, the שׁ was really and originally a ת.
7. How was the ancient mystery of the connection between יָשֵׁן and יָשָׁן finally solved?
8. Give two examples of roots with different ז's.
9. How does צוּר illustrate the three-fold origin of the Hebrew letter צ?
10. Show how Hebrew back-borrowed three Aramaic words in which the צ was a ט, or an ע?
11. Why should the word " בְּרוֹשׁ – cypress " also be spelt בְּרוֹת?
12. Why should the word " זָלַף – drip, drop " also be spelt דָּלַף?

Can you match these columns?

1. עוֹלָם and עֶלֶם are unrelated.	1. Soft English " th " in Sabbath.
2. יָשֵׁן and יָשָׁן are unconnected.	2. Hebrew had a heavy ח and a light ח.
3. קַיְטָנָה is a summer resort.	3. Hebrew has three different צ's.
4. רָעוּעַ broken down, rickety.	4. רַצֵּץ crush.
5. The old Hebrew pronunciation of the ת without a dagesh.	5. They are from different ע's.
6. חָלָל means a) fatally wounded b) profaned, dishonored, a priest of illegitimate descent.	6. Hebrew has two different ש's.
7. Examples of ע gayin.	7. עֲתֶרֶת abundance.
8. צוּר is a) to bind b) be an enemy c) a rock.	8. They are from two different צ's.
9. rich עָשִׁיר	9. Gaza, Gomorrah.
10. צְבִי gazelle and צְבִי delight, ornament, are unrelated.	10. The צ of קַיִץ was originally a ט.

Chapter VII

The Verb and its Patterns

The Hebrew verb can be used in seven different patterns. Each pattern has its own distinctive meaning. These patterns are called binyanim.

The first of these is called Qal; an easier name is פָּעַל. There is not much to say about it. It tells of plain, simple, ordinary action. Its forms and conjugations are familiar to all. A typical example is שָׁמַר – watch.

שׁוֹמֵר – watch
שָׁמַר – watched
אֶשְׁמֹר – I will watch

Here are some important points to bear in mind about the Qal and the way its tenses are formed.

PRESENT TENSE OF QAL

The present tense of the Qal is useable as a noun.

Actually, the statement that this form of the verb can be used as a noun puts the matter in reverse order. The verb was originally a noun. Historically the פּוֹעֵל form was originally and anciently a noun. This noun form indicated the steady and continuous exercise or performance of an action. Thus שׁוֹמֵר was a person who watched regularly, כּוֹתֵב a person who was a writer. It was only much later, when Hebrew needed a present tense form, that they logically enough chose and used the פּוֹעֵל for this purpose. Grammarians call this form a participle. This is a misleading and confusing term and should be avoided. The form פּוֹעֵל at one time in any one sentence is used as either a verb or a noun. It is not both at one and the same time.

אֲנִי שׁוֹמֵר אֶת הַבַּיִת means: I watch the house. שׁוֹמֵר is a present tense verb. But look at the sentence הוּא שׁוֹמֵר, this means, "He is a watcher". In this sentence, the word שׁוֹמֵר is a noun. This use of the present tense as a noun is true for all verb patterns. You will now understand the strange peculiarity of the present tense Hebrew verb; i.e., that its endings for gender and number are the same as those for a noun.

PREFIX LETTERS OF THE FUTURE TENSE

The prefix letters of the future tense are by and large fragments of the personal pronouns; i.e., the

א of אֶשְׁמֹר
ת of תִּשְׁמֹר
י of יִשְׁמֹר
נ of נִשְׁמֹר
ת of תִּשְׁמְרוּ

The ת of תִּשְׁמֹר comes from אַתָּה. The form תִּשְׁמֹר is undoubtedly a telescoped or short way of saying אַתָּה שְׁמֹר. The א is from אֲנִי; the נ is from אֲנַחְנוּ; the י for the third person is probably the result of an interchange with the ו of הוּא. The ת of תִּשְׁמֹר "she will watch," is the ת feminine ending which in ancient times was found at the end of all feminine nouns and adjectives.

IMPERATIVE

The imperative is simply a fragment of the future tense. To derive the imperative, take the second person future and slice off the prefix.

Thus: " תִּשְׁמֹר you will watch " will give " שְׁמֹר watch."
" תִּשְׁמְרִי you will watch " will give " שִׁמְרִי watch."
" תִּשְׁמְרוּ you will watch," will give " שִׁמְרוּ watch."

This is properly so because, after all, when a person gives a command he is simply saying sharply, " You will do this." In Israel today the imperative is hardly used at all. It is felt that it is too curt and in its stead the future is used.

THE אֶפְעַל

Many verbs form their future with the form אֶפְעַל. This is because:

a) The second letter is א, ה, ח, ע or the third letter is ח, ע. These are guttural letters made in the throat and the פַּתַּח or the sound of " ah " is the easiest vowel for them to combine with. Remember what the doctor tells you to do when he wants to look down your throat. So the future of:

סָלַח – forgive	is	אֶסְלַח – I will forgive
שָׂמַח – rejoiced	is	אֶשְׂמַח – I will rejoice
שָׁאַל – asked	is	אֶשְׁאַל – I will ask
פָּחַד – feared	is	אֶפְחַד – I will fear
בָּחַר – chose	is	אֶבְחַר – I will choose

THE REAL FUNCTION OF THE אֶפְעַל

b) The real purpose of the אֶפְעַל future form, though, is to indicate that the verb belongs to the group which would correspond roughly to what is called in English grammar the intransitive. A good word to describe the Hebrew classification would be " stative ". These verbs tell not of action, but rather of a state of being. Thus the future of:

גָּדַל – grew, was big	is	אֶגְדַּל – I will be big
חָכָם – be wise	is	אֶחְכַּם – I will be wise
רָכַב – rode	is	אֶרְכַּב – I will ride
שָׁמֵן – be fat	is	אֶשְׁמַן – I will be fat
חָמֵץ – be sour, fermented	is	יֶחְמַץ – will be sour, fermented
כָּשֵׁר – be fit	is	יִכְשַׁר – will be fit
אָרֵךְ – be long	is	יֶאֱרַךְ – will be long
אָמֵץ – be strong	is	יֶאֱמַץ – will be strong
בָּשֵׁל – be ripe	is	יִבְשַׁל – will be ripe
גָּבַר – be strong	is	יִגְבַּר – will be mighty
דָּבֵק – cling	is	יִדְבַּק – will cling
זָקֵן – old	is	יִזְקַן – will be old
שָׁלֵם – complete	is	יִשְׁלַם – will be completed

VERBS THAT TAKE BOTH אֶפְעֹל AND אֶפְעַל

This point about the transitive verb taking the form אֶפְעֹל and the so called intransitive or stative verbs the form אֶפְעַל will become clear by looking at the following pairs:

From חרש – to plough, to be silent, we get
יַחֲרֹשׁ – he will plow and יֶחֱרַשׁ he will be silent.

The active or transitive verb takes אֶפְעֹל; the intransitive or stative takes אֶפְעַל and this holds true all the way through.

From קצר – harvest, be short
יִקְצֹר – will harvest יִקְצַר – will be short

From חפר – dig, be ashamed
יַחְפֹּר – will dig יֶחְפַּר – will be ashamed

From עצם – to shut, be strong
יַעֲצֹם – will shut יֶעֱצַם – will be strong

From ערב – guarantee, pleasant
יַעֲרֹב – will guarantee יֶעֱרַב – will be pleasant

From חרב – to destroy, be dry
יַחֲרֹב – will destroy יֶחֱרַב – will be dry

THE פָּעֵל VERBS

Some verbs are vowelized with a צֵירֶה i.e. the פָּעֵל. These almost always carry an intransitive meaning, that is, they do not take an object.

Here are a few of these verbs:

כָּבֵד יָרֵא בָּשֵׁל חָפֵץ רָעֵב
שָׁמֵן צָמֵא חָסֵר יָשֵׁן

In the present tense these verbs are not at all difficult. The forms are:

רָעֵב רְעֵבָה רְעֵבִים רְעֵבוֹת
יָרֵא יְרֵאָה יְרֵאִים יְרֵאוֹת

In the past tense most of these verbs have become like the dominant פָּעַל group and we say:

שָׁמַנְתִּי שָׁמַנְתָּ שָׁמַנְתְּ שָׁמַן etc.

However, some still retain their originally correct פָּעֵל form in the third person. The past tense of חָפֵץ desire is חָפֵץ desired.

The most troublesome word is יָשֵׁן, the past tense of which is יָשֵׁן. I recall an amusing incident. A friend slept over in my study. After he left, my daughter, Tamar, Hebrew speaking, and then four years old pointed to the couch on which he had slept and said:

הַדּוֹד יָשַׁן פֹּה.

I corrected her a little doubtfully:

הַדּוֹד יָשֵׁן פֹּה

She looked at me unbelievingly. She looked carefully at the empty couch. She said finally and decisively הַדּוֹד ליאון? לֹא יָשֵׁן פֹּה הוּא יָשַׁן פֹּה and walked out puzzled and annoyed.

Who knows? Some day it may very well officially be יָשַׁן.

Since these verbs are mostly intransitive, it naturally follows that the future will take the form אֶפְעַל. Above we listed a number of verbs in the אֶפְעַל.

These are some others; all from פָּעֵל.

The future of חָסֵר is יֶחְסַר

כָּבֵד is יִכְבַּד

If the פָּעֵל verb ends in an א; such as in the verbs מָלֵא and שָׂנֵא the past tense keeps the צֵירֶה almost all the way through.

שָׂנֵאתִי מָלֵאתִי צָמֵאתִי יָרֵאתִי

To make things really interesting there is still a third form of the verb—פָּעֹל. There is only one common verb יָכֹל in the פָּעֹל. The present tense is:

יָכֹל יְכֹלָה יְכֹלִים יְכֹלוֹת.

The past tense is יָכֹלְתִּי etc. The future is תּוּכַל אוּכַל etc.

WEAK LETTER VERBS IN פָּעַל

As was pointed out above, in the chapter on the Hebrew root, those roots which have weak letters form their tenses differently because the weak letter drops out.

In verbs with last letter ה—for example the verb קָנָה—the present tense singular is קוֹנֶה, קוֹנָה. The plural, however, is קוֹנִים, קוֹנוֹת—the ה has fallen out. In the past tense, some forms lose the ה as in קָנוּ they bought. Everywhere else the old original י is retained. In the future, several forms drop the ה such as in

יִקְנוּ תִּקְנוּ תִּקְנִי.

In verbs middle ו, the ו, which originally had the sound of " w ", usually drops out, thus:

He rises הוּא קָם
He rose קָם
I will rise אָקוּם

Scholars believe that קַמְתִּי was at one time quite regular just like שָׁמַר or כָּתַב and was originally pronounced קָוַמְתִּי " kawamtee " and that it was only in the course of time that the weak " w " dropped out, as it drops out of many English words like sword, answer, etc.

Verbs with middle י are conjugated somewhat in the same way as verbs middle ו. The past tense of שִׁיר is שַׁרְתִּי; the future is אָשִׁיר I will sing. Verbs with first letter י have the י absorbed in the future tense and a long " ay " vowel emerges. Thus the future of

יָשַׁב is אֵשֵׁב
יָרַד is אֵרֵד
יָצָא is אֵצֵא
יָדַע is אֵדַע - the last letter ע

requires a פַּתַּח.

Remember how the gutturals almost always take the " ah " vowel.

Sometimes the first letter י is actually written in the future tense but it remains quite silent. Thus the future of

יָרֵא fear is אִירָא
יָשֵׁן sleep is אִישַׁן

THE STRANGE VERB הָלַךְ

הלך is a sort of verbal Siamese twin; it has two forms namely הלך and ילך. In the present tense the forms used come from הלך; the future though is אֵלֵךְ, תֵּלֵךְ and the infinitive לָלֶכֶת—all from a root ילך. There is אֶהֱלֹךְ I will go and לַהֲלֹךְ to go. They are very rare forms. The הִפְעִיל is הוֹלִיךְ to cause to go, lead; that also comes from ילך. The פִּעֵל is הִלֵּךְ and the הִתְפַּעֵל is הִתְהַלֵּךְ; both, of course, from הָלַךְ.

NIFAL

The passive of the Qal is called the נִפְעַל after the form that the verb takes. Ignorance of grammar these days is so universal that we ought to be sure that we are clear about two things.

1. What is meant by the passive form of the verb?
2. Why do we have it?

Usually when we describe a thing or tell of some experience we know the doer of the action we are describing. Then, normally enough, our sentence will begin with the subject, i.e. the actor, the one who did the action. It will continue with a predicate, and will end with the object, who receives the action. For example:

The man — — — subject
cut — — — predicate
the tree — — — object

However, it will frequently happen that we will want to describe the action that has taken place but *we do not know who did the action.* It is then that we make use of the passive form of the verb. For example:

The man *was murdered.*
The child *was kidnapped.*
The house *was burned.*

You can imagine how George Washington's father came into the house and told his son, " George, a cherry tree was cut down! " He had to use the passive or the NIFAL form of the verb because at the time he did not know who had cut down the tree.

English forms the passive, or the past tense of the passive by putting " was " before the verb; Hebrew by prefixing a נ to the root.

The formation of the nifal pattern really is simplicity itself. You set the נ in front of the root and vowelize it according to the pattern name נִפְעַל. Here are a number of examples of the commonest verbs in the nifal.

was watched	נִשְׁמַר	entered	נִכְנַס
was written	נִכְתַּב	was sworn, swore	נִשְׁבַּע
was finished	נִגְמַר	was remembered	נִזְכַּר
was closed	נִסְגַּר	was broken	נִשְׁבַּר
was opened	נִפְתַּח	was torn	נִקְרַע
was sent	נִשְׁלַח	was buried	נִקְבַּר
was asked	נִשְׁאַל	was cut	נִגְזַר
was heard	נִשְׁמַע	was robbed	נִגְזַל
was studied	נִלְמַד	was tested	נִבְחַן
was stolen	נִגְנַב	was chosen	נִבְחַר
was pardoned	נִסְלַח	was given over	נִמְסַר
was taken	נִלְקַח	was forgotten	נִשְׁכַּח

הַיֶּלֶד כּוֹרֵת
אֶת הָעֵץ

THE BOY CUTS THE TREE

הָעֵץ נִכְרַת.

THE TREE WAS CUT DOWN

נִפְעַל

was sold	נִמְכַּר	was counted	נִסְפַּר
was planted	נִזְרַע	was caused	נִגְרַם
	was burned	נִשְׂרַף	

FIRST LETTER GUTTURALS

was said	נֶאֱמַר	was plowed	נֶחֱרַשׁ
was loved	נֶאֱהַב	was divided	נֶחֱלַק
was arranged	נֶעֱרַךְ	was thought	נֶחֱשַׁב
was killed	נֶהֱרַג	was left	נֶעֱזַב
was gathered	נֶאֱסַף	was helped	נֶעֱזַר
was milked	נֶחְלַב	was done	נַעֲשָׂה
was seized	נֶחְטַף	was answered	נַעֲנָה

In this group the last letter of the root is א—the last vowel is ָ so:

was found	נִמְצָא	was called	נִקְרָא
was created	נִבְרָא	was cured	נִרְפָּא

The same goes for the verbs with last letter ה: the last vowel is ָ .

was built	נִבְנָה	was seen	נִרְאָה
was bought	נִקְנָה	was counted	נִמְנָה

FIRST LETTER " YOD "   FIRST LETTER " NUN "

was known	נוֹדַע	was lifted	נִשָּׂא
was born	נוֹלַד	was damaged	נִזַּק
was added	נוֹסַף	was planted	נִטַּע
was founded	נוֹסַד	was given	נִתַּן

Once the form was created it was used even when we know the actor, just to vary the style.

" The tree was cut by the boy ". A sentence with a passive verb is good English, but normally once we know the cutter we should begin with " the boy ". Arabic calls the NIFAL the BINYAN of the UNKNOWN and never allows it to be used unless the actor is really unknown. Hebrew follows the same practice as English and does allow the use of the nifal for the sake of variation in style even when the actor is known. The sentence is then completed with the added phrase עַל יְדֵי. Thus הַבַּיִת נִשְׁמַר עַל יְדֵי הַיֶּלֶד.

ORIGINAL MEANING OF THE NIFAL

Now after you've taken all the trouble to learn the NIFAL, I have to tell you that the original use of the nifal in ancient days was not as the passive of the QAL at all. The original meaning of the נִפְעַל was as the reflexive of the QAL. Many words in the nifal still retain and are still used in a reflexive sense; witness the following not inconsiderable group all taken from the biblical Hebrew.

הִשָּׁמֵר – A frequently used word, means " watch yourself " and not " be watched "

נֶחְבָּא – means " he hid himself "

נִמְכַּר – sold himself

נִמְלַט – saved himself

נִסְמַךְ – supported himself

נִקַּם – revenged himself

נִחַם – consoled himself

נֶהְפַּךְ – turned himself

הִנָּפֵשׁ – to refresh oneself

נֶחְנַק – choked himself

נִלְחַץ – pressed, squeezed himself
נִכְנַע – humbled himself
נִפְתַּל – twisted himself i.e. wrestled
נִצְמַד – attached himself
נֶעֱגַן – shut himself up
נִשְׁעַן – support himself
נִלְוָה – joined, attached himself
אִכַּף – I shall bow myself (from כָּפַף)

If the נִפְעַל in ancient days was a reflexive of the פָּעַל you may wonder which pattern was then used for passive action. Even in those days they had to have some way of saying " was killed ", " was injured ", " was stolen ", etc.

The answer is that there had been a special verb pattern which was the passive of the פָּעַל. This pattern died out a long time ago. The numerous remnants of it that exist in the Bible have been assigned by the Masoretes to the פֻּעַל and the הָפְעַל patterns.

Thus לֻקַּח now generally regarded as being in the בִּנְיָן פֻּעַל, the passive of פִּעֵל, has really nothing whatsoever to do with the meaning of the פִּעֵל or פֻּעַל. It is a remnant of the passive of the פָּעַל and simply means " was taken. " יֻתַּן generally assigned to the hofal pattern has no connection whatsoever in meaning with הָפְעַל or הִפְעִיל. It is a remnant of the future tense of the passive of the פָּעַל and simply means " will be given ".

However, the present tense of this old, old, passive of the פָּעַל still exists and still flourishes and is frequently used in modern Hebrew. It is the form of the verb known as פָּעוּל.

You ought to know that פָּעוּל just simply does not belong within the framework of our present seven בִּנְיָן structure. It is the solitary survival of a lost eighth בִּנְיָן.

It follows then that we have in modern Hebrew two present tenses of the passive of the פָּעַל. The first is the old, old one—which comes from the long extinct passive. The other is the current one, the commonly used present tense of the נִפְעַל, examples of which are everywhere נִכְתָּב, נִשְׁמָר etc.

Now grammarians in general try to find some distinctions in meaning between these two present tense passives, between the פָּעוּל and נִפְעָל. Really there isn't any at all.

פָּעוּל is most frequently used as an adjective. We say חַלּוֹן שָׁבוּר and we translate it " a broken window ". Here the פָּעוּל is an adjective and not a verb. When the פָּעוּל is used as a verb it has the same meaning as the present tense of the other, the now regularly used passive, the נִפְעָל. There is no difference between these two sentences.

הַבַּיִת שָׁמוּר עַל יְדֵי הַיֶּלֶד
הַבַּיִת נִשְׁמָר עַל יְדֵי הַיֶּלֶד

They both mean the " The house is being watched by the child ". Grammarians who insist on the difference between the פָּעוּל and נִפְעָל usually take a פָּעוּל which is being used as an adjective and compare it with a נִפְעָל which is being used as a verb and announce rather solemnly that the two are not alike. This procedure is rather silly. We don't need grammarians to tell us that an adjective is, of course, different from a verb.

When the פָּעוּל is used as an adjective it is an adjective and that's all there is to it. It is not to be compared to and should not be compared to a verb. When a פָּעוּל is used as a verb, it has the same sense as the present tense of the נִפְעָל.

Incidentally, the נִפְעָל can also be used as an adjective.

That usage is not too common—but nevertheless, we have a fair number of examples:

נֶחְמָד – lovely, desirable	נֶאֱמָן – faithful
נִכְבָּד – honored	נִפְרָד – separate
נֶהְדָּר – magnificent	נִפְרָץ – frequent
נִפְלָא – wonderful	נִרְדָּף – persecuted
נִתְעָב – abominable	נִפְתָּל – twisted
נוֹרָא – fearful	נִסְתָּר – hidden
נִבְזֶה – despised	נִלְבָּב – hearty
נִלְעָג – ridiculous	נִשְׂגָּב – exalted
נִרְגָּשׁ – excited	נָפוֹץ – wide-spread
נָכוֹן – correct	נַעֲנֶה – humble

נִקְלֶה – despised

When the forms פָּעוּל and נִפְעָל are used as adjectives their meanings are quite the same.

חָמוּד־נֶחְמָד – lovely, desireable	אָהוּב־נֶאֱהָב – beloved
כָּבוּד־נִכְבָּד – honored	אָזוּר־נֶאֱזָר – girded
הָדוּר־נֶהְדָּר – magnificent	בָּזוּי־נִבְזֶה – despised

יָדוּעַ־נוֹדָע – known

The only thing we can say about the פָּעוּל and נִפְעָל forms by way of differentiating them is that the פָּעוּל gets used more frequently as an adjective and the נִפְעָל is used more frequently as a verb. But when the same roots are used to indicate the same part of speech, that is, when, both אָמוּר and נֶאֱמָר are used as verbs or חָמוּד and נֶחְמָד are used as adjectives, there just isn't any difference. Individual words may have taken on slightly different shades of meaning.

PIEL

The most difficult of the verb patterns is the פִּעֵל. All other verbs have one definite and specific function.

פָּעַל – simple action

נִפְעַל – passive of פָּעַל.

Later on we will study the hifil, which represents causative action, and the hitpael which tells of reflexive action.

The פִּעֵל is different from these other patterns in that it has two entirely different functions.

It has the fundamental idea of busying oneself eagerly with the action indicated by the root. This intensification of the idea of the root, tho, appears in two rather different ways. Thus the piel has these two different meanings.

THE FIRST WAY IN WHICH IT APPEARS

The action is strengthened or repeated. Here are several examples:

צָחַק	– laugh	צִחֵק	– jest, make sport, laugh repeatedly
פָּתַח	– open	פִּתַּח	– to loose, to open where the opening requires great strength as when opening the gates of a city
שָׁבַר	– break	שִׁבֵּר	– shatter
סָפַר	– count	סִפֵּר	– recount, tell
בָּכָה	– cry	בִּכָּה	– cry and cry, lament
פָּחַד	– fear	פִּחֵד	– fear greatly, to be in great dread
כָּתַב	– write	כִּתֵּב	– write busily
אָהַב	– love	מְאַהֵב	– love many
רָצַח	– murder	רִצַּח	– murder repeatedly
עָבַד	– work	עִבֵּד	– work over, work out, elaborate
הָלַךְ	– go	הִלֵּךְ	– walk
רָמָה	– throw	רִמָּה	– deceive, cheat, to throw someone down in a figurative sense

Often there is no corresponding פָּעַל, the verb existing only in the intensive פִּעֵל. In all likelihood the ancient Hebrews regarded these actions as requiring strength or skill.

זִמֵּר – sang
נִגֵּן – play an instrument
קִנֵּא – jealous
סִיֵּם – graduated
צִוָּה – commanded
קִוָּה – hoped
נִחֵם – comforted
מִהֵר – hurried

THE SECOND WAY IN WHICH IT APPEARS

The eager pursuit of an action may also consist of urging or causing others to do the same: so

לָמַד – study
לִמֵּד – teach

It may be expressed by such phrases as to permit, to declare, to hold, to help,

יָלַד – give birth
יִלֵּד – assist at child birth
צָדַק – be innocent, upright
צִדֵּק – declare innocent

The simplest way to regard this function of the פִּעֵל is to sum it up under the one word CAUSATIVE. It is this function of the piel that is the most vigorous and active now. Practically all new words created in the פִּעֵל in the generations of the revival of Hebrew are used in the פִּעֵל causative sense.

Here then are several examples of causative piel verbs:

דִּבֵּר – he made words, spoke from דָּבָר
שִׂמַּח – he made happy from שָׂמֵחַ
אִחֵד – he made one (unified) from אֶחָד
חִזֵּק – he made strong (strengthened) from חָזָק
יִשֵּׁר – he made straight from יָשָׁר
מִעֵט – he diminished from מְעַט

הַתַּלְמִיד לוֹמֵד

THE PUPIL STUDIES

הַמּוֹרֶה מְלַמֵּד

THE TEACHER TEACHES

פִּעֵל

CAUSATIVE

הַיֶּלֶד פּוֹתֵחַ אֶת הַדֶּלֶת

THE BOY OPENS THE DOOR

הָאֲנָשִׁים פִּתְּחוּ אֶת הַשַּׁעַר

THE MEN OPENED THE GATE

פִּעֵל

INTENSIVE

לִמֵּד	– he made learn (taught)	from	לָמַד
חִדֵּשׁ	– he made new	from	חָדָשׁ
חִלֵּק	– he divided	from	חֵלֶק
יִבֵּשׁ	– he made dry	from	יָבֵשׁ
יִפָּה	– he made beautiful	from	יָפֶה
חִיָּה	– he made live	from	חָיָה
שִׁנָּה	– he made different i.e. changed	from	שׁוֹנֶה
חִמֵּם	– he made warm (heated)	from	חָמֵם
יִסֵּד	– he founded	from	יְסוֹד
גִּדֵּל	– he raised	from	גָּדַל
רִחֵק	– he caused to be distant	from	רָחוֹק
נִקָּה	– he made clean (cleansed)	from	נָקִי
קִלֵּל	– he made light of, cursed	from	קְלָלָה
פִּרְנֵס	– he made a living	from	פַּרְנָסָה
אִפְשֵׁר	– he made possible	from	אֶפְשָׁר
טִהֵר	– he declared it to be clean	from	טָהוֹר
מִלֵּא	– he made full	from	מָלֵא
חִלֵּל	– he made music on a flute	from	חָלִיל
כִּבֵּד	– he made honorable, honored	from	כָּבוֹד
בִּלָּה	– he wore out, spent	from	בָּלָה
כִּלָּה	– he brought to an end, completed	from	כָּלָה

Occasionally a פִּעֵל verb will have what is called a privitative sense, that means depriving or taking away whatever it is that the root means. Often what is being removed or taken away is some unpleasant or objectionable thing. The fundamental sense of the פִּעֵל i.e. to busy oneself eagerly with the object indicated by the root would most naturally in this case mean busying oneself eagerly with removing this thing.

דִּשֵּׁן – remove ashes
זִנֵּב – trim or strike at the back from זָנָב – tail

תִּלֵּעַ – remove worms from תּוֹלָע – worm
שֵׁרֵשׁ – remove, uproot
חִטֵּא – cleanse, remove sin, impurity. The word is now used in the sense of disinfect.
סִקֵּל – remove stones from a field. This word also means to pelt with stones. The word " stone " has the same double meaning in English.

There is a very special and very different form of the פִּעֵל from verbs middle ו and middle י, as well as for the verbs that are כְּפוּלִים. This form could be called פּוֹלֵל. They all have a causative sense.

Thus from:

קוּם	rise we get	קוֹמֵם	cause to rise, raise up
רוּם	be high we get	רוֹמֵם	raise up
עוּר	be awake we get	עוֹרֵר	wake up, rouse
מוּת	die we get	מוֹתֵת	cause death, kill
עוֹד	more we get	עוֹדֵד	encourage, namely to urge someone to go on, to continue
שִׁיר	sing we get	מְשׁוֹרֵר	singer in a choir, a poet

VERBS IN THE PILPEL

A special and highly interesting variety of the piel pattern is the quadriliteral or four lettered verb. They are generally called פִּלְפֵּל and are conjugated quite similarly to piel verbs. There are large numbers of these quadriliterals and they arise in these ways.

THE FIRST WAY:

You remember from the discussion of the root in the last chapter that there are three classes of verbs which frequently drop a letter.

1. Verbs having a ה, ו, י in them.

2. Verbs the first letter of which is נ.

3. כְּפוּלִים verbs in which the last two letters are the same.

These three groups frequently form quadriliteral (4 letter) verbs by dropping one letter and then doubling what is left over.

Thus the following verbs middle ו become פִּלְפֵּל verbs.

עוּף – fly become עִפְעֵף – flutter
נוּעַ – move becomes נִעֲנַע – shake, move repeatedly
נוּם – sleep becomes נִמְנֵם – sleep
נוּף – sprinkle becomes נִפְנֵף – wave
זוֹל – cheap becomes זִלְזֵל – to esteem lightly, to regard with contempt
זוּעַ – move becomes זִעֲזַע – stir
כּוּל – contain becomes כִּלְכֵּל – support

These verbs with last letter ה form פִּלְפֵּל verbs.

תָּעָה – err becomes תִּעְתַּע – make err, to be perverse
עָלֶה – a leaf becomes עִלְעֵל – turn pages
שָׂגָה – grow, flourish becomes שִׂגְשֵׂג – grow, flourish
רָפֶה – weak becomes רִפְרֵף – shake, flutter
תִּוָּה – made marks becomes תִּוְתֵּו – scribble

The following verbs first letter נ become פִּלְפֵּל verbs.

נָטַף – drop becomes טִפְטֵף – drip
נָבַע – gush out, flow becomes בִּעְבַּע – bubble, boil

The following כְּפוּלִים give rise to פִּלְפֵּל verbs. This is the largest group:

גָּלַל – roll becomes גִּלְגֵּל – roll
בָּלַל – mix becomes בִּלְבֵּל – confused

בָּזַז – despoil	becomes	בִּזְבֵּז – to hold in contempt, to waste
צָלַל – ring, sound	becomes	צִלְצֵל – ring
דָּלַל – to swing loosely, be poor	becomes	דִּלְדֵּל – loosen, weaken
נָדַד – wander	becomes	נִדְנֵד – to move back and forth
דָּקַק – be thin, be fine	becomes	דִּקְדֵּק – to be exacting
מִשֵּׁשׁ – feel	becomes	מִשְׁמֵשׁ – feel
מִלֵּל – speak	becomes	מִלְמֵל – speak, mutter
קָלַל – to be light	becomes	קִלְקֵל – destroy, despise
צָחַח – to be dazzling white	becomes	צִחְצֵח – polish

THE SECOND WAY:

Perfectly sound and respectable three letter roots (by that I mean where all three letters are strong and the verbs mostly belong to the category called שְׁלֵמִים whole or complete verbs) often drop one letter and then double what's left over.

סָפֵק – doubt	becomes	פִּקְפֵּק – doubt
לָעַג – mock	becomes	לִגְלֵג – mock, scorn
רַעַשׁ – noise	becomes	רִשְׁרֵשׁ – rustle
חִפֵּשׂ – search	becomes	פִּשְׁפֵּשׁ – search
אָטַם – stop up	becomes	טִמְטֵם – stop up
לַהַב – flame	becomes	הִבְהֵב – flicker

Another thing also happens. Perfectly sound and respectable roots will sometimes double the last letter creating what I guess would be called a פִּעְלֵל verb form.

Thus we have:

רען becoming רַעֲנֵן fresh. We have הִתְרַעְנֵן refreshing one's self.

ערב becoming עִרְבֵּב confuse and from it comes the mouth filling and picturesque word עִרְבּוּבְיָה confusion.

אמל becoming אֻמְלָל unfortunate.

Many foreign words that Hebrew borrowed contained four letters and almost always take on the פִּעְלֵל forms.

Some are:

אִרְגֵּן – organize	קִטְרֵג – prosecute (in court of law)
דִּקְלֵם – declaim	אִקְלֵם – acclimate
אִכְלֵס – populate	פִּרְסֵם – publicise
פִּרְנֵס – support	טִלְפֵּן – telephone
סִנְגֵּר – defend (in court of law)	

Onomatopoeic words imitating natural sounds are frequently formed in the פִּלְפֵּל pattern. These will be discussed below in the chapter on onomatopoeic words.

THE פֻּעַל AND THE מְפֻעָל

The פִּעֵל has a passive form called פֻּעַל. Somehow or other it is not used very much. There are only a few verbs that are used in all tenses. You might ask what does get used as the passive of the פִּעֵל, and the answer is that the reflexive pattern, the הִתְפַּעֵל or נִתְפַּעֵל, often takes the place of the פֻּעַל.

However, the present tense of the פֻּעַל, which has the form מְפֻעָל, has prospered and flourished. There are enormous number of verbs that occur in the מְפֻעָל form. The reason for the great popularity of the מְפֻעָל is that it can be used in three different ways. It is this flexibility that makes it so useful.

It is first of all a verb, the present tense of the passive of the פִּעֵל.

He is honoured by people הוּא מְכֻבָּד עַל הַבְּרִיּוֹת.

Secondly: the present tense of all Hebrew verbs is usable as a noun—so you have מְפֻעָל which functions usually as a noun.

מְשֻׁלָּח – an emissary
מְלֻמָּד – a learned man
מְחֻתָּן – a person related by marriage

Thirdly: Just as the פָּעוּל which is the present tense of the old lost passive of the פָּעַל is frequently used as an adjective so does the מְפֻעָל the present tense of the passive of the פִּעֵל very often serve as an adjective. We have מְבֻגָּר mature.

מְהֻדָּר – magnificent
מְנֻוָּל – villainous

Any word in מְפֻעָל can be used then either as a verb, noun, or adjective. מְלֻמָּד can mean " is taught " (a verb), " a learned person " (a noun), and " learned " (an adjective). A word can have these different meanings only at different times, that is, in different sentences. Don't try to conceive of a word as being at one and the same time a verb and a noun—that way lies madness.

Here are a few examples of the מְפֻעָל.

These are all entirely regular:

מְבֻשָּׁל – cooked, ripe
מְחֻדָּשׁ – renewed
מְחֻיָּב – obliged
מְשֻׁגָּע – mad
מְקֻפָּח – underprivileged

מְהֻלָּל – praised, praiseworthy
מְנֻקָּד – vowelized
מְנֻסֶּה – experienced
מְדֻמֶּה – imagined
מְכֻלֶּה – destroyed

If the second letter is a guttural א ח ע ה ר the vowel is sometimes a holem, thus:

מְבֹרָךְ – blessed
מְפֹרָשׁ – clear, explicit
מְכֹעָר – ugly

Can you guess what these words mean? The roots are well known.

1. מְפֻתָּח
2. מְרֻצֶּה
3. מְקֻצָּר
4. מְעֻשָּׁן
5. מְעֻנָּן

Can you create the מְפֻעָל of the following words and translate them into English?

1. doubt – סָפֵק
2. partner – שֻׁתָּף
3. mark out – צִיֵּן
4. correct – תִּקֵּן
5. arrange – סִדֵּר
6. space – רֶוַח
7. entanglement – סְבָךְ
8. use, serve – שִׁמֵּשׁ
9. furniture – רָהִיטִים
10. color, hue – גּוֹן
11. forge – זִיֵּף

Naturally the פִּלְפֵּל has a passive—the form is מְפֻלְפָּל. Here are some examples:

מְצֻמְצָם – limited
מְסֻכְסָךְ – complicated
מְבֻלְבָּל – confused
מְטֻשְׁטָשׁ – unclear
מְאֻרְגָּן – organized
מְשֻׁכְלָל – perfected
מְתֻרְגָּם – translated
מְנֻמְנָם – drowsy

HIFIL

The next pattern that we shall study is called the הִפְעִיל. It represents causative action. If you want to express the idea that someone caused an action to be done, take the root and put it in the הִפְעִיל pattern; namely, we prefix a ה and insert a י between the second and third letters of the root.

שָׁכַב – lie down
הִשְׁכִּיב – caused to lie down
אָכַל – he ate
הֶאֱכִיל – caused to eat (fed)

If you come across a verb in the הִפְעִיל pattern, extract the root and put before it the phrase " to cause " or " to make " and you will have the meaning of that verb.

Look at the verb הִצְחִיק. If you cut off the prefix ה and cut out the infix י you will see that the root is צָחַק laugh. The meaning therefore must be " he caused or made laugh ". In smoother English we might say " amused ". Very often the הִפְעִיל verb can be rendered by one English word which has in itself the causative idea. Thus " caused to eat " can be expressed in one English word " fed ".

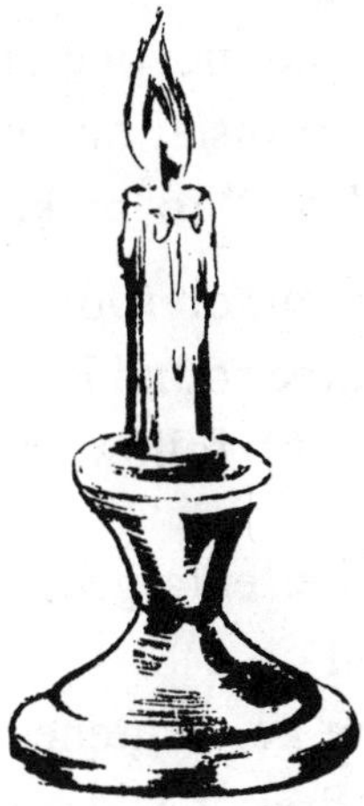

הַנֵּר דּוֹלֵק

THE CANDLE IS AFLAME

הַבָּחוּר מַדְלִיק
אֶת הַנֵּר

THE BOY LIGHTS
(CAUSES FLAME) THE CANDLE

THE HIFIL MAKES THE VERB CAUSATIVE

Sometimes English has no one single word to render the הִפְעִיל word and a translation of the הִפְעִיל requires the phrase " to cause " or " to make ".

Here is a list of common roots in the הִפְעִיל pattern. The regular verbs with three sound letters (called שְׁלֵמִים meaning " whole or complete ") follow closely the form הִפְעִיל.

הִגְדִּיל – made big i.e. enlarged
הִקְטִין – made small
הִלְבִּין – made white i.e. whitened
הִלְבִּישׁ – caused to dress i.e. dressed
הִצְחִיק – made laugh i.e. amused
הִרְעִישׁ – made noise
הִלְהִיב – made enthusiastic
הִשְׁלִים – made peace, made whole
הִשְׁכִּיב – caused to lie down i.e. to lay
הִסְכִּים – made an agreement i.e. agreed
הִבְרִיק – flashed
הִכְשִׁיר – made ready, fit or proper
הִטְבִּיעַ – caused to drown
הִשְׁמִיעַ – caused to hear i.e. announced
הִמְצִיא – invented
הִזְמִין – invited, caused to come at a certain time
הִכְנִיס – caused to enter, brought in
הִרְגִּיז – made angry
הִצְלִיחַ – made a success
הִגְבִּיהַּ – caused to be high i.e. raised
הִגְבִּיר – made strong
הֶעֱבִיר – caused to pass
הֶעֱמִיד – caused to stand
הֶעֱסִיק – made busy
הֶחְכִּים – made wise

הֶחְזִיר - returned i.e. brought back
הֶחְלִיט - decided
הֶחֱשִׁיךְ - made dark i.e. darkened
הֶחְלִישׁ - made weak i.e. weakened
הֶאֱרִיךְ - made long i.e. lengthened
הֶחֱזִיק - made strong, also grasped strongly
הֶרְאָה - caused to see i.e. showed
הֶחֱלָה - made sick
הֶחֱיָה - made live i.e. revived
הִקְשִׁיב - listened
הִרְגִּישׁ - felt
הִשְׁלִיךְ - threw

These last three verbs do not have the idea of causation in their English translation.

HIFIL OF VERBS WITH WEAK LETTERS

These are middle ו or middle י. Note how queer-looking are the verbs in the הִפְעִיל coming from roots with these weak letters.

הֵבִיא - caused to come i.e. brought

The unsuspecting or unanalyzing reader will hardly know that this word comes from בּוֹא - come.

הֵשִׁיב - caused to return, answered
הֵאִיר - caused light i.e. illuminated
הֵרִים - caused to be high i.e. raised
הֵמִית - caused to die i.e. killed
הֵסִיר - caused to step aside i.e. removed
הֵכִין - prepared
הֵבִין - understood

הַיֶּלֶד מִתְרַחֵץ.

THE BOY WASHES HIMSELF

הַיֶּלֶד רוֹחֵץ
אֶת הַכֶּלֶב.

THE BOY WASHES THE DOG

IN THE HITPAEL THINGS HAPPEN TO ONESELF

THESE ARE FIRST LETTER י

הוֹצִיא – caused to go forth, brought forth
הוֹשִׁיב – caused to sit down or dwell
הוֹלִיךְ – caused to go i.e. to lead
הוֹרִישׁ – caused to inherit
הוֹעִיל – was of value
הוֹפִיעַ – appeared
הוֹשִׁיעַ – saved
הוֹכִיחַ – prove, reproved

THESE ARE FIRST LETTER נ

Remember, above we spoke about נ. When it occurs as the second letter of a syllable, it frequently drops out.

הִפִּיל – caused to fall i.e. throw down from נָפַל fall.
הִבִּיעַ – pour forth speech, to express from נָבַע flow
הִגִּיד – tell—from נגד
הִצִּיל – save—from נצל
הִבִּיט – look—from נבט
הִכִּיר – recognize—from נכר
הִזִּיק – damage—from נֶזֶק

The question naturally arises: if the הִפְעִיל represents causative action and the פִּעֵל represents causative action, what is the difference between the two? The answer is, there is none—except in a few special instances.

Thus from the root קָדוֹשׁ holy we can build up:

קִדֵּשׁ – made holy הִקְדִּישׁ – made holy

SIMILARLY

שִׂבַּע – satisfied	הִשְׂבִּיעַ – satisfied
מִתֵּק – sweetened	הִמְתִּיק – sweetened
זִמֵּן – invited	הִזְמִין – invited
רִחֵק – made go far away	הִרְחִיק – made go far away

Occasionally there is a difference between פִּעֵל and הִפְעִיל causative. In the few cases in which this occurs, each has to be learned individually. Thus from the root גדל – big, large we get גִּדֵּל – he raised children הִגְדִּיל – he enlarged. Even when there is a difference you can generally see the connection.

Now that you've had such a large number of examples try to create words in this pattern. Here is a list of fifteen roots. These will help you in forming the הִפְעִיל words.

קָדוֹשׁ – holy	שֶׁקֶט – quiet	בָּטוּחַ – sure
זָכַר – remember	רָאָה – saw	יָדַע – know
קֶסֶם – magic	כַּעַס – anger	צָדַק – right, just
פַּחַד – fear	תְּחִלָּה – beginning	קָפַץ – jump
דָּלַק – be aflame	יָרַד – go down	עָשִׁיר – rich
	פֶּלֶא – wonder	

Here are the words for which you are to find suitable Hebrew words in the hifil pattern.

1. enriched
2. reminded
3. frightened
4. lit
5. began
6. bounce
7. showed
8. angered
9. silenced
10. promised
11. enchanted
12. justified
13. lowered
14. announced
15. sanctified
16. astonished

INTERNALLY CAUSATIVE HIFIL VERBS

Life is never really altogether simple or uncomplicated, and so it is with the hifil. The great mass of the enormous number of Hebrew verbs in the hifil do answer to the simple clear idea of causation. To get the meaning of a verb in the hifil is as simple as one plus one equals two: the word " cause " plus the root equals the meaning of a hifil verb.

However, there are a number of verbs which require a roundabout explanation in order for us to understand why they are in the hifil.

Thus:

הִסְכִּיל act foolishly, really to cause foolish deeds
הִשְׂכִּיל act wisely, really to cause or do wise deeds
הֵיטִיב act well, really to do or cause good deeds
הִזְהִיר shine, really to cause or give forth light
הֶאְדִים become red, really to give forth redness
הֶחֱשָׁה, הֶחֱרִישׁ be silent—the idea is creating silence
הִשְׁמִין grow fat

These are called internally causative verbs.

SHAFEL

Hebrew has a few examples of another form of the הִפְעִיל. It is called שַׁפְעֵל because the prefix letter is ש, but the meaning is basically the same—causative.

שִׁעְבֵּד – to enslave—the root is עָבַד
שִׁכְלֵל – to perfect
שִׁכְנֵעַ – to convince
שִׁעְמֵם – to bore
שִׁרְבֵּב – to enlarge, to prolong
שִׁחְרֵר – to free

HOFAL

The causative הִפְעִיל pattern also has a passive form. More anciently it was called הָפְעַל; lately preference is being given to the vowelization הֻפְעַל. It is not used a great deal. We just do not have too much occasion to say a certain action was caused to be done by someone usually supposed to be unknown.

Again, as with the פֻּעַל pattern, the present tense does get used frequently as an adjective, to a lesser extent as verb and noun.

Here are some examples:

From הִשְׁפִּיעַ – influence we have מֻשְׁפָּע – influenced
" הִבְטִיחַ – promise we have מֻבְטָח – promised, assured
" הִשְׁלִים – perfect we have מֻשְׁלָם – perfect
" הִגְבִּיל – limit, define we have מֻגְבָּל – limited
" הִפְשִׁיט – strip we have מֻפְשָׁט – stripped of corporeality, abstract

Several types of irregularities in verbs assume somewhat the same form in the מֻפְעָל—verbs having a middle ו or י, a first letter "nun" and the כְּפוּלִים group. Thus from הֵאִיר lit up (root אור) we have מוּאָר illuminated.

הִכִּיר – recognized (root נכר) מֻכָּר – recognized
הֵבִין – understood (root בין) מוּבָן – understood
הֵכִין – prepared (root כון) מוּכָן – prepared
הִכָּה – strike (root נכה) מֻכֶּה – struck
הֵסֵב – surround (root סבב) מוּסָב – surrounded

Now try to create the מֻפְעָל forms for the following הִפְעִיל verbs and give the correct English meaning.

1. הִצְדִּיק – justified
2. הִכְרִיחַ – forced
3. הִרְגִּישׁ – felt
4. הִצְלִיחַ – succeeded
5. הֶחְלִיט – decided
6. הִכְתִּיר – crowned

First letter נ

7. הִקִּיף – surrounded
8. הִתִּיר – permitted
9. הִנִּיחַ – placed

First letter י

10. הוֹכִיחַ – proved

REFLEXIVE VERBS הִתְפַּעֵל

A reflexive verb carries the meaning of action happening to one's self. Thus in the sentence " he warmed himself ", " warmed himself " is in the reflexive; namely, the action falls on the actor, the one doing the action.

In Hebrew a verb is put into the reflexive by prefixing הִתְ to the root. Thus לָבַשׁ means dressed; הִתְלַבֵּשׁ he dressed himself. רָחַץ he washed; הִתְרַחֵץ he washed himself. This הִתְ is in all likelihood a fragment of the personal pronoun אַתָּה.

If the root begins with an שׁ then the ת of the prefix is placed after the שׁ. Thus the reflexive of the root שָׁלֵם is " הִשְׁתַּלֵּם, he perfected himself "; the reflexive of שִׁכּוֹר drunk, is " הִשְׁתַּכֵּר became drunk ".

This introduces us to one of the most interesting of all language principles. The ת was placed after the שׁ, instead of before it, where it would normally belong, because the Hebrews of old experienced a slight difficulty in pronouncing הִתְשַׁלֵּם and found it much easier to say הִשְׁתַּלֵּם.

The important principle that is operating here can be stated briefly in this way. Whenever in the course of the conjugation we should be compelled to make a combination of sounds that is difficult to pronounce or harsh, or unmusical, the language changes the sounds so as to make it easier on the throat and pleasanter to the ear.

Please look upon all departures from the regular conjugations in the light of this principle. It is not really correct to call הִשְׁתַּלֵּם an irregular reflexive because it places the ת after the שׁ; this is done to make Hebrew a more beautiful and musical language.

Similarly, the ת of the prefix הִתְ is placed after the first letter of the root if it is שׁ or ס. סָרַק he combed, הִסְתָּרֵק he combed himself, שָׂכָר wages, הִשְׂתַּכֵּר he earned wages for himself.

If the first of the letters of the root is a צ, the heavier " t " sound i.e. the ט is used. Thus צַעַר sorrow, becomes הִצְטַעֵר " he was filled with sorrow ". The word צִיֵּן he made a mark became הִצְטַיֵּן, he made a mark for himself, he excelled.

If the first letter of the root is a ז then the ת of the prefix הת not only skips over the ז but becomes changed to a ד. " T " frequently is " D " in the neighborhood of a voiced sound. We often pronounce the " T " of " butter " or " city "—incorrectly, of course—with a " D " sound. In Hebrew this change is correct and necessary. So:

זַיִן – weapon becomes הִזְדַּיֵּן – armed oneself
זְמַן – time הִזְדַּמֵּן – agreed or chanced to be at a certain time.

Here is a list of common words in the reflexive.

הִתְחַמֵּם – warmed himself
הִתְרַחֵץ – washed himself
הִתְלַבֵּשׁ – dressed himself
הִתְלַמֵּד – taught himself
הִתְחַכֵּם – acted wisely
הִתְאַמֵּר – boasted
הִתְקָרֵב – drew near
הִתְנַשֵּׂא – raised himself
הִתְעַסֵּק – busied himself
הִתְעַשֵּׁר – became rich
הִתְפַּלֵּא – wondered

פָּעַל

PLAIN, SIMPLE, ORDINARY ACTION

נִפְעַל

PASSIVE OF THE פָּעַל ACTION WAS DONE BY SOMEONE—

OFTEN WE DON'T KNOW WHO

פִּעֵל

MAY INDICATE INTENSIVE ACTION OR CAUSATIVE ACTION

UNTIE, LOOSEN—פִּתַּח MADE STRONG— חִזֵּק

הִפְעִיל

CAUSATIVE ACTION

CAUSED TO LAUGH, AMUSED—הִצְחִיק

הִתְפַּעֵל

INDICATES ACTION HAPPENING TO ONE-SELF

HE WASHED HIMSELF—הִתְרַחֵץ

THE FIVE MAJOR . . . . בִּנְיָנִים

הִתְקַדֵּשׁ – sanctified himself
הִתְרַפֵּא – healed himself
הִתְאַמֵּץ – strained himself
הִתְבּוֹדֵד – isolated himself
הִתְוַדַּע – made himself known

THESE ARE MUTUAL

In this group the action is mutual. That means first of all that it is reflexive, that it does happen to oneself; but at the very same time, in addition, it also is happening to someone else. הִתְנַשְּׁקוּ means that you are being kissed—but at the same time that you are kissing the other person.

הִתְלַחֲשׁוּ – whispered among themselves
הִתְחַבְּקוּ – they embraced one another
הִתְיַעֲצוּ – they took council with one another
הִתְאַהֲבוּ – they loved one another
הִתְוַכְּחוּ – they debated with each other
הִתְרָאוּ – they saw one another

THE FIRST LETTER IS SIBILANT

הִשְׁתַּלֵּם – perfected himself
הִשְׁתַּכֵּר – he became drunk
הִשְׁתַּמֵּשׁ – he used
הִשְׁתַּגֵּעַ – he became mad
הִשְׁתַּטָּה – acted foolishly
הִסְתַּתֵּר – he hid himself
הִצְטָעֵר – was filled with grief
הִסְתּוֹבֵב – went around
הִצְטַלֵּם – had himself photographed

THESE ARE LAST LETTER ה

הִתְכַּסָּה – covered himself

הִתְחַלָּה – pretended sickness

הִתְרַצָּה – was satisfied

הִתְעַלָּה – raised himself up

The following group are interesting. They mean " to give oneself over to, to devote oneself ". נְדָבָה is a gift so הִתְנַדֵּב really means to make a gift of oneself; מָסַר is to hand over, הִתְמַסֵּר is to hand oneself over. מָכַר is to sell, so הִתְמַכֵּר is to devote oneself with zeal to a cause.

Now that you've read so many examples of the הִתְפַּעֵל you should, without too much difficulty, be able to create words in the reflexive by yourself.

THESE ARE THE ROOTS THAT YOU WILL WORK WITH

סַדֵּר – arrange

אֶבֶן – stone

צַדִּיק – a righteous person

לַהַב – a flame

אָדֹם – red

רָאָה – see

נֶגֶד – against

אֶחָד – one

אֱמֶת – truth

צִיּוּן – mark

נָפַל – fell

אִבֵּד – destroy

גָּנַב – steal

נָהַג – lead

לָבָן – white

חָתָן – groom

Here are the words for which you are to find suitable Hebrew words in the hitpael pattern.

1. blushed
2. was verified
3. came in quietly, stealthily
4. conducted oneself
5. became enthusiastic
6. commited suicide
7. opposed
8. to settle oneself, to arrange one's affairs
9. became petrified
10. excelled
11. justified
12. said... au revoir
13. attacked
14. paled
15. married
16. become united

ANSWERS TO QUESTIONS ON VERBS

GUESSING WORDS IN THE מְפֻעָּל

1. מְפֻתָּח means developed, from the root פָּתַח open and פִּתַּח developed.
2. מְרֻצֶּה means satisfied, from the root רָצָה be pleased with.
3. מְקֻצָּר means shortened, from the verb קָצַר shortened.
4. מְעֻשָּׁן means smoked, from the verb עָשֵׁן smoke.
5. מְעֻנָּן means cloudy, from the word עָנָן cloud.

CREATING WORDS IN THE מְפֻעָּל

1. מְסֻפָּק – doubtful
2. מְשֻׁתָּף – common, having in common or in partnership
3. מְצֻיָּן – excellent, marked out
4. מְתֻקָּן – corrected
5. מְסֻדָּר – arranged

6. מְרֻוָּח – spacious
7. מְסֻבָּךְ – entangled, complicated
8. מְשֻׁמָּשׁ – used, second-hand
9. מְרֻהָט – furnished
10. מְגֻוָּן – many-colored
11. מְזֻיָּף – forged

CREATING WORDS IN THE הִפְעִיל PATTERN

1. enriched	הֶעֱשִׁיר	
2. reminded	הִזְכִּיר	really, "made remember"
3. frightened	הִפְחִיד	
4. lit	הִדְלִיק	
5. began	הִתְחִיל	really, "made a beginning"
6. bounce	הִקְפִּיץ	really, "made to jump"
7. showed	הֶרְאָה	
8. angered	הִכְעִיס	
9. silenced	הִשְׁקִיט	
10. promised	הִבְטִיחַ	
11. enchanted	הִקְסִים	
12. justified	הִצְדִּיק	
13. lowered	הוֹרִיד	
14. announced	הוֹדִיעַ	
15. sanctified	הִקְדִּישׁ	
16. astonished	הִפְלִיא	

CREATING WORDS IN THE מֻפְעָל FORM

1. from הִצְדִּיק – he justified we get מֻצְדָּק – justified.
2. " הִכְרִיחַ – he forced we get מֻכְרָח – forced.
3. " הִרְגִּישׁ – he felt we get מֻרְגָּשׁ – felt.

4. from הִצְלִיחַ – he succeeded we get מֻצְלָח – successful.
5. ” הֶחְלִיט – he decided we get מֻחְלָט – decided.
6. ” הִכְתִּיר – he crowned we get מֻכְתָּר – crowned.
7. ” הִקִּיף – he surrounded we get מֻקָּף – surrounded.
8. ” הִתִּיר – he permitted we get מֻתָּר – permitted.
9. ” הֵנִּיחַ – he placed we get מֻנָּח – placed, lying.
10. ” הוֹכִיחַ – he proved we get מוּכָח – proven.

CREATING WORDS IN THE הִתְפַּעֵל PATTERNS

1. blushed הִתְאַדֵּם
2. was verified הִתְאַמֵּת
3. came in quietly, stealthily הִתְגַּנֵּב
4. conducted oneself הִתְנַהֵג
5. became enthusiastic הִתְלַהֵב
6. committed suicide הִתְאַבֵּד
7. opposed הִתְנַגֵּד
8. settled oneself הִסְתַּדֵּר
9. became petrified הִתְאַבֵּן
10. excelled הִצְטַיֵּן
11. justified oneself הִצְטַדֵּק
12. to see each other again לְהִתְרָאוֹת
13. attacked הִתְנַפֵּל
14. paled הִתְלַבֵּן
15. married הִתְחַתֵּן
16. become united הִתְאַחֵד

QUESTIONS ON CHAPTER SEVEN

1. How may the present tense of the qal also be used? Why?
2. Give the origin of the prefix letters of the future tense.
3. How is the imperative formed in Hebrew?
4. How does the presence of a א, ה, ח, ע as a second letter or ח, ע as the third letter affect the verb in the future?
5. What is the real function of the אֶפְעַל? Give three examples.
6. Give three verbs that form their future with both אֶפְעֹל and אֶפְעַל and explain why.
7. What function does the nifal or passive form of the verb serve?
8. Give two examples of each a) regular verbs in the nifal b) last letter א c) last letter ה d) first letter guttural e) first letter י.
9. What was the meaning of the nifal originally in ancient days? Give three examples.
10. Where does our present פָּעוּל come from?
11. Why is it wrong to insist on a different meaning for all פָּעוּל and present tense nifal verbs? Give three pairs of נִפְעָל and פָּעוּל words the meaning of which is exactly the same.
12. What makes the פִּעֵל more difficult than any other binyan? Give three examples of each of the two functions of the פִּעֵל.

13. Show how verbs middle ו, last letter ה, first letter נ, and כְּפוּלִים form the פִּלְפֵּל. Give two examples of each kind.
14. Give two examples of sound verbs becoming פִּלְפֵּל by a) dropping a letter and doubling what's left b) simply adding a fourth letter.
15. Give three examples of foreign words in the פִּלְפֵּל.
16. In what three ways can מְפָעֶל be used? Illustrate with the word מְלֻמָּד.
17. Give two examples of a) regular מְפָעֶל b) with ל״ה c) with second letter guttural.
18. What is the function of the hifil? Give two examples of each of a) a regular hifil b) first letter guttural c) first letter י.
19. Give two examples of verbs in the shafel.
20. Give two examples of a) regular מְפָעֶל b) irregular.
21. What is the function of the הִתְפַּעֵל?
22. Explain a) the form הִשְׁתַּלֵּם b) the form הִזְדַּיֵּן.
23. Give three examples of regular reflexive verbs.
24. Give two examples of reflexive verbs where the action is mutual.

THESE QUESTIONS HAVE TO DO WITH THE פָּעַל

Can you fill in the missing word or words?

1. The endings for the present tense of the Hebrew verb for gender and number are similar to the noun endings for the very simple reason that the present tense was originally a ———.
2. The prefix letters for the future tense are largely fragments of the ———.
3. The imperative is logically a curt, short form of the future tense, because a command simply says sharply ———.
4. The guttural letters ע, ח, ה, א combine most easily with the ——— vowel because the guttural letters are formed in the ——— and the ——— comes up from the ———.
5. The future of גָּדַל is יִגְדַּל because it is a ——— verb.
6. קצר has a future in both אֶפְעֹל and אֶפְעַל because it has both a ——— and ——— meaning.
7. The third person past tense of חפץ and ישן is troublesome because the form is the same as in the ———.
8. The one common verb in פָּעֹל is ———.
9. The ה drops out of a ל״ה future tense verb such as קנה in these three forms a) ——— b) ——— and c) ———.
10. הלך is a sort of verbal twin because in the present and past tense conjugation it follows the root ——— and in the future and infinitive it follows a root ———.

THIS EXERCISE DEALS WITH THE NIFAL

Can you match these two columns?

1. was forgotten	1. נוֹדַע
2. ancient original meaning of nifal	2. נִשָּׂא
3. יֻתַּן לֻקַּח	3. to describe the action when the actor was unknown.
4. בָּזוּי—נִבְזֶה חָמוּד־נֶחְמָד	4. to vary the style
5. was known	5. reflexive of פָּעַל as in הִשָּׁמֵר
6. was done	6. two present tenses of the passive of the פָּעַל
7. chief function of the nifal	7. shows that the נִפְעָל is also used as an adjective.
8. פָּעוּל and נִפְעָל	8. נִשְׁכַּח
9. was lifted	9. נַעֲשָׂה
10. a secondary minor function of the nifal.	10. verbs that are remnants of the ancient passive of the פָּעַל

THESE DEAL WITH פִּעֵל AND פֻּעַל

Can you match these two columns?

1. two different meanings of פִּעֵל	1. busy oneself eagerly with the action indicated by the root.
2. נִעְנֵעַ, זִלְזֵל	2. examples of intensive פִּעֵל
3. מְבַכֶּה, מְעַבֵּד	3. can be verb, noun or adjective
4. שִׂגְשֵׂג, תִּעְתַּע	4. privitative פִּעֵל
5. the fundamental meaning of the פִּעֵל	5. שְׁלֵמִים becomes פִּלְפֵּל
6. גִּלְגֵּל, בִּלְבֵּל	6. examples of causative פִּעֵל
7. סִקֵּל, חִטֵּא	7. כְּפוּלִים becomes פִּלְפֵּל
8. לִגְלֵג, פִּקְפֵּק	8. causative and intensive
9. מְלֻמָּד	9. ל״ה becomes פִּלְפֵּל
10. בִּיֵּשׁ, שִׂמַּח	10. ע״ו becomes פִּלְפֵּל

THESE DEAL WITH THE HIFIL, HOFAL, HITPAEL

Can you match these two columns?

1. hifil of נֵזֶק damage	1. הוֹשִׁיב
2. רִחֵק הִרְחִיק	2. two examples of shafel
3. הִשְׂכִּיל־הֶאֱדִים	3. causative
4. hifil of בּוֹא	4. פִּעֵל and hifil with the same meaning
5. שִׁחְרֵר, שִׁעְבֵּד	5. מוּבָן
6. הִזְדַּיֵּן־הִשְׁתַּלֵּם	6. mutual reflexive
7. basic meaning of hifil	7. הִזִּיק
8. hifil of יָשַׁב	8. these unusual forms arise because they are easier to pronounce
9. hofal of הֵבִין	9. הֵבִיא
10. הִתְנַשְּׁקוּ	10. internally causative hifil verbs.

Chapter VIII

The Patterns of the Noun

When it comes to noun patterns, Hebrew has an enormous flexibility. There are only seven regular verb patterns, but a very large number of noun patterns. At one time their meanings were probably clearly differentiated; today, only a limited number have a sharply defined meaning.

These we will study very carefully and for this reason: when a noun pattern does have a definite meaning it is important to learn it, for then we will have a clue to the meaning of any noun in that pattern. If we see a verb in the hifil we know that the meaning is causative, or if in the hitpael that the meaning is reflexive. In exactly the same way, if we know that the noun pattern מַפְעֵל represents an instrument of some sort, or that the פַּעֶלֶת is frequently used to indicate disease, we are able—if we know the root—to work out the meaning of a new word by ourselves without recourse to a dictionary. If you work out the meaning of a word by yourself it gets fixed in your mind a whole lot more deeply than if it was told you, or if you looked it up.

VERBAL NOUNS

Each of the active verb patterns forms nouns in a simple regular way. They are called verbal nouns because of their close connection with the parent verb. Almost all active verbs can form this corresponding verbal noun.

פְּעִילָה

First of all let us look over the nouns that are derived from the qal. Nouns formed from the qal for the most part follow the pattern פְּעִילָה.

From:	we get:
שָׁמַר – watched	שְׁמִירָה – watching
כָּתַב – wrote	כְּתִיבָה – writing
סָגַר – closed	סְגִירָה – closing
אָכַל – ate	אֲכִילָה – eating
פָּגַשׁ – met	פְּגִישָׁה – meeting
יָצָא – went forth	יְצִיאָה – going forth, departure
יָדַע – knew	יְדִיעָה – knowing
זָכַר – remembered	זְכִירָה – remembering
מָצָא – found	מְצִיאָה – finding (In Yiddish, a " bargain ")
קָרָא – read, called	קְרִיאָה – reading, calling
הָלַךְ – went	הֲלִיכָה – walking
שָׁמַע – heard	שְׁמִיעָה – hearing
לָקַח – took	לְקִיחָה – taking
שָׁחַט – slaughtered	שְׁחִיטָה – slaughtering
עָמַד – stood	עֲמִידָה – standing
יָשַׁב – sat	יְשִׁיבָה – sitting
יָרַד – went down	יְרִידָה – descent
מָכַר – sold	מְכִירָה – selling
נָפַל – fell	נְפִילָה – falling
סָלַח – forgave	סְלִיחָה – forgiving

This can go on endlessly. The list is drawn up just to make sure you get the idea.

Naturally, if the root has a weak letter the noun pattern will be somewhat different because of the loss of the weak letter. Here are the verbs last letter ה.

These really have the י as their last letter. There is a dagesh in the י, to indicate that it is to be pronounced twice: once for the original י and once for the י of the noun pattern. Remember that we told you way back that the last letter ה verbs once ended in י.

From:	we get:
קָנָה – bought	קְנִיָּה – buying
רָאָה – saw	רְאִיָּה – seeing
עָלָה – went up	עֲלִיָּה – going up
מָנָה – counted	מְנִיָּה – counting
עָשָׂה – did, made	עֲשִׂיָּה – doing
בָּכָה – cried	בְּכִיָּה – crying
פָּנָה – faced	פְּנִיָּה – facing

From the roots middle ו and י.

From:	we get:
מוּת – die	מִיתָה – death
שׁוּב – return	שִׁיבָה – return
בּוֹא – come	בִּיאָה – coming
קוּם – rise	קִימָה – rising
שִׁיר – sing	שִׁירָה – singing

Verbs whose last two letters are the same—the group called ע״ע or כְּפוּלִים—are conjugated both as regular verbs and defectively. Similarly in the formation of their verbal nouns we have the same two alternatives, namely, the regular formation and a somewhat shortened form.

The regular formation:

From מָדַד – measured, we get מְדִידָה – measurement.

From סָבַב – went around, we get סְבִיבָה – surroundings, environment.

The somewhat shortened form:

From מָדַד – measured, we get מִדָּה – measurement, also a measurement of character, namely a quality of personality.

From סָבַב – went around, we get סִבָּה – a cause, that which makes something go around.

From חָבַב – loved, we get חִבָּה – love.

From בָּזַז – despoiled, plundered, we get בִּזָּה – spoil, booty.

From צָנַן – was cold, we get צִנָּה – cold.

From זָמַם – considered, devised, we get זִמָּה – plan, device, evil device, wickedness.

From גָּזַז – sheared, we get גִּזָּה – sheared wool.

A few verbs form their nouns in a slightly different way.

Thus from:	we get:
שָׂרַף – burned	שְׂרֵפָה – burning
גָּנַב – stole	גְּנֵבָה – theft
אָסַף – gathered	אֲסֵפָה – gathering
שָׁאַל – asked	שְׁאֵלָה – question
הָרַג – killed	הֲרֵגָה – killing
בָּעַר – burned	בְּעֵרָה – burning
אָבַד – was lost	אֲבֵדָה – loss
עָבַד – worked	עֲבוֹדָה – work

פִּעוּל

The noun pattern for the פִּעֵל verb follows the form פִּעוּל.

Thus from:	we get:
סִפֵּר – told	סִפּוּר – a story
דִּבֵּר – spoke	דִּבּוּר – speech, speaking
חִזֵּק – strengthened	חִזּוּק – strengthening
כִּבֵּד – honored	כִּבּוּד – honoring
לִמֵּד – taught	לִמּוּד – teaching, study
אִחֵד – united	אִחוּד – unification
נִחֵם – comforted	נִחוּם – consolation
צִוָּה – commanded	צִוּוּי – imperative
נִקָּה – cleaned	נִקּוּי – cleaning
גִּדֵּל – raised	גִּדּוּל – raising

פִּלְפּוּל

The פִּלְפֵּל—forms nouns in a closely similar way—the pattern is פִּלְפּוּל.

Thus from:	we get:
גִּלְגֵּל – rolled	גִּלְגּוּל – rolling
פִּקְפֵּק – doubted	פִּקְפּוּק – doubting, doubt
בִּלְבֵּל – confused	בִּלְבּוּל – confusion
צִלְצֵל – rang	צִלְצוּל – ringing
רִשְׁרֵשׁ – rustled	רִשְׁרוּשׁ – rustling

הַפְעָלָה

The noun pattern for הִפְעִיל is הַפְעָלָה.

Thus from:	we get:
הִדְלִיק – kindled	הַדְלָקָה – kindling
הִלְבִּישׁ – dressed (causative)	הַלְבָּשָׁה – dressing
הִכְנִיס – brought in	הַכְנָסָה – bringing in, income

הִבְדִּיל – separated	הַבְדָּלָה – distinction, distinguishing
הִזְכִּיר – reminded	הַזְכָּרָה – making mention
הִשְׁפִּיעַ – influenced	הַשְׁפָּעָה – influence
הִבְטִיחַ – promised	הַבְטָחָה – promise
הִתְחִיל – began	הַתְחָלָה – beginning
הִצְלִיחַ – succeeded	הַצְלָחָה – succeeding, success
הִשְׁלִים – completed, made peace	הַשְׁלָמָה – completing
הִזְמִין – invited	הַזְמָנָה – inviting, invitation
הִלְבִּין – whitened	הַלְבָּנָה – whitening
הֵבִיא – brought	הֲבָאָה – bringing
הֵטִיב – improved	הֲטָבָה – improving
הוֹצִיא – brought out	הוֹצָאָה – taking out
הוֹדִיעַ – made known	הוֹדָעָה – making known
הִגִּיד – told	הַגָּדָה – telling
הִצִּיל – rescued	הַצָּלָה – rescuing

הִתְפַּעֲלוּת

The noun pattern for הִתְפַּעֵל is הִתְפַּעֲלוּת.

Thus from:	we get:
הִתְלַהֵב – became enthusiastic	הִתְלַהֲבוּת – enthusiasm
הִתְנַפֵּל – attacked	הִתְנַפְּלוּת – attack
הִתְאַחֵד – became united	הִתְאַחֲדוּת – unification
הִתְנַגֵּד – opposed	הִתְנַגְּדוּת – opposition
הִתְוַדֵּעַ – made oneself known	הִתְוַדְּעוּת – making oneself known
הִשְׁתַּלֵּם – perfected oneself	הִשְׁתַּלְּמוּת – perfecting oneself
הִשְׁתַּתֵּף – participated	הִשְׁתַּתְּפוּת – participation
הִסְתַּדֵּר – arranged one's affairs	הִסְתַּדְּרוּת – organization

הִצְטַיֵּן – excelled הִצְטַיְּנוּת – excelling

הִצְטַדֵּק – justified oneself הִצְטַדְּקוּת – justifying oneself

פַּעָל – MAKING A LIVING

All the noun patterns that we have studied so far, describe directly and simply the action of the verb from which they are derived. In Hebrew these patterns are all called שֵׁם הַפְּעוּלָּה meaning the noun which tells of the action. The first of the next group of noun patterns that we shall study is called פַּעָל and indicates usually a profession or way of making a living. Thus דַּיָּן is a judge; סַבָּל is a porter.

Any verb or noun which describes something that can be the basis of making a livelihood can be put into this pattern. The coming of the Industrial Revolution has increased greatly the division of labor, and with it has grown the need for words which indicate the large number of highly specialized crafts and new professions that have sprung up. Where in days of old a few words would have sufficed to describe the men engaged in building, we now need literally dozens to describe the enormous number of building operations carried on by as many separate individuals. The same division of labor applies in agriculture.

If the last letter of the root or word is ה, the ה will become a י. This is not a strictly accurate statement because י was the original ending of most of these words. What we really mean is that the original י was retained. To make sure the י is pronounced and does not get lost an א is added. Thus בָּנָה he built becomes בַּנַּאי builder; מְדִינָה state; מְדִינַאי statesman.

Here are a few examples of nouns in the פַּעָל pattern:

From:	we get:
קֶשֶׁת – bow	קַשָּׁת – archer
נָטַע – planted	נַטָּע – planter
בֹּשֶׂם – perfume, spice	בַּשָּׂם – spice dealer
דִּין – law	דַּיָּן – judge
רָכַב – rode	רַכָּב – coachman
סָבַל – bore, carried	סַבָּל – porter
חוּט – thread	חַיָּט – tailor
צוּד – hunt	צַיָּד – hunter
צֶלֶם – image	צַלָּם – photographer
שֶׁמֶן – oil	שַׁמָּן – dealer in oils
נָפַח – blew	נַפָּח – blacksmith
זְכוּכִית – glass (כ changes to ג)	זַגָּג – glazier
ספר – originally to cut	סַפָּר – barber
לְטֵשׁ – polished	לַטָּשׁ – diamond cutter
חַיִל – power, strength	חַיָּל – soldier
טוּס – fly	טַיָּס – aviator
קְדֵרָה – a pot	קַדָּר – potter

Here are a group of words in the פַּעָל pattern. Without too much trouble you can recognize the roots, and should be able to get their meaning.

1. כַּסָּף	6. כַּנָּר
2. זֶהָב	7. מַיָּן
3. גַּנָּב	8. צַמָּר
4. דַּיָּג	9. פַּסָּל
5. חַמָּר	10. סַפָּן

סַבָּל

PORTER

דַּיָּן

JUDGE

דַּיָּג

FISHERMAN

חַיָּט

TAILOR

פַּעָּל

THIS PATTERN TELLS OF WAYS OF MAKING A LIVING

Can you create the word in the פַּעָל pattern from the following group of words. They are all connected somehow with buildings and homes.

לְבֵנָה – brick	שִׁפֵּר – beautify
חָצַב – hew	סִיד – whitewash
זֶפֶת – tar	תַּנּוּר – stove
רִפֵּד – upholster	לַכָּה – lacquer
צֶבַע – color	טִיחַ – plaster

1. upholsterer
2. brickmaker
3. plasterer
4. interior decorator
5. painter (house)
6. lacquerer
7. tarrer
8. whitewasher
9. worker in quarry
10. stove maker

Can you create words for the following occupations associated with agriculture? The Hebrew words will help you.

גָּזַז – cut, shear	בָּקָר – cattle
גַּן – garden	גְּבִינָה – cheese

דוּשׁ – thresh

1. gardener
2. cowherd
3. thresher
4. cheesemaker
5. sheepshearer

פַּעְלָן – PERSONAL CHARACTERISTIC

Our next pattern פַּעְלָן is very easy to comprehend and also widely used. It tells usually of personal characteristics. We like to talk about people, and particularly do we like to pass judgment upon them and characterize them in a few well chosen words. So we have many of these פַּעְלָן words. Any time you feel like it, just make one up for somebody. You have a perfect right to do so, as long as the form is correct, and the whole thing makes sense.

פַּעְלָן will also indicate one who does something customarily not as a profession or as a means of livelihood; so רַקְדָן – a dancer; שַׂחְיָן – a swimmer.

Here are a few examples:

רַחֲמָן – a merciful person
כַּעֲסָן – a short tempered person, a person easily angered
פַּחְדָן – a coward
לַמְדָן – a learned person
דַּיְקָן – an exact person
סַקְרָן – a curious person (to look at, ogle סקר)
יַחְסָן – one from distinguished family
קַפְּדָן – like קִפּוֹד, a porcupine, having little patience, quick to anger
קַנְתְּרָן – nagger, teaser
פַּהֲקָן – one who yawns a lot
שַׁדְכָן – marriage broker; it comes from שדך which means to smooth over, settle, negotiate
הַסְסָן – one who hesitates a lot
רַשְׁלָן – a negligent person
חַמְקָן – shirker, from חָמַק – slip away
שְׁתַּדְלָן – one who tries on your behalf; הִשְׁתַּדֵּל means " to try "
פַּקְפְּקָן – one who doubts, a skeptic
קַשְׁקְשָׁן – a pest, nuisance; קִשְׁקֵשׁ – to knock at

Again; if the last letter of the root is ה it resumes its original י so that בָּכָה cry becomes בַּכְיָן, one who cries a lot.

Can you guess by examining the root the meaning of each word in the following group?

1. יַדְעָן
2. גַּזְלָן
3. בַּיְשָׁן (from בּוּשָׁה – shame)
4. לַגְלְגָן (from לִגְלֵג – mock)
5. עַסְקָן (from עֵסֶק – occupation)
6. גַּבְהָן
7. רַגְזָן (think of בְּרֹגֶז)
8. שַׁקְרָן
9. חַשְׁדָן (from חֲשַׁד – suspicion)

Human characteristics so very often come in opposite pairs. We think of people being loud or quiet, truthful or liars, economical or spendthrifty. I wonder whether you would like to try—with appropriate hints—to work out a set of opposites to the following group. Here are a few of the more difficult words you'll need.

עָצֵל – lazy
פָּשׁוּט – simple
עִקֵּשׁ – stubborn
קָמַץ – hold tightly to
תָּבַע – demand

1. זַכְרָן – a person with a good memory. The opposite is?
2. בַּכְיָן – one who is accustomed to cry. The opposite is?
3. נַדְבָן – a generous person, one who gives charity freely. The opposite is?
4. פַּשְׁרָן – a person who likes to compromise. The opposite is?
5. נַקְמָן – a person who seeks revenge. The opposite is?
6. וַתְּרָן – one who is always willing to give in. The opposite is?
7. חַדְשָׁן – one who likes new things. The opposite is?
8. שַׁקְדָן – a diligent, hardworking person. The opposite is?
9. עַמְקָן – a person who goes deeply into matters. The opposite is?

Occasionally פַּעְלָן will be used to designate occupations, where we would more usually expect the form פַּעָל. This will be done when:

1. The פַּעָל form is already taken over by some other word.
   סַפָּר is a barber so a librarian is סַפְרָן.
   חַלָּף is a knife so חַלְפָן is a money changer.
2. If the פַּעָל were used it would sound too much like other forms of the word. יַעְרָן is a forester; the פַּעָל form of the word would sound too much like יַעַר. The word חַלְבָן is used for dairyman for the same reason.
3. Sometimes the פַּעְלָן is used for no particular reason at all. קַבְּלָן is a contractor, from קִבֵּל one who receives or accepts projects to carry out. רַקְדָן is a dancer.

מַפְעֵל - INSTRUMENT OR UTENSIL

Our next noun pattern is מַפְעֵל and it is largely used for instruments or utensils. The prefix מ in Hebrew nouns usually come from the word מַה what; that is why so many nouns begin with מ.

The letter מ which is the first letter of the present tense of the פִּעֵל, of הִפְעִיל and of הִתְפַּעֵל is probably an abbreviation of the word מִי who—in other words מְדַבֵּר is really " one who speaks," מִתְלַבֵּשׁ is really " one who dresses himself."

Just see how neatly the מַפְעֵל words break up.

מַפְתֵּחַ - a key is really	מַה פּוֹתֵחַ - what opens
מַעֲשֶׂה - a deed is really	מַה נַּעֲשֶׂה - what is done
מַסְרֵק - a comb is really	מַה סּוֹרֵק - what combs
מַסְפֵּג - a blotter is really	מַה סּוֹפֵג - what absorbs
מַעְדֵּר - a hoe is really	מָה עוֹדֵר - what hoes
מַרְאֶה - a sight is really	מַה נִּרְאָה - what is seen
מַעְצֵר - a brake is really	מָה עוֹצֵר - what restrains, what holds back
מַרְצֵעַ - an awl is really	מָה רוֹצֵעַ - what bores, pierces

מַשְׁעֵן – a staff is really עַל מַה נִשְׁעָן – on what one leans
מַצְרֵף – a crucible is really מַה צוֹרֵף – what smelts
מַגְלֵחַ – a razor is really מַה מְגַלֵּחַ – what shaves
מַקְלֵף – a peeler is really מַה מְקַלֵּף – what peels

Can you work out the following words by recognizing the root and putting the word " what " in front of the root? These Hebrew words will give you a clue.

בֹּרֶג – screw גָּרַף – sweep in אָפָה – bake
טָחַן – grind קָדַח – make a hole גֵּרֵד – file
צָפוֹן – north

1. מַבְרֵג 3. מַקְדֵּחַ 5. מַגְרֵף
2. מַטְחֵן 4. מַאֲפֶה 6. מַצְפֵּן
7. מַגְרֵד

Kitchen utensils and household gadgetry have given rise to a large number of words. Here is a list of words and their meanings. From them create the terms for the kitchen utensils listed below.

פִּצַּח – cracked סָחַט – squeezed
שָׁפַךְ – poured גִּהֵץ – ironed
קָצַף – foam חָלַץ – pulled out
פִּלַּח – cleaved כָּתַשׁ – crushed
טָרַף – mixed רִסֵּק – mashed

1. funnel
2. potato masher
3. corkscrew
4. ironer
5. egg beater
6. egg slicer
7. mixing machine (for mixing cakes, etcetera)
8. orange squeezer
9. nutcracker
10. mortar (in which spices are pulverized)

There are many technical words which use the מַפְעֵל which you might know if you studied science.

מַסְרֵק
COMB

מַפְתֵּחַ
KEY

מַשְׁפֵּךְ
FUNNEL

מַקְדֵּחַ
DRILL

מַפְעֵל

THIS PATTERN TELLS OF UTENSILS OR INSTRUMENTS

Some are:

מַבְדֵד – isolater	מַקְלֵט – receiver
מַצְבֵּר – accumulator	מַתְאֵם – adapter
מַלְחֵם – solderer	מַסְנֵן – filter
מַגְבֵּר – amplifier	

THE מִפְעָל

There is a slightly different pattern, where the " mem " is vowelized מִ. The meaning, though, is exactly the same.

Thus מִקְדָשׁ is temple; really it means מַה קָדוֹשׁ what is holy; מִכְתָּב a letter; that which is written.

Here are a few words in the מִפְעָל pattern.

מִפְעָל – a project, undertaking—literally what one is doing.

מִשְׁפָּט – judgement	מִשְׁכָּן – dwelling, tabernacle
מִשְׁקָל – weight	מִסְחָר – business
מִשְׂרָה – office	מִנְהָג – custom
מִשְׁכָּב – couch, bed	מִצְוָה – commandment
מִגְדָל – tower	מִקְרָא – Bible, i.e. what is read
מִשְׂחָק – game	מִשְׁנָה – Mishna, i.e., what is studied

מַפְעֵלָה

The pattern מַפְעֵלָה is somewhat similar to מַפְעֵל, the prefix מַ indicating " what ". However, this time, the "what", i.e., the utensil or the machinery, is more pretentious, and that is in harmony with the greater size of the word. After all, מַפְעֵלָה has an additional הָ and there are three syllables instead of two. This pattern is also used frequently to indicate the factory where the machinery is used or a place of business. Some examples are:

From:	we get:
חָרַשׁ – plough	מַחְרֵשָׁה – a plough
חָתַךְ – cut	מַחְתֵּכָה – slicing machine
שַׁחֵז – sharpen	מַשְׁחֵזָה – sharpener (of tools)
כָּתַב – write	מַכְתֵּבָה – writing table
סִדֵּר – arrange	מַסְדֵּרָה – linotype machine
זָרַע – sow (seed)	מַזְרֵעָה – machine for sowing seed

Can you create words in the מַפְעֵלָה pattern?

זָמַר – prune	עֵשֶׂב – grass, herb
שָׁתַל – plant	שָׁאַב – draw water
שִׂדֵּד – harrow	חָלַב – milk
קָצַר – cut	חָצַב – hew
דָּגַר – hatch	זָרַק – throw

1. harvesting machine
2. tree nursery
3. chicken incubator
4. a harrow
5. pruning hook
6. herbarium
7. pump
8. dairy
9. quarry
10. water fountain

מִפְעָלָה

Many words occur in a slighty different form—מִפְעָלָה.

Some are:

מִרְפָּאָה – clinic
מִבְדָּקָה – an experimental station
מִבְרָאָה – a sanitarium
מִנְסָרָה – a saw mill

Related to מַפְעֵלָה in meaning is a group of nouns ending in יָה and indicating generally a place of business of some sort.

מַחְרֵשָׁה

PLOUGH

מַחְלֵבָה

DAIRY

מַשְׁאֵבָה

PUMP

מַשְׁתֵּלָה

NURSERY

מַפְעֵלָה

Thus:

From:		we get:	
נַקְנִיק	– frankfurter	נַקְנִיקִיָּה	– delicatessen store
אָפָה	– bake	מַאֲפִיָּה	– bakery
רִפֵּד	– upholster	מַרְפֵּדִיָּה	– upholsterer's shop
נַגָּר	– carpenter	נַגָּרִיָּה	– carpenter shop
סַנְדְּלָר	– shoemaker	סַנְדְּלָרִיָּה	– shoe repair shop
סֵפֶר	– book	סִפְרִיָּה	– library
מַסְגֵּר	– locksmith	מַסְגֵּרִיָּה	– locksmith's shop
כְּרִיכָה	– bookbinding	כְּרִיכִיָּה	– book bindery
גְּלִידָה	– ice cream	גְּלִידִיָּה	– ice cream parlor
עִיר	– city	עִירִיָּה	– city hall
צֹרֶךְ	– need	צַרְכָנִיָּה	– food store—generally a combination of groceries and fruits

This sort of thing can go on without end. All around Tel Aviv there are signs on shop windows and each sign has a word ending in יָּה telling what is sold or done there.

There were so many of these words made, and in so short a time, that this pattern has been sharply criticized by conservative scholars. However, I think it is quite a healthy, normal development. It is silly and clumsy to say חֲנוּת לְנַקְנִיקִים a store for frankfurters, when you can say נַקְנִיקִיָּה, or חֲנוּת לִגְלִידָה an ice cream parlor when one can say with equal clarity and much economy the one word גְּלִידִיָּה. Certainly, for spoken Hebrew in America, where ice cream parlors and delicatessen stores abound, we need these particular words.

פַּעֶלֶת – DISEASES

The pattern פַּעֶלֶת is frequently used for names of diseases. That there should be a large number of words in

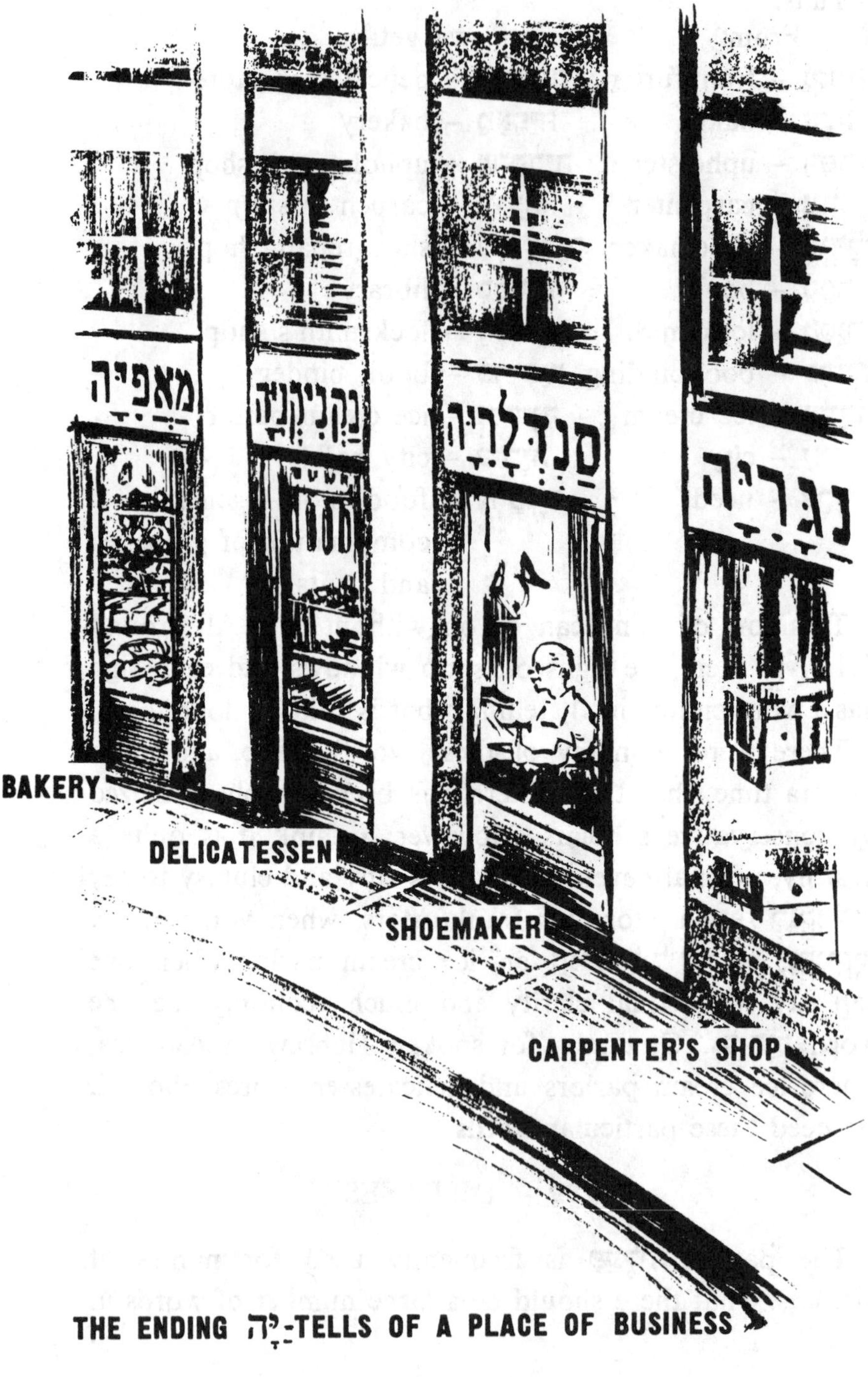

THE ENDING ־ִיָּה-TELLS OF A PLACE OF BUSINESS

פַּעֶלֶת would be expected from the enormous variety of ailments that can afflict man. Many of these have highly technical names and you wouldn't recognize even the English names if you saw them, much less the Hebrew.

However, there are a goodly number of the common diseases that you should know and we will play around with these.

אַדֶּמֶת is measles. Why?	בַּהֶרֶת is white spots on skin. Why?
דַּלֶּקֶת is inflammation. Why?	עַשֶּׁשֶׁת is tooth decay
	עָשַׁשׁ is to decay
נַזֶּלֶת is a running nose. Why?	שַׁחֶפֶת is consumption
צָרֶבֶת is heartburn. Why?	שַׁהֶקֶת is hiccups
מַתֶּנֶת is lumbago. Why?	שַׁפַּעַת is influenza
מָתְנַיִם are thighs	שָׁפַע is to flow
שַׁעֶלֶת is whooping cough	קַדַּחַת is fever
שִׁעוּל is a cough	קָדַח is to burn
צַלֶּקֶת is a scar	צָרַעַת is leprosy

גַּבַּחַת is baldness (front of head)

In the last four words the presence of a guttural letter changes the vowels of this pattern to " ah "!

Try your hand at creating words for illnesses. You will get appropriate hints from either the chief symptom or the chief cause or from the part of the body affected.

1. Hydrophobia is usually caused by dogs, of course, the bite of the mad dog. What's the word?
2. The chief symptom of jaundice is the yellowing of the skin. What's the word?
3. צָרוּד means hoarse. How would you say hoarseness?

4. The chief symptom of rickets is softening of the bones.
5. The chief symptom of asthma is shortening of the breath.

Once my daughter Tamar instead of saying יֵשׁ לִי כְּאֵב בֶּטֶן said quite naturally יֵשׁ לִי בַּטֶּנֶת.

פִּעֵל - BODILY DEFECTS

The pattern, פִּעֵל (it has nothing to do at all with the verb pattern, פִּעֵל) tells of bodily, occasionally, mental defects. Thus we have:

עִוֵּר – blind
גִּבֵּן – hunch backed
קִטֵּעַ – crippled (קָטַע is to cut)
פִּסֵּחַ – lame
אִלֵּם – dumb (אָלַם is to bind—it is as though the mouth were bound up)
חִגֵּר – lame (חָגַר is to bind—it is as though the feet were bound up)
אִטֵּר – left handed—(it is a short way of saying אִטֵּר יַד יָמִין with the right hand closed, or shut up)
גִּדֵּם – one armed (גָּדַם is to cut)
גִּבֵּחַ – bald—front part of the head
קֵרֵחַ – bald (the vowel is ‥ because of the ר which takes no dagesh)
חֵרֵשׁ – deaf (again the vowel is ‥ because of the ר which takes no dagesh); חָרַשׁ is to be quiet
עִקֵּשׁ – perverse; עִקֵּשׁ רַגְלַיִם is used for knock-kneed
טִפֵּשׁ – a fool

DIMINUTIVES

There are two chief ways of creating diminutive words in Hebrew. One is by repeating either the last letter or the last syllable of the word. Some examples are:

כֶּלֶב – dog	puppy – כְּלַבְלַב
חָתוּל – cat	kitten – חֲתַלְתּוּל
זָקָן – beard	small beard – זְקַנְקַן
מַר – bitter	slightly bitter – מָרִיר
קַר – cold	cool – קָרִיר
חַם – warm	warmish – חָמִים
זָנָב – tail	small tail – זְנַבְנַב
חוֹר – hole	small hole – חָרִיר
עָב – cloudy	light cloud – עָבִיב
בָּצָל – onion	small onion – בְּצַלְצוּל

This is frequently done with color words. We have:

אָדֹם – red	אֲדַמְדַּם – reddish
יָרוֹק – green	יְרַקְרַק – greenish
כָּחֹל – blue	כְּחַלְחַל – bluish
זָהָב – gold	זְהַבְהַב – having a gold hue
חִוֵּר – pale	חֲוַרְוַר – palish, somewhat pale
לָבָן – white	לְבַנְבַּן – whitish
שָׁחוֹר – black, dark	שְׁחַרְחַר – darkish, swarthy

An interesting word is " אֲסַפְסֻף – rabble " from אָסַף – gather. The implication here is that the quality is diminutive. אֱלִיל is a contemptuous way of referring to the other gods—much as though to call them " little gods " or godlings.

The Vaad ha Lashon has begun to use this method with verbs, that is, when they wish to indicate a lesser degree of the action of the verb. These two are very effective and much-needed new words.

עָקַץ – sting	עִקְצוּץ – itching
דָּקַר – stab, pierce	דִּקְרוּר – pricking

The other way of creating diminutives is by adding the suffix ית to the noun. ית is a form of the feminine ending, and things feminine probably suggested smallness, diminutive size, or general weakness. At any rate here are a number of examples.

כַּף – spoon	כַּפִּית – teaspoon
עֻגָּה – cake	עֻגִּית – cookie
בֻּבָּה – doll	בֻּבִּית – small doll
כַּד – pitcher	כַּדִּית – small pitcher
כּוֹבַע – hat	כּוֹבָעִית – cap
תֹּף – drum	תֻּפִּית – small drum
צְנוֹן – radish	צְנוֹנִית – small radish

The suffix ית way of forming diminutives differs in one important respect from the first method in which the last letter or syllable is doubled. When the last letter or syllable is doubled the diminutized word must be the same as the word from which it came, only smaller in size or degree. כְּלַבְלַב must be a dog, only a smaller one; עִקְצוּץ must be stinging, but to a lesser degree.

However, words ending in ית, while they signify being smaller in size than the words from which they are formed may be different in kind with only a general resemblance remaining between them and the parent word.

Thus:

כְּרוּב – is cabbage	כְּרוּבִית – is cauliflower

It is smaller but it is not cabbage; it merely looks something like it.

קָטִיף
PICKING ORANGES

נָשִׁיר
FALLING OF LEAVES

פָּעִיל
PATTERN INDICATES SEASON

כֶּלֶב
DOG

כְּלַבְלָב
PUPPY

מַפִּית
NAPKIN

מַפָּה
TABLECLOTH

DIMINUITIVE IN HEBREW

מַפָּה – is tablecloth	מַפִּית – is napkin
לֶחֶם – bread	לַחְמָנִית – roll
שַׁרְווּל – sleeve	שַׁרְווּלִית – cuff
צֵל – shadow	צְלָלִית – silhouette
אֶשְׁכּוֹל – cluster	אֶשְׁכּוֹלִית – grapefruit

ABSTRACT NOUNS END IN וּת

וּת is a magic syllable in Hebrew word building. Just tack it on to a noun—nouns of any kind, shape or form and the word loses all concreteness and becomes an abstract or immaterial thing. All the vast array of words that are created in English by adding the suffixes " dom ", " ness ", " hood ", are formed in Hebrew by the one single simple syllable וּת.

There are thousands of them and you form them yourself at any time that the need arises.

Here are some few examples:

יֶלֶד – child	gives rise to	יַלְדוּת – childhood
מֶלֶךְ – king	"	מַלְכוּת – kingdom
עֶבֶד – slave	"	עַבְדוּת – slavery
אַלְמָנָה – widow	"	אַלְמָנוּת – widowhood
נַגָּר – carpenter	"	נַגָּרוּת – carpentry
יָתוֹם – orphan	"	יַתְמוּת – orphanhood
חַקְלַאי – farmer	"	חַקְלָאוּת – agriculture
רַחֲמָן – merciful	"	רַחְמָנוּת – mercy
דַּרְשָׁן – preacher	"	דַּרְשָׁנוּת – preaching
מַזְכִּיר – secretary	"	מַזְכִּירוּת – secretariat
מֵבִין – understand	"	מְבִינוּת – understanding
נָחוּץ – necessary	"	נְחִיצוּת – necessity
סֵפֶר – book	"	סִפְרוּת – literature

מָהִיר - swift gives rises to מְהִירוּת - speed
יְדִיד - friend " יְדִידוּת - friendship
יָנַק - suckled (תִּינוֹק is infant) יַנְקוּת - infancy

and so on without any end.

Added Letters.

Quite a number of nouns and verbs in Hebrew are formed by the addition of a fourth letter. These words are called quadriliterals. The additional letter may be ר, ל, שׁ or occasionally some other. This additional letter may be in the middle or at the end of the word.

Some examples are:

Additional ר

סַרְעַפָּה - branch from סְעִיף - branch
כִּרְסֵם - gnaw " כָּסַם - cut
סְנַפִּיר - fin " סָנַף - branch out
קִרְטֵם - cut " קָטַם - cut

Additional שׁ

חַלָּמִישׁ - flint from חָלַם - be sound, hard
רְטַפַּשׁ - moist " רָטֹב - moist (פ = ב)
עַכָּבִישׁ - spider, probably from עִכֵּב - hold back, detain –the insects caught in the web

Additional ל

זַלְעָפָה - raging heat from זָעַף - be hot, angry
עִנְבָּל - clapper of a bell " עֵנָב - grape; it resembles a grape

Can you guess the roots of the following words? The point is to recognize which is the additional letter.

1. שַׁרְבִיט - sceptre
2. עַרְסָל - hammock
3. חַרְטוֹם - beak
4. כַּרְמֶל - garden land
5. כֻּרְסָה - armchair
6. גִּבְעֹל - flower cup

SUFFIX וֹן

A very common suffix in Hebrew is וֹן. It doesn't indicate anything in particular, as do the patterns that we have just studied about. However, it occurs very frequently and you ought to recognize at once that it is a suffix. In trying to get the meaning of a word that has וֹן attached to it, the first thing to do is mentally cut off the וֹן, and examine carefully what is left of the word which is generally then the root.

Here is a representative group of words with the suffix וֹן:

חַלוֹן – window	from	חלל – pierce
גָּאוֹן – pride	"	גָּאָה – be proud
שָׁעוֹן – clock, watch	"	שָׁעָה – hour
עִתּוֹן – newspaper	"	עֵת – time
מִלּוֹן – dictionary	"	מִלָּה – word
לָצוֹן – scorning, jesting	"	לֵץ – jester
זָדוֹן – arrogance	"	זוד – seethe
שָׁאוֹן – noise, sound of crashing	"	שָׁאָה – be ruined, ruin
רָצוֹן – desire	"	רָצָה – want
עִפָּרוֹן – pencil	"	עוֹפֶרֶת – lead

The וֹן suffix has been and is being used in Israel now as a diminutive ending. It is a sort of fad and people attach it to any noun they feel like diminutizing. Some that are widely used are:

ספרון – booklet	יַלְדוֹן – a little child
דִּגְלוֹן – a little flag	גַּגּוֹן – an awning

פָּעִיל FOR SEASONS

The noun pattern פָּעִיל frequently indicates season—usually connected with some aspect of agriculture. It forms a small group.

אָבִיב – spring
חָרִישׁ – plowing
קָצִיר – harvest, also harvest time
בָּצִיר – vintage
אָסִיף – ingathering
עָדִיר – hoeing time
קָטִיף – orange picking season
נָשִׁיר – time of the falling of the leaves
זָמִיר – time of the pruning
מָסִיק – time of the olive harvest

ANSWERS TO QUESTIONS ON NOUN PATTERNS

MEANING OF WORDS IN פַּעָל PATTERN – page 170

1. כַּסָּף – silversmith
2. זֶהָב – goldsmith
3. גַּנָּב – thief
4. דַּיָּג – fisherman
5. חַמָּר – donkey driver
6. כַּנָּר – violinist
7. מַיָּן – sorter from מִין – kind
8. צַמָּר – wool dealer
9. פַּסָּל – sculptor from פֶּסֶל – image
10. סַפָּן – sailor from סְפִינָה – boat

CREATING WORDS IN פַּעָל PATTERNS – page 172

1. upholsterer רַפָּד
2. brickmaker לַבָּן
3. plasterer טַיָּח
4. interior decorater שַׁפָּר
5. painter צַבָּע
6. lacquerer לַכַּאי
7. tarrer זַפָּת
8. whitewasher סַיָּד
9. worker in a quarry חַצָּב
10. stove maker תַּנָּר

CREATING WORDS IN פַּעָל PATTERNS – page 172

1. gardener גַּנָּן
2. cowherd בַּקָּר
3. thresher דַּיָּשׁ
4. cheesemaker גַּבָּן
5. sheepshearer גַּזָּז

GUESSING WORDS IN פַּעְלָן PATTERN

1. יַדְעָן – one who knows a great deal
2. גַּזְלָן – a robber
3. בַּיְשָׁן – a bashful person
4. לַגְלְגָן – a scornful mocking person
5. עַסְקָן – one who busies himself generally with communal affairs
6. גַּבְהָן – arrogant person
7. רַגְזָן – one who gets angry easily and often
8. שַׁקְרָן – liar
9. חַשְׁדָן – suspicious person

OPPOSITES OF WORDS IN פַּעְלָן PATTERNS

1. The opposite of זַכְרָן is שַׁכְחָן – a forgetful person
2. " בַּכְיָן " צַחֲקָן – a laughter-loving person
3. " נַדְבָן " קַמְצָן – a miser
4. " פַּשְׁרָן " עַקְשָׁן – a stubborn person
5. " נַקְמָן " סַלְחָן – a forgiving person
6. " וַתְּרָן " תַּבְעָן – a demanding person
7. " חַדְשָׁן " שַׁמְרָן – a conservative person
8. " שַׁקְדָן " עַצְלָן – a lazy person
9. " עַמְקָן " פַּשְׁטָן – a simple person

GUESSING WORDS IN THE מַפְעֵל PATTERN

1. מַבְרֵג – a screwdriver or in other words: what screws
2. מַטְחֵן – a grinder or in other words: what grinds
3. מַקְדֵּחַ – a drill or in other words: what drills
4. מַאֲפֶה – baked things
5. מַגְרֵף – shovel
6. מַצְפֵּן – compass—namely what points to the north
7. מַגְרֵד – a file or what scrapes

KITCHEN UTENSILS IN THE מַפְעֵל PATTERN

1. funnel מַשְׁפֵּךְ
2. potato masher מַרְסֵק
3. corkscrew מַחְלֵץ
4. iron i.e. what one irons with מַגְהֵץ
5. egg beater מַקְצֵף
6. egg slicer מַפְלֵחַ
7. mixing machine מַטְרֵף
8. orange squeezer מַסְחֵט
9. nut cracker מַפְצֵחַ
10. mortar מַכְתֵּשׁ

CREATING WORDS IN THE מַפְעֵלָה PATTERN

1. harvesting machine מַקְצֵרָה
2. tree nursery מַשְׁתֵּלָה (some say this word should be) מִשְׁתָּלָה
3. chicken incubator מַדְגֵּרָה
4. a harrow מַשְׂדֵּדָה
5. pruning hook מַזְמֵרָה
6. herbarium מַעְשֵׂבָה
7. pump מַשְׁאֵבָה
8. dairy מַחְלֵבָה
9. quarry מַחְצֵבָה
10. water fountain מַזְרֵקָה

CREATING WORDS IN THE פַּעֶלֶת

1. אַדֶּמֶת is measles because of the enormous number of tiny red spots that the disease brings out.
2. דַּלֶּקֶת is inflammation—דָּלַק is to be aflame.
3. נַזֶּלֶת is a running nose for the simple reason that נָזַל means to flow.
4. צָרֶבֶת is heartburn because צָרַב is burn. In the Bible the word is used for scab, the scab left by a sore.

CREATING WORDS IN THE פַּעֶלֶת

1. Hydrophobia is כַּלֶּבֶת
2. Jaundice is צַהֶבֶת
3. Hoarseness is צָרֶדֶת
4. Rickets is רַכֶּכֶת
5. Asthma is קַצֶּרֶת

ADDITIONAL LETTERS

1. The root of	שַׁרְבִיט – sceptre	is	שֵׁבֶט – rod
2. ”	עַרְסָל – hammock	”	עֶרֶשׂ – couch
3. ”	חַרְטוֹם – beak	”	חֹטֶם – nose
4. ”	כַּרְמֶל – garden land	”	כֶּרֶם – vineyard
5. ”	כֻּרְסָה – armchair	”	כִּסֵּא – chair
6. ”	גִּבְעֹל – flower cup	”	גֶּבַע – hill

QUESTIONS ON CHAPTER EIGHT

1. How do the number of noun patterns and verb patterns differ in Hebrew?
2. Why is it important to know the meaning of a noun pattern?
3. What is the regular verbal noun pattern for a) פָּעַל b) פִּעֵל c) הִפְעִיל d) הִתְפַּעֵל. Give examples of each.
4. How do פַּעָל and פַּעְלָן essentially differ? Give five examples of each.
5. Where does the מ of the מַפְעֵל come from? Give three examples of words in the מַפְעֵל.
6. Give five examples of words in the מַפְעֵלָה·
7. Why is כַּלֶּבֶת hydrophobia; קַדַּחַת fever; and צָרֶדֶת hoarseness?
8. Give three examples of words in the pattern telling of bodily defects.
9. What are the two chief ways of creating diminutives in Hebrew? Give three examples of each.
10. What is the great usefulness of the suffix וּת for Hebrew nouns?
11. Give an example of a Hebrew word formed with additional ר; with an additional שׁ; with an additional ל.
12. Give the roots of five Hebrew nouns ending in וֹן.
13. What is the significance of the noun pattern פָּעִיל? Give two examples.

Can you match these two columns?

1. measles	1. סַבְלָן - סַבָּל
2. professional pattern from חוט thread	2. סִפְרוּת – literature
3. abstract noun from book	3. כְּרוּבִית – cauliflower
4. שַׁרְבִיט sceptre	4. מָרִיר
5. example of pattern of bodily defects	5. חַיָּט
6. noun from סָבַב	6. גִּבֵּן
7. a patient man—a porter from the same root	7. אֲדֶמֶת
8. season for picking oranges	8. from שֵׁבֶט – rod
9. slightly bitter	9. קָטִיף
10. diminuitive word from cabbage	10. סִבָּה – cause

Chapter IX

All the other Parts of Speech

ADJECTIVES

Hebrew has a goodly number of primitive adjectives such as גָּדוֹל, קָטָן, רַע, טוֹב, חָכָם etc. Large numbers of adjectives are built from the present tense passive verb forms.

Thus in the	פָּעוּל	we have	שָׁבוּר, פָּתוּחַ	etc.
"	נִפְעַל	"	נֶאְדָּר, נִפְלָא	etc.
"	מְפֻעָּל	"	מְלֻמָּד, מְבֻגָּר	etc.
"	מֻפְעָל	"	מֻפְלָג, מֻצְלָח	etc.

English forms adjectives—great numbers of them—by adding "y" to the noun. Thus from "rust" we get "rusty"; from " milk " we get " milky ", etc. Hebrew, curiously enough, forms enormous numbers of adjectives—hundreds of them—in precisely the same way, i.e., by adding "י" to the noun.

Here is a sampling:

From:	we get:
חֹדֶשׁ – month	חָדְשִׁי – monthly
חֹק – law	חֻקִּי – legal
יוֹם – day	יוֹמִי – daily
חֵלֶק – part	חֶלְקִי – partial
חֹפֶשׁ – freedom	חָפְשִׁי – free

From:	we get:
טִפֵּשׁ – fool	טִפְּשִׁי – foolish
שֵׂכֶל – intelligence	שִׂכְלִי – intelligent
סְפָרַד – Spain	סְפָרַדִי – Spanish
כְּלָל – rule	כְּלָלִי – general, common
מְסֹרֶת – tradition	מְסָרְתִּי – traditional
עֵת – time	עִתִּי – timely
צַד – side	צְדָדִי – side (adj.)
מָקוֹר – origin	מְקוֹרִי – original
אֶרֶץ – earth	אַרְצִי – regional

If there is a ה at the end of the noun, the most correct practice is to drop it, so:

From:	we get:
אַגָּדָה – legend	אַגָּדִי – legendary
חֲגִיגָה – celebration	חֲגִיגִי – festive
מִשְׁנָה – Mishna	מִשְׁנִי – Mishnaic

Suppose you now create adjectives this way. Work with the following nouns:

מָקוֹם – place	חִנּוּךְ – education	עֲנָק – giant
כַּלְכָּלָה – livelihood	חֲלוּדָה – rust	נֵס – miracle
נוֹצָה – feather	חֹמֶר – material	מַמָּשׁ – actuality
	יְסוֹד – basis	

Now give the Hebrew for these ten adjectives.

1. miraculous
2. fundamental
3. feathery
4. economic
5. educational
6. gigantic
7. material
8. actual
9. rusty
10. local

ADJECTIVES IN פָּעִיל

Very interesting is the extensive development of the פָּעִיל form to indicate in a general way adjectives that in English would end in "ible" or "able". The early Hebrew dictionaries had the clumsiest circumlocutions to indicate this idea in Hebrew. They would say for inflammable אֶפְשָׁר לְהִשָּׂרֵף or for meltable בַּר תְּמִסָּה. These are certainly pathetically inadequate. But now some very bright people have thought of using the פָּעִיל to express this extremely common idea. So now we have a large and rapidly growing group of words in this form.

רָחִיץ – washable

מָסִיס – meltable

שָׁבִיר – breakable

דָּלִיק – inflammable

חָדִיר – penetrable

כָּוִיץ – contractable

דָּבִיק – sticky

עָבִיר – passable, in the sense that it is possible to cross over; navigable

שָׁמִיעַ – audible

צָמִיג – adhesive

נָזִיל – liquid, something that can flow.

Would you like to try and create adjectives in this pattern?

Here is a list of roots: סָפַר – count; כָּפַף – bend; רָפָא – cure; מָדַד – measure; מָתַח – stretch; קָשַׁר – bind, tie; עָנַשׁ – punish; פָּגַע – hurt, wound.

Can you work out the Hebrew words for the following adjectives?

1. punishable
2. bendable
3. numerable
4. attachable
5. stretchable
6. vulnerable
7. curable
8. measurable

ADVERBS

The oldest way of forming adverbs in Hebrew was by adding a " מ " to a noun or adjective. We have about six of these. Thus:

from יוֹם – day, we form the adverb יוֹמָם – by day

" רֵיק – empty, we form the adverb רֵיקָם – empty, vainly

" חֵן – charm, we form the adverb חִנָּם; somewhat equivalent to the English word " gratis", which means because of one's charm

" אָמֵן – true, established, we form the adverb אָמְנָם – truly

" דְמָמָה – silence, we form the adverb דוּמָם – silently

" פֶּתַע – suddenness, we get the adverb פִּתְאֹם – suddenly

ADVERBS WITH THE LETTER בְּ

The commonest way at present of forming adverbs in Hebrew is to prefix the letter בְּ to a noun. Thus we have: בְּאַהֲבָה literally, " with love ". It serves in Hebrew as the adverb " lovingly ". In other words the Hebrew letter ב meaning " with ", has the force of the adverb ending " ly " in English.

Some examples are:

בְּגָאוֹן – with pride or proudly

בֶּאֱמוּנָה – with faith or faithfully

בְּעָרְמָה – with cunning or cunningly
בְּכֹחַ – with strength or strongly
בִּמְהִירוּת – with rapidity or rapidly
בְּטָעוּת – by mistake or mistakenly
בְּגָלוּי – openly
בְּרַע – with evil intentions
בְּסֵתֶר – secretly
בִּצְנִעָה – quietly, without fanfare
בְּכַוָּנָה – intentionally
בְּקוֹל – with voice or loudly
בְּזוֹל – with cheapness or cheaply
בְּרֹגֶז – with anger or angrily (this expression is commonly used in Yiddish)

You have the perfect right to create any adverb at all in Hebrew in this way—if it makes sense and expresses what is in your mind. No one can say to you that the adverb you created was not used before and therefore is not correct.

Another way of forming adverbs, much less frequently used, is prefixing a כּ. For example:

כַּהֲלָכָה according to the law or legally. (Although this word is used mostly to indicate someone who is up to or above standard, the famous phrase is בָּחוּר כַּהֲלָכָה meaning a splendid young man.)

כְּהֹגֶן – properly
כְּשׁוּרָה – according to regulation
כָּרָאוּי – worthily

Sometimes a ל is the prefix letter. We have:

לְבַטָּלָה – vainly
לָשֹׂבַע – in abundance or abundantly
לְמַכְבִּיר – plentifully

The suffix ית also forms adverbs. We have:
אֲחוֹרַנִּית – backwards
קְדוֹרַנִּית – gloomily

Of course, you can always use the helping word בְּאֹפֶן which means " in the manner of "; or בְּצוּרָה, which means " in the form of ". We can say בְּאֹפֶן מְצֻיָּן to mean " in an excellent way, in an excellent manner; " בְּצוּרָה מְכֹעֶרֶת – in an ugly way ". These are somewhat clumsy.

A common way of forming adverbs used frequently in all periods is to add וֹת to the adjective. Here are some examples:

דִּבֵּר קָשׁוֹת – spoke harshly
דִּבֵּר טוֹבוֹת – spoke well (of some one)
עָנָה עַזּוֹת – answered impudently
מִתְאַנֵּחַ תְּכוּפוֹת – sigh frequently

PREPOSITIONS

A preposition is a word that is placed before a noun or a pronoun and which tells of its relation to some other word in the sentence.

He placed the book on the chair. " On " is a preposition.

The words for prepositions in Hebrew come largely from nouns, and because they are no longer or very rarely used as nouns their true origin may come as something of a surprise.

Here are some:

עַל " on " is a noun meaning " height, upper part ". The name of the Israeli Airline El-Al simply means " to the heights ".

תַּחַת – is the under part – under
אַחַר – hind or back part – behind, after

בֵּין – intermediate space – between
עַד – duration – during, until (related to the word עוֹד)
אֵצֶל – side, i.e., close by
לִפְנֵי – in the face of – before
לְפִי – according to the mouth, i.e., the command of or simply according to
מֵחֲמַת – through the fury of, the energy or activity of, or simply " through, by "
עַל גַּב – upon the back of or simply " on "
עַל מְנָת – on the portion of, for the sake of
כְּדֵי – sufficient for, in order that.

ANSWERS

Creating Adjectives – page 198

1. נִסִּי	6. עֲנָקִי
2. יְסוֹדִי	7. חָמְרִי
3. נוֹצִי	8. מַמָּשִׁי
4. כַּלְכָּלִי	9. חֲלוּדִי
5. חִנּוּכִי	10. מְקוֹמִי

Creating adjectives in the פָּעִיל pattern – page 200

1. עָנִישׁ	5. מָתִיחַ
2. כָּפִיף	6. פָּגִיעַ
3. סָפִיר	7. רָפִיא
4. קָשִׁיר	8. מָדִיד

QUESTIONS ON CHAPTER NINE

1. What four present tense verbs are useable as adjectives? Give one example of each.
2. What curious similarity exists between Hebrew and English in one important method of creating adjectives. Give four examples.
3. How was the פָּעִיל adjective form which expresses the idea of adjectives ending in " ible " or " able " a great improvement over the early way of expressing this thought.
4. What six adverbs are formed by adding ם to a noun or adjective?
5. Explain how adverbs are created in Hebrew with the letter ב. Illustrate.
6. Explain how adverbs are created in Hebrew with the letter כ. Illustrate.

Chapter X

Verbs Come From Nouns

One of the commonest and oldest privileges that men took for themselves is that of turning a noun into a verb. It was the most natural thing in the world once they have the noun " hand "—for men to say " Please hand this over ". To " book " someone is to write charges in a book; to " floor " is to knock to the floor and so on quite endlessly. Verbs that we can clearly see come from or are built from nouns are called de-nominatives—" de " is " from ", " nom " means name or noun. De-nom-inative means coming from a noun.

The matter may be as simple as this. חָלָב is milk, a noun, the thing milk. חָלַב, he milked, is a verb coming from the noun. גֶּשֶׁר is a bridge. From it we have גִּשֵּׁר he made a bridge. שַׁבָּת Sabbath; שָׁבַת he rested or spent the Sabbath.

Of course, all of these nouns must have roots that mean something; however, we can usually only guess at what the roots of the word mean. חָלָב is milk: it must come from a root which means something; possibly something having to do with white. Scholars aren't too sure what the root of שַׁבָּת Sabbath is. One plausible suggestion is that it comes from שֶׁבַע seven.

The point is that these words as we see them first used in Hebrew are nouns; the verbs חָלַב milked, גִּשֵּׁר he bridged, שָׁבַת he rested, come later than and directly from the nouns.

One of the most famous denominatives is the verb תָּרַם – found in the Mishnah and created from the noun תְּרוּמָה, a contribution, an offering for sacred uses. תְּרוּמָה comes from the verb הֵרִים (root רום) and means something lifted off, separated. There are denominative verbs in almost all of the בִּנְיָנִים.

VERBS IN THE QAL FROM NOUNS

In the qal we have the following group:

From:	we have:
אֹהֶל – tent	אָהַל – he pitched a tent
דֶּרֶךְ – road	דָּרַךְ – he stepped
גְּבוּל – boundary	גָּבַל – bordered on
פְּרִי – fruit	פָּרָה – was fruitful
כְּבָרָה – sieve	כָּבַר – he sieved
חֹרֶף – winter	חָרַף – spent winter
כֹּפֶר – pitch, tar	כָּפַר – tarred
חֻלְדָּה – weasel	חָלַד – he dug
אֵצֶל – side, near	אָצַל – set aside
הֶבֶל – vanity	הָבַל – acted in a vain manner
מֶלַח – salt	מָלַח – salted
קֶרֶן – ray of light	קָרַן – shone

Try these: 1. Why should בָּעַר mean " be stupid "? In other words from what noun does בָּעַר come? 2. From what noun does סָפַג absorb come? 3. What two verbs come from דָּג fish?

Often enough a noun from which a verb comes itself comes from a verb and then we have a really interesting series of words. For example:

לָבַן – is white; לְבֵנָה – a brick (bricks were cream colored in the Orient) לָבַן – made bricks

עָלָה - go up; עָלֶה - a leaf; עַלְעֵל - turn leaves i.e. pages of a book

נָעַל - close in, enclose; נַעַל - shoe; נָעַל - put on a shoe

לָבָן meaning to be white, and לָבַן meaning to make bricks would be a complete puzzle without one having as a clue the intermediate noun which is the child of the one and the father of the other.

4. Can you work out the noun and the verb from which the verb נָשַׁךְ " he took interest " comes?

DENOMINATIVE VERBS IN פִּעֵל

Denominative verbs occur most frequently in the piel. A large percentage of the new verbs formed in recent years are in this binyan. Some are very ancient occurring in the Bible—thus from כֹּהֵן we have כִּהֵן officiated as a priest; others such as בִּיֵּם he directed a theatrical production (from בִּימָה) are from a recent issue of the Leshonenu—the quarterly of the Hebrew Academy of Israel.

Again, we often do not know the root meaning of the noun from which the verb comes and we tell all we know by two columns.

יָבָם - a brother-in-law; יִבֵּם - to do the duty of the brother-in-law, i.e. to marry the childless widow of a deceased brother.

קֵן - nest	קִנֵּן - make a nest
נָחָשׁ - snake	נִחֵשׁ - he divined (apparently using snakes)
זָנָב - tail	זִנֵּב - strike at the rear (tail)
עָשָׁן - smoke	עִשֵּׁן - he smoked
זֶפֶת - tar	זִפֵּת - he tarred

סֵמֶל – sign, symbol	סִמֵּל – symbolized	
גָּדֵר – fence	גִּדֵּר – he made a fence	
אֵימָה – fear	אִיֵּם – threatened, caused to fear	
יְצוּא – export (from יָצָא)	יִצֵּא – he exported	two very important words in Israel
יְבוּא – import (from בּוֹא)	יִבֵּא – he imported	
מִין – kind	מִיֵּן – classified	
זֶה – this one	זִהָה – he identified	
סְגֻלָּה – precious thing, property	סִגֵּל – acquired, adapted	
אוֹת – a sign	אוֹתֵת – signaled	

Now that you have the idea, try and create verbs—in the piel from the following nouns.

		How would you say?
5.	דּוֹנַג – wax	— he waxed
6.	סַבּוֹן – soap	— he soaped
7.	תּוֹךְ – midst	— he acted as intermediary or go between
8.	שׁוּק – market	— he created markets
9.	מָמוֹן – money, capital	— he financed
10.	סַיִף – a sword	— he fenced
11.	יַעַר – forest	— he afforested
12.	בָּסִיס – a base	— he based
13.	אֱמֶת – truth	— he verified
14.	פַּךְ – flask	— water gurgling or bubbling
15.	סִכּוּם – sum	— summed up, summarized

Can you work out the following cookery terms:

16. Flavor with onions
17. Sprinkle with flour
18. Flavor with egg
19. Stew (from אד vapor)

With this group of denominative verbs in the piel we know the meaning of the verb from which the noun comes and therefore to give a complete picture we have to have three columns:

בכר – to break through	בְּכוֹר – first born	בִּכֵּר – he preferred (it seems there is a human tendency, recognized by law too, to show preference to the first born)
פָּתָה – be open	פֶּתִי – fool	פִּתָּה – he enticed, deceived
שָׁכַב – lie	שִׁכְבָה – a layer	שִׁכֵּב – arrange in layers
חלל – pierce	חָלִיל – a flute	חִלֵּל – play flute
מָשַׁשׁ – feel	מַמָּשׁ – real, actual	מִמֵּשׁ – he made real

DENOMINATIVE VERBS IN HIFIL

The denominative verbs in the hifil form a smaller but very interesting group.

עֲנָק – necklace	הֶעֱנִיק – richly loaded with gifts
תְּנַאי – condition	הִתְנָה – made a condition
אֱלוֹהַּ – God	הֶאֱלִיהַּ – deify
יָמִין – right	הֵימִין – turn right
שְׂמֹאל – left	הִשְׂמְאִיל – turn left
גֶּשֶׁם – rain	הִגְשִׁים – cause or send rain

Can you create verbs from the following nouns in the hifil pattern?

20.	תְּאוֹם – twin	to fit, or mate together
21.	פֶּתַע – suddenness	he surprised, came suddenly upon
22.	תְּחִלָּה – beginning	he made a beginning
23.	זֵעָה – sweat	he sweated
24.	תּוֹרָה – Torah	he told what Torah or law was, warned
25.	כְּרוּז – announcement	he announced

26. קִפּוֹד	porcupine (who bristles all over)	he acted irritably, he was fussy
27. דֶּרֶךְ	– road	guide, counsel, to show someone the right path

DENOMINATIVE VERBS IN HITPAEL

The denominative verbs in the הִתְפַּעֵל are all very easy to grasp.

אַפִּיקוֹרוֹס – Epicurean, one who denied God	הִתְפַּקֵּר – became irreligious
צֵידָה – provisions	הִצְטַיֵּד – provided himself with food
יְהוּדִי – Jew	הִתְיַהֵד – became a Jew
סַף – threshhold	הִסְתּוֹפֵף – stood at the threshhold
מַזָּל – luck	הִתְמַזֵּל – became lucky
שַׂר – ruler	הִשְׂתָּרֵר – acted as a ruler or prince

Can you create verbs in the הִתְפַּעֵל from the following nouns?

28. אֶזְרָח – citizen	— he became a citizen
29. סִנָּר – apron	— he put on an apron
30. כַּרְכֹּם – saffron (pale yellow)	— he paled
31. נָכְרִי – stranger	— he acted like a stranger
32. רֶגֶל – foot	— he became accustomed

In the following two denominative verbs in hitpael we know the meaning of the root of the noun.

עָבַר – cross over	עֶבְרָה – anger	הִתְעַבֵּר – he became furious
גּוּר – live	גֵּר – a resident alien, later, a proselyte	הִתְגַּיֵּר – became a proselyte

DENOMINATIVES FROM NOUNS WITH ADDITIONAL LETTERS

As we noted above, Hebrew nouns are formed by the addition of prefix, suffix, or infix letters, particularly, מ, וֹן or ת. Often verbs are formed from these nouns, which will then have four letters instead of the regular three. From שִׁכֵּן " cause to dwell " we get מַשְׁכּוֹן – a pledge; something held as security. From מַשְׁכּוֹן we now have the new denominative verb מִשְׁכֵּן – he gave as a pledge or guarantee.

סִקֵּר – ogle, eye	סַקְרָן – curious person	סִקְרֵן – he aroused curiosity
חוּשׁ – feel	מוּחָשׁ – concrete	הִמְחִישׁ – he made concrete
רוּעַ – make noise	תְּרוּעָה – blast	הִתְרִיעַ – he blew shofar, made noise
רָעַם – make noise, grumble	תַּרְעֹמֶת – grievance	תַּרְעֵם – aggrieve
כָּזָב – lie	אַכְזָבָה – disappointment	הִתְאַכְזֵב – he was disappointed i.e. hopes were given the lie
גָּבַר – strong	תִּגְבֹּרֶת – re-inforcement	תִּגְבֵּר – re-inforced
בָּחַן – examine	אַבְחָנָה – diagnosis	אִבְחֵן – diagnosed

Here is a curious creation אַל אֲתַר – on the spot (this is Aramaic) אִלְתֵּר – he improvised.

Would you like to try your hand at creating some of these verbs with additional noun letters attached?

זִמֵּר – sing or play an instrument תִּזְמֹרֶת – orchestra

33. How would you say he orchestrated, that is he arranged a song for an orchestra to play?

How would you say?

34. נַסֵּה – try; נִסָּיוֹן – experiment — to conduct experiments?
35. עֲמִילָן – starch — to starch?
36. עַצְבָּן – nervous — to make nervous?

DENOMINATIVE VERBS FROM PARTS OF THE BODY

English denominatizes, that is, uses as a verb practically all parts of the body. We face, we hand over, we eye, we thumb, we shoulder, etc. It is interesting to note that Hebrew does exactly the same thing.

In Hebrew:

From:	we have:
פָּנִים – face	פָּנָה – he faced
אֹזֶן – ear	הֶאֱזִין – he listened, a poetic word
לָשׁוֹן – tongue	הִלְשִׁין – he slandered (this is an interesting commentary on human nature that the word for using the tongue should mean telling tales, slandering)
עַיִן – eye	עוֹיֵן – he eyed, also the word עַיֵּן – to look

37. There are two other denominative verbs coming from עַיִן. Can you guess them?
    רֶגֶל – foot, רָגַל – went about maliciously, slander, מְרַגֵּל – spy; also there is רָגִיל – accustomed.
38. There is still another verb from רֶגֶל with one letter changed. Can you guess it?
39. And yet another in a very strange and unusual verb pattern.

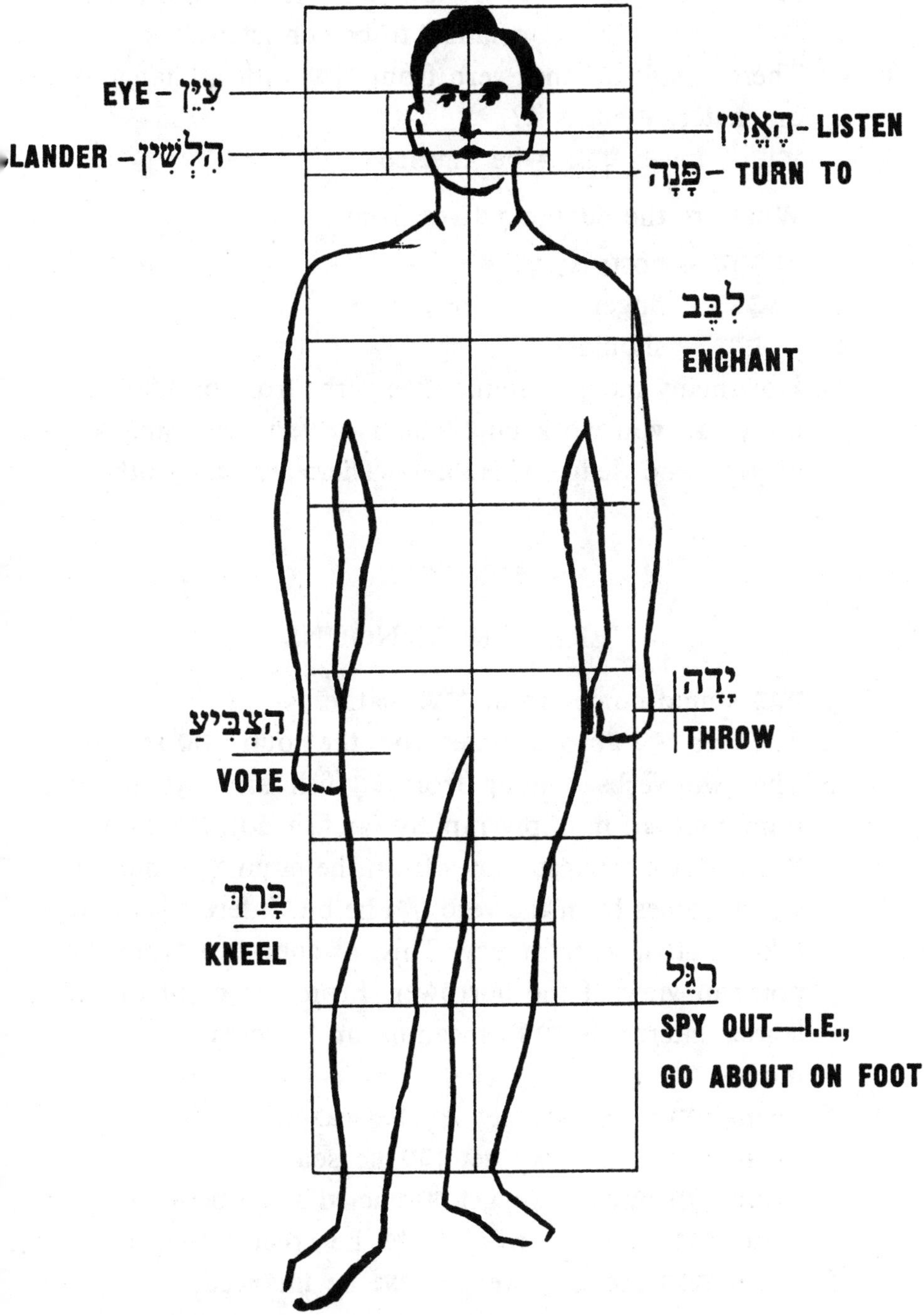

VERBS FROM NAMES OF THE PARTS OF THE BODY

עָקֵב - heel; עָקַב - to follow on the heels of, also means " to be consistent ".

40. There is still another verb from עָקֵב with a change of one letter. What is it?

בֶּרֶךְ - knee; בָּרַךְ - he kneeled

What are the denominatives from:

41. נְחִירַיִם - nostrils
42. אֶצְבַּע - finger
43. כָּתֵף - shoulder
44. How many more denominative verbs from parts of the body can you work out? This is a very searching test of your knowledge of Hebrew. There are many others.

ANSWERS

VERBS FROM NOUNS

1. בַּעַר stupid comes from בְּעִיר cattle.
2. The verb סָפַג absorb comes from the noun סְפוֹג sponge.
3. The two verbs coming from דָּג fish are: דָּגָה to be numerous, to multiply rapidly (as fish do); דוּג to fish.
4. נָשַׁךְ he took interest comes from the noun נֶשֶׁךְ interest, which comes from the verb נָשַׁךְ he bit. Interest is a bite taken out of your money. This, of course, is from the point of view of the borrower. From the point of the lender interest is רִבִּית meaning an " increase " of his money.
5. From דּוֹנַג wax we get דִּנֵּג he waxed.
6. From סַבּוֹן soap we get סִבֵּן he soaped.
7. From תּוֹךְ midst we get תִּוֵּךְ acted as go-between.
8. From שׁוּק market we get שִׁוֵּק he created markets.
9. From מָמוֹן money we get מִמֵּן he financed.

10. From סַיִף sword we get סַיֵּף he fenced.
11. From יַעַר forest we get יִעֵר forested.
12. From בָּסִיס base we get בִּסֵּס he based.
13. From אֱמֶת truth we get אִמֵּת he verified.
14. From פַּךְ flask we get פִּכָּה water bubbling or flowing.
15. From סִכּוּם sum we get סִכֵּם summarized, summed up.
16. Flavor with onions is בִּצֵּל.
17. Sprinkle with flour is קִמַּח.
18. Flavor with egg is בִּיֵּץ.
19. Stew is אִדָּה.
20. The verb coming from תְּאוֹם twin is הִתְאִים fit, be suitable for.
21. The verb coming from פֶּתַע sudden is הִפְתִּיעַ surprise.
22. The verb from תְּחִלָּה a beginning is הִתְחִיל he began.
23. The verb coming from זֵעָה perspiration is הֵזִיעַ he sweated.
24. The word coming from תּוֹרָה is הִתְרָה he warned, or really, he told, what the law תּוֹרָה was. This may be a little difficult for us to understand—until we realize that in the Mishna—where the word הַתְרָאָה was first used it referred specifically to a warning by two men that a certain act was a violation of the law—of the Torah and indicated the penalties for this violation.
25. From כְּרוּז announcement we get הִכְרִיז announced.
26. From קִפּוֹד porcupine we get הִקְפִּיד he was fussy.
27. From דֶּרֶךְ road we get הִדְרִיךְ he guided.
28. From אֶזְרָח citizen we get הִתְאַזְרֵחַ he became a citizen.
29. From סִנָּר apron we have הִסְתַּנֵּר he put on an apron.
30. From כַּרְכֹּם saffron we get הִתְכַּרְכֵּם he paled.
31. From נָכְרִי stranger we get הִתְנַכֵּר acted like a stranger.
32. From רֶגֶל foot we get הִתְרַגֵּל became accustomed.
33. תִּזְמֵר he orchestrated.

34. נִסֵּין he experimented.
35. עִמְלֵן he starched.
36. עִצְבֵּן made nervous.

DENOMINATIVE VERBS FROM PARTS OF THE BODY

37. Two other denominatives from עַיִן eye, are מְעַנְיֵין interesting and מְעוֹנֵן a soothsayer, one who looked in the crystal ball.
38. Another denominative from רֶגֶל foot is רוֹכֵל a peddlar (the ג has changed to a כ). The peddlars must have also been the tale bearers because רְכִילוּת is the regular Hebrew word for slander or gossip. There is the famous verse "Thou shalt not go about as a tale bearer" לֹא תֵלֵךְ רָכִיל.
39. Still another denominative from רֶגֶל is found in the very beautiful verse from Hosea, תִּרְגַּלְתִּי לְאֶפְרַיִם "I taught Ephraim to walk".
40. Another word from עָקֵב heel is עָקַב more usually spelled עִכֵּב to seize the heel, to hinder, to restrain.
41. The denominative from נְחִירַיִם nostrils is נָחַר snort.
42. The denominative from אֶצְבַּע finger is הִצְבִּיעַ he voted.
43. The denominative from כָּתֵף shoulder is כִּתֵּף he shouldered.
44. Here are some other denominative verbs from parts of the body:

From יָד hand we get יָדָה he threw.

From לֵבָב heart we get לִבֵּב he enchanted (literally he captured the heart of).

From גָּחוֹן belly we get גָּחַן he bent down.

With an interchange of two letters the guttural ח to ה

and the liquid נ to ר we get the word גָּהַר having the same sense “ he bent down ”.

From חֹפֶן hollow of hand we get חֹפֶן handful חָפַן he took a handful.

From גֶּלֶד skin we get הִגְלִיד form a skin or crust.

From טֶפַח handbreadth we get טִפַּח carry on palms, dandle, to help develop or bring to maturity. The qal טָפַח means to tap, to give a light blow—also using the hand.

From עֶצֶם bone we get עִצֵּם break bones.

From גֶּרֶם bone we get גָּרַם break bones.

From עֹרֶף back of neck we get עָרַף break the back of the neck.

From שֵׂעָר hair we get שָׂעַר bristle up.

From גֶּשֶׁם body we get הִתְגַּשֵּׁם materialize.

From חֹטֶם nose we get with metathasis מָחַט he wiped the nose.

From אַף nose we have אָנַף snort in anger, be angry.

From שְׁכֶם shoulder we get הִשְׁכִּים rise early. In the morning the shoulder of the beast of burden was loaded.

From צֶדַע temple we get הִצְדִּיעַ saluted.

From יָמִין right hand we get הֵימִין he went to the right.

From שְׂמֹאל left hand we get הִשְׂמְאִיל he went to the left.

From קָדְקֹד crown of the head we get קָדַד to bow one’s head. The usual form of this verb is וַיִּקֹּד.

QUESTIONS ON CHAPTER TEN

1. What is meant by saying that a verb is a denominative?
2. Trace the origin of the denominative verb תָּרַם?
3. Give three denominative verbs in the qal.
4. Why should לָבַן mean " made bricks "?
5. Give three denominative verbs in the פִּעֵל.
6. Why does הִקְפִּיד mean "act irritatedly"; הִפְתִּיעַ mean "he surprised"; and הִתְאִים mean " fit, to be suitable for "?
7. Give two reflexive denominative verbs.
8. Trace " הִתְעַבֵּר be furious " all the way back to its root.
9. Trace הִתְאַכְזֵב all the way back to its root.
10. Draw a picture of a man and label all the parts of the body from which Hebrew has created verbs (at least 12).
11. In music books and military manuals in Israel today the verb תִּרְגֵּל is used with the meaning " do exercises ". Can you trace this verb back to its root? You should have an equation with four words in it.

Can you match these two columns?

1. נָשַׁךְ – bit	1. דוּג – to fish דָּגָה – be numerous
2. קִפּוֹד – a porcupine	2. הִצְדִּיעַ – saluted
3. תַּרְגִּילִים – exercises	3. goes back to root רום
4. בְּכוֹר – first born	4. רֶגֶל
5. תּוֹרָה	5. is from פֶּתַע suddeness
6. הִפְתִּיעַ – surprised	6. הִתְחִיל made a beginning
7. two verbs from דָּג fish	7. gave rise to בִּכֵּר prefer
8. verb תָּרַם	8. הִקְפִּיד – acted fussily
9. תְּחִלָּה – a beginning	9. הִתְרָה warned-said this is the law
10. denominative from צֶדַע temple	10. נָשַׁךְ – took interest

Chapter XI

Why Lions Roar, Bees Buzz and Brooks Babble

Time: Many thousands of years ago.

A man came running in from the forest—breathless, wild-eyed, white with fear. He had seen a lion in the woods and heard its deep-throated roar. The man was now in the village and he wanted to tell his fellows of the danger that would soon be upon them. So he too screamed out to them the lion's roar: RI—RI—RI—. They heard him and they knew what he told them.

From this man's scream, from his attempt to imitate the lion's roar arose the Hebrew word for lion — אֲרִי.

The little children were playing at the edge of the clearing in front of their house. Suddenly their mother, horror struck, saw a snake near them, with lifted head, poised to strike. She hissed out to them sharply the warning sound חַשׁ imitating the very hiss of the snake. The children heard. They understood and ran to safety.

From this warning syllable חַשׁ arose the Hebrew word for snake נָחָשׁ.

The great poet Bialik listened to the music of the rustling leaves and with the poetic genius that was his, he created from the Hebrew word רַעַשׁ the word רִשְׁרוּשׁ rustling. So perfect and so beautiful was this word and so rapidly did its use spread that in later years people could hardly believe it was newly created, but were sure it must be a word from the Hebrew of thousands of years ago.

Onomatopoeia is a long and clumsy word but you have got to learn it, for it tells of one of the easiest and most interesting elements of language study. Onomatopoeia is man's attempt to imitate the sounds he hears about him in nature. Some of our most beautiful and poetic words arose out of these fumbling efforts to reproduce what was heard in jungle, forest, and field. The bee " buzzed ". There was " clanging ", " howling ", " yelling ", " wailing ", etc.

It was the most natural thing in the world to do, to describe the phenomena of life about by imitating the sounds one heard made. These words are among the most ancient in any language and Hebrew has an unusually large number of them. We do not know how language began. It is only this one group of words in each language, i.e., the onomatopoeic, whose origin is not in the least puzzling, in fact, it is so clear that even a child can readily understand how the words arose.

SOUNDS MADE BY MAN

Man himself is responsible for a variety of fairly strange noises which are reproduced more or less exactly. When he has a cold he will sneeze עָטַשׁ or spit כּוּחַ or clear his throat כַּעְכֵּעַ. He will probably gargle his throat גַּרְגֵּר and speak through his nose אַנְפֵּף. When with friends he will talk idly פַּטְפֵּט or chatter מַלְמֵל. If embarrased he may גַּמְגֵּם stammer, he may grumble לַמְלֵם. If cheerful he will whistle שָׁרַק; or hum הָמָה. When eating he may sip מַצְמֵץ or smack his lips פַּמְפֵּם. If greedy one may lick לִקְלֵק the plate. If an Oriental, and a guest, he will belch גִּהֵק in appreciation of his host. He would be remiss—if he did not offer this—to our mind—strange thanks. He may hiccup שָׁהַק. If in pain he may נָנַח groan. When asleep he will snore נָחַר. If sleepy he will פִּהֵק yawn.

SOUNDS MADE BY ANIMALS

In the animal world both the animals and the sounds they make are frequently onomatopoeic. A lion cub is גור (compare the English word " growl " or the sound grrrrr); the lion roars שָׁאַג; a donkey brays נָעַר; a cow moos גָּעָה (so mournful is the sound of a cow's mooing that this word has in an expanded form become הִתְגַּעְגֵּעַ to long for); the horse gallops דָּהַר; the dog barks נָבַח. The word bird צִפּוֹר is onomatopoeic as are, of course, the words for its chirping צִפְצֵף or צִוֵּץ. The Hebrew word for dove is תּוֹר named for its cooing. Geese cackle קִרְקֵר; chickens cluck קִדְקֵד. A bee buzzes זִמְזֵם. The word for a fly is זְבוּב.

MUSICAL AND OTHER

Naturally there will be onomatopoeic words to indicate musical instruments and the sounds they make. From the shofar we have the calls תְּקִיעָה and תְּרוּעָה; from the drum תֹּף we have the verb תּוֹפֵף; cymbals are צֶלְצְלִים; a trumpet is a חֲצוֹצְרָה.

The gurgle of water coming from a bottle gave בַּקְבּוּק bottle its name. A drop is טִפָּה; the verbs " to drop or to drip " are נָטַף and טִפְטֵף. The clock's ticking is תִּקְתֵּק, from זִמְזֵם buzz we have the noun זַמְזָם a buzzer. The verb הֵרִיעוּ they shouted, sounds just like the English verb hurrahed and means pretty much the same; one can hear a hissing sound in the word " תְּסִיסָה bubbling, fermenting ".

נְחִירָה
SNORING

אֲרִי
LION

צִפְצוּף
CHIRPING

תֹּף
DRUM

WORDS COME FROM SOUNDS

Many words are not so obviously onomatopoeic. Their forms have in the course of centuries become so conventionalized that we hardly recognize their true origin; they nevertheless quite definitely belong to this group. Some such words are:

קָצַץ – cut, in imitation of the ax striking against a tree (note how it resembles the English word " cut "). The words for scratching or scraping such as גָּרַד, חָרַט and שָׂרַט. To blow is פּוּחַ and נָפַח; these imitate the expulsion of breath. קָרָא to cry out, קוֹל a sound or a call are onomatopoeic in both Hebrew and English. רַעַם means thunder. הֵידָד is hurrah.

There are sometimes whole families coming from one onomatopoeic word. Along with הָמָה hum, which comes from the humming noise one makes with the mouth shut, we also have הוּם with the same meaning. Sounding like it are נָהַם to moan, and נָאַם to speak. There is הֲמוּלָּה noise. All these words are obviously based on the syllable הַם.

Another family centers around the nasal sound of "n" mostly the words mean sighing, groaning, grumbling.

sigh – אָנַח (also נֶאֱנַח and הִתְאַנֵּחַ)
sigh – אָנַק
sigh – נָהַק
sigh – נוּק
complain – רָגַן
complain – הִתְאוֹנֵן
lament, wail – קִינָה־קוֹנֵן

Still another family centers around ל and indicates yelling or wailing. We have:

אָלָה – mourn. Most Jews who chant the beautiful Tisha

B'Av lament אֱלִי צִיּוֹן hardly realize that it means "Mourn or lament O' Zion".

wail – אָלַל

The common expression is אַלְלַי לִי which means "woe is to me".

wail – יָלַל
wail – הֵילִיל

There is a group which could be called "knock" words. They are:

to strike – נָקַף
strike – נָגַף
to knock or strike – נָקַשׁ – נִקֵּשׁ
to hit – נָגַד
touch – נָגַע

Onomatopoeic words frequently occur in the פִּלְפֵּל form because they reproduce sounds that go on and on. It is natural to attempt to imitate this repetitive quality in the word; it makes for a much more effective and adequate picture of the sound. Some examples are:

ring – צִלְצֵל
knock at – קִשְׁקֵשׁ
chatter – פִּטְפֵּט
drop – טִפְטֵף — from טִפָּה a drop
knock at door – קִרְקֵשׁ
knocker or clapper – קַרְקַשׁ

One of the most interesting of the onomatopoeic groups is the "sh" group, indicating silence—interesting because it is to be found almost all over the world.

Hebrew has:

quiet – שֶׁקֶט
he was silent – שָׁתַק
he whispered – לָחַשׁ
softly, quietly – חֶרֶשׁ
silently – חֲשַׁאי
hush – הַס

he whispered very quietly לְחֻשֵׁשׁ

QUESTIONS ON CHAPTER ELEVEN

1. What Hebrew words come from the roaring of the lion, the hissing of the snake and the rustling of the leaves?
2. In what important way are onomatopoeic words different from all other Hebrew words?
3. What are some of the rather weird noises that man himself makes and for which we have onomatopoeic words?
4. What are some of the onomatopoeic words given to us by the animal world?
5. What are some words whose onomatopoeic origin is not so obvious?
6. What Hebrew onomatopoeic words sound very much like to hum, to wail and to knock?
7. Give four Hebrew " sh " words.

Can you match these two columns?

1. hissing of a snake	1. צִפּוֹר
2. water gurgling from a bottle	2. שָׂרַט־חָרַט
3. two shofar calls	3. נָחַר־עָטַשׁ
4. a lion's cub makes a sound of gurr	4. תֹּף
5. Hebrew verb sounding like hurrah	5. שָׁתַק־לָחַשׁ
6. two words for scratching	6. גּוּר
7. two sounds made frequently by men	7. shouted – הֵרִיעוּ
8. two silence words	8. בַּקְבּוּק
9. birds make chirping sounds	9. תְּרוּעָה־תְּקִיעָה
10. sound of a drum	10. נָחָשׁ

Chapter XII

With "Dragger Dawn" or Sounds Do Get Mixed Up

I wrote a book of Hebrew stories that is used in the public high schools. In the English introduction to one of them a line which tells how the murderer entered a room has the words " with dagger drawn ". A great many of the students who read this line aloud say: " With dragger dawn ".

In a vocabulary test, when I give the word לְשָׁוְא at least three or four students will write " He dressed ". So natural and so common is the phenomenon of mixing up the order of sounds.

There is a word for this—that is, when we misplace sounds within a word—it is " METATHESIS ". Take a few seconds off, look at the word and learn it. The accent is on the syllable " tath " and the " a " is pronounced like the " a " in fat.

The classic illustration of this in English is the word butterfly. This beautiful insect, it is said, has nothing to do with butter; the word was originally and sensibly " flutter-by ". However, the sounds were metathesised, mixed up so often, that the correct form " flutterby " after a while became incorrect.

We smile when we hear a person say, " I will akse him ",

but the really funny thing is that " akse " is probably the originally correct form of the word. The present " ask " at one time was an ignorant metathesis of " akse ". Similarly " bird " was originally " bridd ". A curl was originally " crul " and " third " was " thrid ". " Wrought " is another form of " worked ".

English is a comparatively young language. Essentially, it is a mixture of Anglo-Saxon and French. This mixture became recognizable as English only in the 1300's. Not long after this, printing was invented and this stabilized and made fairly permanent the forms of words. Once printing had fixed the spelling forms there were only few examples of words having alternate, metathetic forms.

Not so with Hebrew. Hebrew is a very ancient language having a history going back thousands of years. During by far the greatest part of this time there was no printing and so large numbers of words are current in two forms; the originally correct form and a metathesized one. There were many different tribes in Israel, many geographical centers quite isolated and for these reasons different forms of the same word would be in use in the various parts of Israel.

In the largest number of examples of metathesis in Hebrew, not the faintest difference in meaning exists between the two forms of the word. Often we do not even know which was the originally correct form and often it is not really important. Many metatheses present two forms of a word with but one meaning.

Here is a group of common examples. After you have grasped the idea, we will let you guess at some others.

In Hebrew we have both:

כֶּבֶשׂ – a lamb   כֶּשֶׂב

יָעֵף – weary   עָיֵף

עַוְלָה	עַלְוָה	– unrighteousness
מַתְלְעוֹת	מַלְתְּעוֹת	– jaw teeth
גָּזַר	גָּרַז	– cut (the word גַּרְזֶן axe is from גָּרַז)
עָרַף	רָעַף	– drop down
בֶּהָלָה	בַּלָּהָה	– confusion, fear
שַׁלְפּוּחִית	שַׁלְחוּפִית	– bladder
תּוֹאֲנָה – occasion	תְּאוּנָה	– accident
תְּאוֹ	תּוֹא	– buffalo
זָקַר	זָרַק	– throw, fling
לַמְלֵם	מַלְמֵל	– mutter
סָחִישׁ	שָׁחִיס	– aftermath, aftergrowth
אַגְמוֹן – bulrush	גֹּמֶא	– rush, reed

The Hebrew word כְּתֹנֶת has become " tunic " in Latin and English.

Can you work out the following, that is, can you find another word with the same letters in a different order but which has essentially the same meaning?

1. לַהֲקָה – a company
2. לָבָה – a flame
3. סָכָל – a fool
4. שִׂמְלָה – dress
5. נֶאֱלָח – filthy (get the root first by dropping the נ)
6. נְאָקָה – sigh
7. זַעֲוָה – terror
8. הָדַךְ – thrust at, strike
9. אָבָה – desire

The next group is more interesting. Not only are the spellings different but also different meanings have developed.

כֶּבֶשׂ כֶּשֶׂב

LAMB

לַבָּה לַהַב

FLAME

חֵלֶק חַקְלָא

FIELD

כְּתֹנֶת

TUNIC

LETTERS CHANGE PLACES IN HEBREW

חֵלֶק portion; חַקְלָא field is one's portion of land which is, of course, the real source of all wealth. From חַקְלָא we have developed חַקְלַאי a farmer and חַקְלָאִי agricultural and חַקְלָאוּת agriculture. גַּמָּד a dwarf גָּדַם cut off. Words meaning short usually come from roots meaning cut. Thus קָצָר short is from קָצַר cut. קָטָן small; the primitive root קט means cut. The English word " short " means " sheared or cut off ". חִתּוּל wrapping, diaper מֶלְתָּחָה (root לתח) is wearing apparel—it is now used in sense of suitcase. עֵרֶב cross or woof line in weaving. The common Hebrew expression is שְׁתִי וָעֵרֶב. The original word was, of course, עָבַר.

Can you work out the following—that is find words which are the metatheses of these?

10. tie packages אָרַז
11. forget שָׁכַח
12. blow, breathe נָשַׁף
13. great rift of the Jordan and the Dead Sea to the Gulf of Akaba עֲרָבָה
14. midst עֶצֶם
15. speaking inarticulately עִלֵּג

Each word in this group presents two problems. First there has been an interchange of letters—in each case it is a guttural that has interchanged—and in addition a metathesis. What can you do with these?

16. tremble רָעַד
17. have a bad odor עָבַשׁ
18. be strong אָמַץ
19. be dark עָלַף

This group offers a very unusual difficulty. In addition to a metathesis the word you must find is also opposite in meaning to the given word.

Think now—metathesis plus opposite meaning.

20. uproot תָּלַשׁ
21. move עָתַק
22. slip מָעַד
23. vagrant צָעַן

Answers to the questions in the chapter.

With " Dragger Dawn "—or Sounds do get mixed up.

1. The doublet of לַהֲקָה – a company is קְהִלָּה – community.
2. The doublet of לֶבָה – a flame is לַהַב – a flame.
3. The doublet of סָכָל – a fool is כְּסִיל – a fool.
4. The doublet of שַׂלְמָה – a dress is שִׂמְלָה – a dress
5. The doublet of נֶאֱלַח – filthy is חֶלְאָה – filth
6. The doublet of נְאָקָה – sigh is אֲנָקָה – sigh
7. The doublet of זַעֲוָה – terror is זְוָעָה – terror
8. The doublet of הָדַךְ – thrust at, strike is דָּכָה – thrust at.
9. The doublet of אָבָה – desire is אָהַב – love.
10. The doublet of אָרַז – tie packages is אָזַר – bind, girdle.
11. The doublet of שָׁכַח – forget is חֹשֶׁךְ – darkness.
12. The doublet of נָשַׁף – blow, breathe is נֶפֶשׁ – soul.
13. The עֲרָבָה – the great rift, from the Dead Sea to the gulf of Akaba is from עָבַר.
14. The doublet of עֶצֶם – midst is אֶמְצַע – midst.
15. The doublet of עִלֵּג – speaking inarticulately is לַעַג – mockery.
16. The doublet of רָעַד – tremble is חָרַד – tremble.
17. The doublet of עָבַשׁ – have a bad odor is בָּאַשׁ – malodorous.

18. The doublet of אָמַץ – be strong is עָצַם – be strong.
19. The doublet of עָלַף – be dark is אָפֵל – darkness.
20. The doublet of תָּלַשׁ – uproot is שָׁתַל – plant.
21. The doublet of עָתַק – move is תָּקַע – stick in.
22. The doublet of מָעַד – slip, totter is עָמַד – stand.
23. The doublet of צָעַן – vagrant is נָעַץ – fix, set firmly.

QUESTIONS ON CHAPTER XII

1. Give some examples of metathesis in English words.
2. Why should Hebrew have many more examples of metathesis than English?
3. Give five examples of metathesis in Hebrew.
4. How does the Hebrew word for farmer חַקְלַאי arise?
5. Why is גַּמָּד a dwarf?

Can you match these two columns?

1. agriculture – חַקְלָאוּת	1. metathesis with interchange of one letter
2. עָתַק־תָּקַע	2. עַלְוָה־עַוְלָה
3. two words for lamb	3. tunic
4. אָבָה – desire	4. metathesis plus opposite meaning
5. two words for unrighteousness	5. חֹשֶׁךְ – darkness
6. עָצַם – be strong	6. גִּדֵּם – cut off
7. גַּמָּד – dwarf	7. כֶּשֶׂב־כֶּבֶשׂ
8. שָׁכַח – forget	8. אָהַב
9. כֻּתֹּנֶת – metathesized in English	9. חֵלֶק – one's portion in life
10. רָעַד־חָרַד	10. אָמַץ

Chapter XIII

Beel=Meel=Veel=Peel or Sounds do Interchange

My little son Carmi, almost two years old, dropped a toy elephant from his crib. He tried unsuccessfully to.retrieve it. He then turned to me to enlist my aid. He cried excitedly, אַבָּא אַבָּא בִּיל בִּיל. I feigned indifference. He continued, אַבָּא וִיל וִיל. I did not stir. He then yelled, אַבָּא מִיל מִיל. I still did not move. Finally his lips framed the correct sound, אַבָּא פִּיל פִּיל. I rewarded him by reaching down for the elephant. The young man was certainly a living example of how people interchange labial sounds.

There is an extremely important law or principle of words that you must learn thoroughly and master before you can really have any fun with words. It is called " interchange of letters " and simply means this:

Sounds made in the same part of the mouth or made in the same way, tend to change with one another. This occurs in every language and before we illustrate in Hebrew we will give several examples showing how this happens in English words.

The sounds that interchange come in groups. The name we give the groups depends on where in the mouth they are formed. You must learn these groups because almost all the work we will be doing requires a knowledge of them, and they will help in the study of any language.

LABIAL OR LIP LETTERS INTERCHANGE

The first of these groups is called labial and consists of B, V, M, P, F; in Hebrew ב, ו, מ, פ. It is called labial because the sounds are framed at the lips. The lips coming together try to stop the air coming out of the mouth. Put your finger on your lips and you will feel very quickly that these letters B, V, M, P, F, or ב, ו, מ, פ are made in practically the same way.

In English we have the following pairs of words—pairs which had one origin and later developed differences in one or two letters. We can recognize without too much difficulty and that the differences belong to the group B, V, M, P, F that the meanings are essentially the same. Thus we have:

sever–separate	telegram–telegraph
triple–treble	robber-rover
kidnap really is kid–nab	lip–labial

Probate means to prove that a will is authentic.

We say " I haf to go " not " have ", changing the " V " to " F ". You won't find it in the dictionary but you would have to go far and wide to find a person who does not say it; " of " is usually pronounced " ov ".

In Hebrew, far more anciently than in English we have numerous examples of this phenomenon. Thus we have the series:

נָשַׁף - נָשַׁב - נָשַׁם

All three of these words have the same meaning—to breathe or to blow—the only difference is that one has ב the other מ and the other פ.

From נָשַׁם we have the well known word נְשָׁמָה – soul; from נָשַׁף with change of place of the last two letters we have נֶפֶשׁ – soul; also the verb הִנָּפֵשׁ – take breath, be refreshed.

239 *Beel = Meel = Veel = Peel or Sounds do interchange*

BEEL - MEEL - VEEL - FEEL - PEEL

SOUNDS MADE BY THE LIPS INTERCHANGE

Illustrations of individual interchanges are as follows: מ = ב מָרִיא – stout, fat בָּרִיא – now mostly used in the sense of healthy. בָּרָא means create and בָּרִיא is healthy. These two words look alike but really are not because בָּרִיא is simply a variant pronunciation or variant form of מָרִיא. Jacob was also pronounced Jacome.

	רָבָה – shoot	רָמָה – throw
ב = פ	רִפֵּד – pad, upholster	רבד – is the root of מַרְבָד – rug
ב = ו	לִבְלֵב – blossom gives rise to	לוּלָב – branch of palm tree
	גַּב – back	גֵּו – back

Scholars say that קוֹל gave rise to קָבַל complain. קַבַל in Arabic means " to protest, to complain ". The word קָבַל basically means " to raise one's voice in angry protest and complaint ".

פ = מ	זָעַף – gets angry	זָעַם – get angry
פ = מ	פָּלַט – get out, escape	מָלַט – escape
פ = ו	גוּף – body, another form is the word גְּוִיָּה	
ו = מ	אַרְגָּמָן – purple	אַרְגְּוָן – purple

To work out the doublet of other forms of the following words should not be too hard because there is only one change to watch out for, i.e.; ב may equal מ = פ = ו and the words you have to find are closely related in meaning to the words given you.

1. שָׁלוֹם – another word meaning quiet, peaceful
2. טָמַע – vanish without a trace. The word טְמִיעָה means assimilation
3. פּוּרָה – wine vat-hole dug in the ground
4. פָּרַח – fly away
5. נַוְלוּת – wickedness

6. אָבָה – desire
7. אָבִיק – channel
8. בָּצַע – cut
9. בִּזֵּר – scatter
10. רָפַס – stamp down
11. פָּקַע – split, burst
12. סֶמֶל – statue, symbol. There is also a metathesis, i.e., the letters change places in this word
13. חָפָא – cover over

DENTAL LETTERS INTERCHANGE

The next group of letters that interchange are the dentals. The tongue presses either against the upper teeth or a little above them. In English, this group is D, T and TH. If you listen carefully to your ordinary pronunciation of words like city and butter you will find that the sound of " T " is practically " D ". You will thus see how easily a " T " can pass into a " D ". The familiar German word Brot is bread in English. In English, the past tense of kiss, i.e. kissed is pronounced kist. The name of the Spanish language spoken by the Sephardic Jews is Ladino, a way of pronouncing the word Latin. Spanish came from Latin.

In Hebrew the letters of this group are ד, ת and ט. The roots טוּר, דּוּר, תּוּר have the sense of going around, surrounding.

Other examples are:

תָּעָה־טָעָה – err
נוּט – to move נוּד to move to and fro, to wander
חָתַף־חָטַף – seize
רֶתֶת־רֶטֶט – tremble
שָׁתַק־שָׁקַט – be silent, there is also a metathesis
14. נְדָן – is the gift that goes with the bride

To what very common Hebrew word is it related? A common form of this word is נְדוּנְיָה.

THE SIBILANT OR HISSING LETTERS INTERCHANGE

The next group is called the sibilants, a word which means whistling or hissing. In English they are the sounds S, Z, SH. How readily they interchange in English can be noted from the fact that the letter "s" has among others these three sibilant sounds:

"s" as in seat
"s" as in birds—it has here the sound of "z"
"s" as in sugar—it has here the sound of "sh"

Hebrew is rich in sibilants which also frequently interchange. We pronounce some of them quite alike, though in ancient times they were quite different. This, of course, makes for errors in spelling. The Hebrew sibilants are ז, ס, שׂ, שׁ and צ. צ is now pronounced ts, originally it was an "s" sound pronounced deep back in the throat. The Yemenite Jews still pronounce the צ that way.

Thus we have in Hebrew עָלַץ, עָלַז and עָלַס. All these three words mean to be happy, exult.

סָפַן – צָפַן – שָׂפַן – all mean to hide
סוּר – זוּר – צוּר – all mean go around, surround.

ז = צ	זָעַק	– cry	צָעַק	– cry
	צָרַב	– burn, scald	זָרַב	– burn, scald
ס = צ	חָמַס	– do violence	חָמַץ	– be ruthless
	רִצֵּץ	– crush in pieces	רִסֵּס	– to crush, to sprinkle
שׂ = ס	שָׂרַט	– scratch	סָרַט	– scratch
שׂ = צ	שָׂחַק	– laugh	צָחַק	– laugh
שׁ = ז	נָשַׁף	– blow at	נָזַף	– scold, rebuke

See if you can work out the following. There is only one change to watch out for—an interchange of sibilants, that is ס may equal ז = שׁ = שׂ = צ.

15. זָהָב – gold. What word sounds like it and has something of its meaning?
16. כָּבַשׁ – press down, later it meant to subdue, conquer. Why should the word כִּבֵּס wash, be related to it?
17. שְׂדֵרָה is a row, and orderly arrangement. From what word does it come?
18. צָרַף – to refine metals. Think what the process of refining metals chiefly consists of. Then find the related word.
19. Why should צָרַב to be parched, be related to שָׂרַף burned? What additional interchange is there in this word?
20. זָעִיר – small, insignificant. What is the related word?
21. צֹהַר – window. צָהֳרַיִם – noon. How are these two words related? To what other word are they both related?

The commonest interchange by far in the sibilant group is between שׂ and ס. There must have been at one time a distinction between שׂ and ס. However by Mishnaic times and perhaps even earlier it was lost and we find the rabbis writing practically all biblical words that have שׂ in them with a ס. In almost all cases where שׂ and ס both occur the שׂ is original. It has been suggested that except for sacred literature and poetry we drop the שׂ entirely and write only ס. Schoolchildren would welcome this innovation.

These are the commonest words in which this variant spelling occurs,

תָּפַס־תָּפַשׂ – grasp	סוּחַ־שׂוּחַ – talk
סַכִּין־שַׂכִּין – knife	סִיד־שִׂיד – calcium

חֶרֶס־חֶרֶשׁ – clay
סָחַט־שָׁחַט – press
שֶׂכֶל־הִסְתַּכֵּל – intelligence, look attentively
סָתַם־שָׁתַם – stop up
שַׂהֲרוֹנִית – ornaments shaped like moon
מַשּׂוֹר – a saw, same root as נְסֹרֶת – sawdust
סוּט־שָׂטָה־שׂוּט – turn aside
אָרַס־אָרַשׂ – betroth
סֵבֶר־שֵׂבֶר – hope
חָסַךְ־חָשַׂךְ – held back
סַהַר – moon

פָּרַס, פָּרַשׂ – spread. (There is really a פָּרַס not a variant spelling of פָּרַשׂ which means " to tear "; from that פָּרַס which means tear we get פְּרוּסַת לֶחֶם piece of bread).

The fortress near the Dead Sea to which the Jews fled when Jerusalem was conquered by the Romans in the year 70 C.E. was called simply מְצוּדָה, the Hebrew word for fortress. The Romans wrote this in Latin Masada and Hebrew simply and unthinkingly borrowed it back in the form מְסָדָה.

PALATALS

The fourth group is called the palatals and consists of the letters K, G (hard), Y. They are formed by the tongue pressing against the palate and trying (unsuccessfully, of course, or otherwise there would be no sound) to stop the breath. Y hardly sounds as though it would be closely related to G and K yet we have many words in English that show this relationship.

Some doublets in English which show this palatal interchange are:

G = Y royal – regal
garden – yard
frail – fragile
G = K intrigue – intricate

K = Y Jacome (a later form of Jacob) was also pronounced Jaime. This is how James arose out of Jacob.

In German and Yiddish we have:

German Auge is equivalent to English eye.

German sagen is equivalent to English say.

German gern is equivalent to English yearn.

In Hebrew the palatal group consists of ג, כ, ק and י.

In addition ח may sometime equal כ or ק.

זָכַךְ equals זָקַק equals זַגָּג to be or make clear. From זָכַךְ we have זְכוּכִית glass etc.; זַגָּג is a glazier; זָקַק is to distill, to make a liquid clear.

כ equals י—כָּשֵׁר fit, proper equals יָשָׁר straight, honest.

ק equals ג—נָקַף strike equals נָגַף strike, knock

קֶשֶׁר connection, gives rise to גֶּשֶׁר bridge

שָׂרַג entangle, intertwine שָׂרַךְ intertwine

תִּכֵּן ordain, arrange, establish equals תִּקֵּן ordain, establish

לִקֵּק lick לִחֵךְ lick (here a ק equals ח as well)

See what you can do with these:

22. From רֶגֶל. What business man went around mostly on foot?
23. קוֹבַע – a helmet. What is the related word?
24. כַּבִּיר – strong. What is the related word?
25. שׂוּךְ – to enclose. What is the related word?
26. קִפֵּל – fold. What is the related word?
27. קֵהָה – dull, blunted. What is the related word?
28. לְחֹלַח – wet. What is the related word?
29. קָשִׁישׁ – old. What is the related word?
30. סָגַר – close. What is the related word? This particular word occurs in the story of the flood.
31. מָסַךְ – pour. The related word has two interchanges —a sibilant as well as a palatal.

GUTTURALS

The next group ע, ח, ה, א are called gutturals because they are made deep in the throat (guttar-throat in Latin).

Some examples are:

ע equals ח פָּצַע – cut, split = פָּצַח – split, crack
ע equals א גָּעַל – soil, dirty = גָּאַל – soil
תָּעַב – despise = תָּאַב – despise, abominate
ע equals ה פָּדַע – redeem = פָּדָה – redeem
ה equals א נֶאְדָּר – glorious = נֶהְדָּר – magnificent
ה equals א חָפָה – cover over = חָפָא – cover
לאה – be weary = להה – be weary as in
וַתֵּלַהּ הָאָרֶץ Gen. 47:13
ה equals ח מָחָה – wipe, rub = נִמְהָה – was worn out
ח equals א חוֹכֵר – farmer = אִכָּר – farmer. This is the Assyrian form of the word; they reduced gutturals to א.

Now you can work these out:

32. חוג – a circle. What is the related word?
33. פֶּתַע – suddenness. What is the related word?
34. קָרָה – to meet. What is the related word meaning toward?

The next two words involve changes of two letters.

35. עָקַד – bind. There is a palatal as well as a guttural change.
36. אָבַר – lead. A labial as well as a guttural change.
37. What obviously does עִכֵּל digest, come from?
38. With what word is עָפָר dust usually combined?
39. אָרִיס – a tenant farmer. From what Hebrew word does it come?

There is a sibilant as well as a guttural change.

40. To what common Hebrew adjective is גִּבְעָה hill related?
41. מֹהַר – the gift a groom paid to obtain a bride. What is the related word?

LIQUIDS

The next group is called the liquids. They are l, m, n, r or in Hebrew ר, נ, מ, ל. These letters just flow on. They can be prolonged and sounded for as long as one has breath. L and R are made very close one to the other; and in almost the same way, so much so that the Chinese pronounces all r's as l's and the Japanese vice versa i.e.; they sound all l's as r's. The Chinese pronunciation of American as Amelican is well known. In both " m " and " n " the breath comes through the nose.

Some examples of interchanges of liquid letters in Hebrew are:

ל = נ	לִשְׁכָּה – office, chamber	נִשְׁכָּה – office, chamber
ל = נ	לָקַט – pick up	נָקַט – take
נ = מ	מַשְׂטֵמָה – hatred	שִׂטְנָה – hatred
נ = מ	טָמַן – hide	טָמִיר – hidden
נ = מ	רֵיקָם – empty—also written	רֵיקָן – empty
ל = ר	צֹהַר – skylight, window	הִצְהִיל – make shine

מ = נ frequently in plural endings in Mishnaic Hebrew.

We commonly pronounce the Hebrew phrase יום טוב holiday, as " yuntif " changing the מ to נ (and also the ב to פ). זָנַק is burst forth. Another form of the word is זָרַק throw.

The Aramaic form of the word אַלְמָנָה is אַרְמַלְתָּא-the ל became ר and the נ became ל.

Now let's see what you can do with these:

42. What are two closely related words in Hebrew for chain?

43. גָּמַל – weaning-the close of the nursing period. What is the related word?

44. לון – to lodge. From what common Hebrew noun does it come?
45. נָשַׁל – to slip off. What is the related word?
46. חֶבֶל – a rope. What is the related word?
47. נָחַץ – is to press. What is the related word?
48. קֻמְקוּם – a teakettle. What is the related word?
49. שָׂטַם – to hate. What is the related word?
50. בָּחַן – to examine. What is the related word?
51. מוט – move, shake. What is the related word?
52. גַּלְעִין – seed. What is the related word?
53. כָּמַס – hide. What is the related word?
54. The בַּר of בַּר מִצְוָה really equals?
55. גָּחַן – bend over. To what Biblical verb is it closely related?

There is a guttural as well as liquid interchange.

THE SEMI-VOWELS ו AND י

Letters of the alphabet are divided into two groups—consonants and vowels. The essence of the distinction is very simple. What makes a letter a consonant is that something, somewhere in the mouth tries to stop the breath from coming out. It may be the lips coming together, and then we call it a labial consonant, one of the group B, V, M, P, F. It may be the tongue pressing against the upper teeth and then we call the letters dentals such as T, D. It may be the tongue pressing the palate and then we have the palatals K, G, Y. In all cases it is of the essence of the consonant that something, somewhere, obstructs or tries to stop the breath coming out. This obstruction of the breath is what helps to give strength, body and force to the consonants.

With the vowels on the other hand it is just the opposite.

In the vowel the breath comes pouring out of the mouth—and nothing whatsoever stops it. Repeat aloud A, E, I, O, U, and you will see how true it is.

ו AND י ARE SEMI-VOWELS

Two of the consonants ו and י (ו really and anciently equals w) are called semi-vowels. They are halfway between the categories of a consonant and vowel for this reason. *While the breath is obstructed* (making it a consonant) *the obstruction is verv slight* and these two letters can very readily become vowels—the ו becoming " oo " and the consonant י becoming the vowel " ee ".

These two letters interchange very frequently in Hebrew. Almost all verbs, now first letter י, were originally first letter ו, and in many of the binyanim still retain the original ו. This we can see by the verb יָדַע.

The נִפְעַל is נוֹדַע
The הִפְעִיל is הוֹדִיעַ
The הִתְפַּעֵל is הִתְוַדַּע

In Hebrew ו passes into י and י passes into ו with perfectly astonishing ease. Many verbs middle ו exist in two forms—middle ו and middle י. Thus we have both לון and לִין; דון and דִּין; שׂום and שִׂים etc.

Verbs middle ו frequently form their פִּעֵל with a middle י thus:

From קום – rise we get קִיֵּם – fulfil (cause to rise).
From חוב – debt we get חִיֵּב cause to be in debt.
From בּוּשָׁה – shame we get בִּיֵּשׁ – shamed.

Verbs middle ו will form nouns in the פַּעָל pattern by changing ו to י. Thus:

from חוט – thread we get חַיָּט – tailor.

from דוּג – to fish we get דַּיָּג – fisherman.
from בּוֹר – pit we get בַּיָּר – well digger.
The word רַוָּק – bachelor comes from the word רֵיק – empty.

ANSWERS

SOUNDS DO INTERCHANGE

LABIALS

1. שַׁלְוָה means peace, quiet, and it is the same as the word שָׁלוֹם except for the interchange of מ to ו.
2. The doublet of טָמַע is טָבַע – to sink.
3. The doublet of פּוּרָה – wine vat is בּוֹר – pit.
4. The doublet of פָּרַח – fly away is בָּרַח – flee.
5. The doublet of נַוְלוּת wickedness is נְבָלָה – wickedness.
6. The doublet of אָבָה – desire is אָוָה – desire.
7. The doublet of אָבִיק – outlet is אָפִיק – channel.
8. The doublet of בָּצַע – cut is פָּצַע – wounded.
9. The doublet of בִּזֵּר – scatter is פִּזֵּר – scatter.
10. The doublet of רָפַס – stamp down is רָמַס – tread.
11. The doublet of פָּקַע – split is בָּקַע – split.
12. The doublet of סֵמֶל – statue, symbol is פֶּסֶל – idol.
13. The doublet of חָפָא – cover over is חָבָא – hide.

DENTAL

14. The doublet of נָדָן – the gift that goes with the bride is נָתַן – he gave.

SIBILANT

15. The doublet of זָהָב – gold is צָהֹב – yellow.
16. כִּבֵּס is related to כָּבַשׁ to press down, because in washing, the clothing was pressed upon.

17. The doublet of שְׂדֵרָה – row, orderly arrangement is סִדֵּר – arrange.
18. The word related to צָרַף – refine metals is שָׂרַף – burn. Metals are refined by subjecting them to heat sufficient to melt them.
19. When a person is שָׁרַב parched it seems as though he is burning up שָׂרַף.

Note the large group of words that belong to this family of burning, being parched, smelting, refining etc.

שָׂרַף – burn
צָרַף – refined metals
צָרַב – to be burned, to be scorched
זָרַב – to be burnt, to be scorched
שָׁרַב – to be parched. In the last three words in addition to the sibilant change there is a labial ב = פ

20. The doublet of זָעִיר – small, insignificant is צָעִיר – young.
21. צֹהַר – window, from which the זֹהַר light comes. צָהֳרַיִם noon, is the time of the greatest light.

PALATALS

22. The doublet of רֶגֶל is רוֹכֵל – a peddlar.
23. The doublet of קוֹבַע – helmet is כּוֹבַע – hat.
24. The doublet of כַּבִּיר – strong is גִּבּוֹר – mighty.
25. The doublet of שׂוּךְ – inclose is סִיָג – fence.
26. The doublet of קִפֵּל – fold is כִּפֵּל – fold, double.
27. The doublet of כֵּהֶה – dull, blunted is קֵהֶה – dim.
28. The doublet of לַחְלֵחַ – wet is לִכְלֵךְ – soil, dirty.
29. The doublet of קָשִׁישׁ – old is יָשִׁישׁ – old.
30. The doublet of סָגַר – closed is סָכַר – shut.
31. The doublet of מָסַךְ – pour is מָזַג – pour.

GUTTURALS

32. The doublet of חוּג – circle is עוּג – circle.
33. The doublet of פֶּתַע – suddenness is פִּתְאֹם – suddenly.
34. The word לִקְרַאת – toward.
35. The doublet of עָקַד – bind is אָגַד – bind.
36. The doublet of אָבָר – lead is עוֹפֶרֶת – lead.
37. The doublet of עִכֵּל – digest is the word אָכַל – ate.
38. The word עָפָר – dust is associated with and is the original form of אֵפֶר – ashes.
39. The word אָרִיס – tenant farmer is a doublet of חָרַשׁ – plough.
40. גִּבְעָה is a doublet of גָּבוֹהַּ.
41. The doublet of מֹהַר – the gift paid to obtain a bride is מְחִיר – price.

LIQUIDS

42. Two closely related Hebrew words for chain are שַׁרְשֶׁרֶת and שַׁלְשֶׁלֶת.
43. The doublet of גָּמַל – wean, close of the nursing period is גָּמַר.
44. The verb לוּן – to lodge comes from the common Hebrew word לַיִל – night.
45. The doublet of נָשַׁל – to slip off is נָשַׁר – to fall out of.
46. The doublet of חֶבֶל – rope is the root חָבַר – to be joined together.
47. The doublet of נָחַץ – press is לָחַץ – press.
48. The doublet of קֻמְקוּם – teakettle is קַנְקַן – container.
49. The doublet of שָׂטַם – hate is שָׂטָן – adversary, more

popularly known as Satan. Some scholars, tho, think שָׂטָן is from שׂוּט to roam.

50. The doublet of בָּחַן – examined is בָּחַר – chose.
51. The doublet of מוּט – move, shake, is נוּט – move.
52. The doublet of גַּלְעִין – seed is גַּרְעִין – seed.
53. The doublet of כָּמַס – hide is כָּנַס – gather.
54. The בַּר of בַּר מִצְוָה really means בֵּן – son.
55. The word גָּחַן – bend over is related to the Biblical verb גָּהַר also bend over.

QUESTIONS ON CHAPTER THIRTEEN

1. How did the little Hebrew-speaking baby illustrate the interchange of labial or lip sounds?
2. What are some English words in which labial sounds interchange?
3. Show that נֶפֶשׁ and נְשָׁמָה are really variant pronunciations of the same word.
4. Give five examples of Hebrew words in which there is interchange of labial letters.
5. Give five examples of Hebrew words in which there is interchange of dental letters.
6. How do the Hebrew words for laugh, cry out and rejoice illustrate the interchange of sibilants?
7. Give five examples of ס = שׂ, the commonest sibilant interchange.
8. Give some examples of the interchange of palatal letters in English and Yiddish.
9. Where does the Hebrew word for bridge come from?
10. Give five examples of the interchange of guttural letters in Hebrew.
11. How were American intelligence officers able to pick out Japanese trying to pass as Chinese during the second world war? What did they simply ask them to pronounce?
12. Give some examples of liquid interchanges in Hebrew words.
13. How does a consonant differ from a vowel?
14. Why are ו and י called half vowels?
15. Give several examples of how ו and י interchange.

Can you match these two columns?

1. שָׂרַף, שָׂרַב, צָרַף, זָרַב, צָרַב	1. an example of three sibilants interchanging
2. ו and י are semi vowels	2. are the liquids that can be prolonged for as long as one has breath
3. nothing stops the breath coming out of the mouth	3. lip letters interchange
4. ל, מ, נ, ר	4. נָשַׁר – fall out חָבֵר – friend
5. לִקְרַאת	5. they obstruct the breath only slightly
6. אָרִיס – tenant-farmer	6. חָרַשׁ represents a guttural and sibilant change
7. א, ה, ח, ע	7. comes from קָרָה – meet, happen
8. ב, ו, מ, פ	8. these are palatal interchanges
9. represents a palatal and sibilant interchange	9. all variants on one theme "burning"
10. נָשַׁל – slip off חֶבֶל – rope	10. מָסַךְ and מָזַג mean pour
11. נָגַף, נָקַף – knock גִּבּוֹר־כַּבִּיר – strong	11. the four guttural letters
12. עָלַז, עָלַס, עָלַץ – rejoice	12. the vowels a, e, i, o, u

Chapter XIV

Hebrew Borrows Words

The Hebrews form what is probably the oldest cultural group in the world, and during the course of the four thousand years of their history they were in contact with practically all the peoples of the earth. And as they taught the other peoples and made important contributions to their lives so, too, they were profoundly influenced by them, and absorbed important elements of their culture. They used the products of all the known world, and as was customary, would frequently keep the foreign name of the product. Israel, too, was a crossroad of the ancient world, it was a bridge over which kings with their armies, and merchants with their wares crossed out of, and into the great continent of Asia.

All these long and intimate contacts left their traces. Hebrew has been hospitable to, and has welcomed the strange words of their neighbors. Often the strange words were made to feel so much at home that the average student would hardly suspect that they were not ancient Hebrew words, so perfectly were they fitted in.

HEBREW WORDS FROM EGYPTIAN

Hebrew borrowed only a few words from Egyptian; few considering the long years that Israel sojourned there. We have פַּרְעֹה the Egyptian name for king (which means " big house"); יְאוֹר the name for the Nile River; אָחוּ meadow, גֹּמֶא papyrus, שִׁטָּה acacia, צִי ship, and סוּף reeds, rushes.

FROM SANSKRIT

From Sanskrit, the mother of the languages of India come words which tell of the products coming from and through that land. Some are:

פִּלְפֵּל – pepper
נֵרְדְּ – nard
פִּטְדָה – chrysolite

ASSYRIAN AND HEBREW

In the fairy tale the children read of a beautiful princess who was asleep for one hundred years until the prince charming came and awoke her.

Something like this actually happened in real life. The prince charming was Sir Henry Rawlinson, a gallant soldier, gentleman and, oddly enough, a brilliant scholar.

The princess—well that's more involved. For three thousand years the empires of Assyria and Babylon sprawled over the fertile crescent; their far flung armies tramped all the dusty roads of the Near East. They developed a great culture and civilization; this culture they recorded with curious wedge shaped marks on clay tablets—their cuneiform writing. These tablets were left about by the thousands and became covered with the dust of the centuries. Gradually all knowledge of the Assyrian language faded and its place was taken in all the lands by Aramaic. Sometime in the second or third century died the last man who was able to read this strange writing. Almost all clear knowledge of this mighty empire that had lived so long and been so great and feared passed from the minds of men.

Until, in 1840 Henry Rawlinson, an officer of the East India Company passed by the great inscriptions in three languages—Persian, Susian, and Babylonian. (Assyrian and Babylonian are dialects of the same language). It flashed upon Henry Rawlinson that it should be possible to work out from the Persian, a known language, the meaning of the unknown cuneiform, and he burned with scholarly passion to solve the great mystery of this writing.

With incredible exertion and at considerable risk he obtained an impression of the Behistun inscription. After a few years of intense application he emerged with the key to practically the whole cuneiform alphabet.

And then, what a great, wide, brave, new world was opened to the eyes of man. All the life and loves and hates, the dreams of world conquest, the struggles for power of the Babylonians and Assyrians and of the strange medley of peoples who used their writing became known to scholars. A whole new science was born—the science of Assyriology—and great scholars read and interpreted this vast literature in innumerable magazines and scholarly publications.

Now Assyrian is quite a close sister language of Hebrew. The Hebrews were greatly influenced by the Assyrians and Babylonians over the course of many centuries. Students of Hebrew are most grateful for the bright light that the opening of this cuneiform recorded civilization has thrown upon many mysteries of the Hebrew language.

PHONETIC CHANGES

In giving you these examples of how Assyrian helps us in the study of Hebrew, it is necessary that you watch out for a few phonetic changes. Mostly they center around the fact that the Assyrians didn't like the guttural letters and cavalierly reduced them to an א sound. The only guttural letter that stood up against this general ban was the strong ח. (Remember the chapter on twin letters; we pointed out there that there are two different ח's in Hebrew, one strong and one weak). Thus Hebrew borrowed אָרִיס tenant-farmer from Assyrian. This was originally the same as the Hebrew חָרַשׁ plough. Similarly borrowed from Assyrian was אִכָּר, equivalent in Hebrew to חוֹכֵר tenant-farmer. Also, Assyrian אֵפֶר ashes is equivalent to original Hebrew עָפָר dust.

Here are some other examples of how Assyrian drops gutturals. Hebrew בַּעַל became בֵּל in Assyrian, a common idol name. Hebrew borrowed נִמֵּק "to find a good reason for" from Assyrian—the root though is עָמֹק from which the Assyrians had dropped out the ע.

Also they changed the Hebrew מ to Assyrian ו and strangely enough, vice versa; that is Hebrew ו became Assyrian מ. These two changes explain a word that had hitherto been quite inexplicable, i.e. מַרְחֶשְׁוָן the Hebrew name of the eighth month of the year; that is the eighth counting Nisan as the first. This is the usual way of counting Hebrew months. מַרְחֶשְׁוָן is really two words; the two words are שמן - ורח namely, i.e., the eighth month. The ו of ורח (equals יֶרַח) became מ and the מ of שמן (equals שְׁמִינִי) became ו. In this way the word מַרְחֶשְׁוָן emerges. All our presently used Hebrew names of months were borrowed from Assyrian and Babylonian.

ASSYRIAN THROWS LIGHT UPON HEBREW

Here then are just a few examples of the light that Assyrian throws upon Hebrew. I will give you the question or the difficulty that has bothered scholars for many generations, and the simple clear answer that Assyrian gives.

Why should the Hebrew word קַת mean a handle? קַת is the regular Assyrian word for hand—and from hand to handle is a very short step.

What is a רְאֵם? From the Bible we gather that it is some sort of wild animal. Some translators render it " unicorn " which could not be correct because the Bible speaks of קַרְנֵי רְאֵם implying more than one horn. We know from Assyrian texts that it is the wild buffalo.

Why is דֶּגֶל a flag? From the Assyrian we know that דגל means to look at.

What is the meaning of the sentence סֹחֵרָה אֲמִתּוֹ? From Assyrian we know that סֹחֵרָה is the wall around the city.

There are too many Assyrian words in Hebrew to give a complete list. Here, however, is a representative group of them. Officials and officers of administration of a foreign power would usually and naturally retain their native titles of office.

סְגָן – prefect. We now use it in the phrase סְגַן נָשִׂיא vice president. (The common Hebrew word סוֹכֵן – agent is from סְגָן with a change of ג to כ).

פֶּחָה – official. This word ultimately made its way to English in the form pasha.

תַּרְתָּן – commander—the one who issues laws or decrees—the one who tells what the Torah—the law is.

שׁוֹטֵר – in Assyrian is an officer whose function it is to write—really a scribe. שְׁטָר – a document is what he writes. Nowadays שׁוֹטֵר is used for policemen whose writing is usually confined to summonses for erring motorists.

מֶלְצַר – we now use it for waiter—it is from the same

root as Hebrew נָצַר – watch (the נ has become a ל, a frequent interchange). The waiter watches out for us.

רַב מָג – an officer
תְּחוּם – famous for its use in the phrase תְּחוּם שַׁבָּת – the limits of a Sabbath day journey
בִּירָה – capital city
חַסָּה – lettuce
מַזָּל – position of the stars or the constellation. We now use it for luck, fortune
תַּגָּר – merchant
בֵּית נְכוֹת – in Assyrian a treasure house. We now use it for a museum
מִנְזָר – we now use it for the word monastery
נְכָסִים – property
מִסְכֵּן – poor fellow
מַשְׁכּוֹן – a pledge. שְׁכֵּן means " to place ". A מַשְׁכּוֹן is what is placed in the hands of the creditor to assure him that the loan will be repaid
שֶׁלֶד – skeleton

Strangely enough this word comes from the root שלם whole, complete. The word in Assyrian is שַׁלַמְתּוּ, meaning " the whole body ". In passing through Aramaic the מַ dropped out and ת hardened to a ד.

SUMERIAN

A mysterious people lived in the land between two rivers, the Tigris and Euphrates, in very ancient days. No one knows who they were or from where they came. This people was called the Sumerians. Their language Sumerian is not related to any known family of languages.

Into their land came a Semitic people, the Assyrians,

settled among them, took over their wedge-shaped writing, the cuneiform, (the Sumerians were the inventors of it) borrowed their culture, and, of course, a very large number of their words.

Now Hebrew, when it borrowed from Assyrian, borrowed a large number of these originally Sumerian words. They are somewhat different from the other Assyrian words that Hebrew took over.

Other Assyrian words are often only distantly related but ultimately they are kin with Hebrew. The Sumerian words form a special group a little stranger than the other borrowings. Some sense of their strangeness persists, for very rarely are other words built from them. They usually stand alone.

Here are some of the words that come ultimately from this people that is surrounded with so much mystery.

הֵיכָל – big house—used in Hebrew for temple or palace
אַשָּׁף – magician
מַלָּח – in Sumerian לח=go and ma=ship—and so מַלָּח – a sailor—one who goes to sea in ships
סְאָה – a vegetable measure
אַסְיָא – a doctor; אָסוּתָא means " to your good health "
אַשְׁלָג – an alkali
נַחְתּוֹם – a baker
טַפְסָר – scribe; " sar " is " write " and " tap " is " board "
תַּרְנְגוֹל – rooster
גֵּט – an official document

ARAMAIC

The second language that Hebrew borrowed from extensively was Aramaic.

The story of the Aramaic contribution to Hebrew is not

quite so dramatic as the story of the relation of Assyrian and Hebrew. Aramaic is the closest sister language of Hebrew. For almost a thousand years Aramaic was an international language used by the close neighbors of the Jews; and for many centuries Aramaic was the language spoken by the Jews of Babylon and Palestine. It was during these years that it became a second national and second sacred language of the Jews, and it influenced Hebrew profoundly. The influence was on the whole a healthy one, for Aramaic was highly developed, and a practical language; simple in its grammatical structure.

Whatever Hebrew needed, they helped themselves to from the Aramaic. Just as Latin and Greek serve English as a storehouse of additional words available for all purposes, scientific, philosophical, et cetera; so Aramaic would be drawn upon by Hebrew when new words were needed. It is a happy thing that we have so close a sister language of Hebrew in view of the fact that so much of our ancient Hebrew language is lost beyond hope of recovery. There is no doubt in the world that many or most of the words regarded as being borrowed by Hebrew from the Aramaic were part of the ancient Hebrew word stock.

PERSIAN, GREEK AND LATIN

Three empires in succession ruled over Palestine; the Persian, Greek and Roman. From all of these peoples Hebrew borrowed words. The three languages are all members of the Indo-European group (see chapter one) to which English also belongs. Most of the words that Hebrew borrowed from these languages are also found in English. We will constantly be asking you to give the English word parallel, or similar to the one that Hebrew borrowed. Sometimes knowing this will help you remember the Hebrew word better; at other times it will at least be an interesting curiosity.

A brief historical note is in order. Persia, the first of these three empires ruled over Israel from the days of Cyrus the Great. Cyrus was the ruler, who in 538 B.C.E., permitted the Jews to return to Israel from the Babylonian exile. In 332 B.C.E. Alexander the Great took over Israel. The Greek language and culture swept through the Orient. There was a long, peaceful period of Greek influence on Hebrew culture before the head-on clash in the time of the Maccabees. During the quiet days of peaceful co-existence the Bible was translated into Greek at the behest of Ptolemy Philadelphus, ruler of Egypt, so tradition has it. Rome, the last of these three world empires was in practical control of Israel from the time of Pompey's visit to Jerusalem in 64 B.C.E., and for many centuries afterwards.

To sum up then:

Persian rule over Palestine—538 B.C.E. to 332 B.C.E.
Greek rule—332 B.C.E. to 141 B.C.E.
Roman rule—64 B.C.E. to 635 C.E.

HEBREW WORDS FROM PERSIAN

There are only a few Persian words in Hebrew—some of unusual interest. Many of them you would naturally find in the book of Esther, the events of which took place in the land of Persia.

1. דָּת - law—now the word is used for religion in Hebrew. It meant in Persian, that which is given, that which is set down, an ordinance. Pronounce the word דָּת - using the Sephardic pronunciation, and then give two common English words that come from the same root.

2. פַּרְדֵּס – in Persian it is a park—in modern Hebrew an orange grove. What common English word come from it? (This word passed through Greek into English).

וֶרֶד – rose
אֹרֶז – rice
כַּוֶּרֶת – beehive
זַרְנִיךְ – arsenic
כַּרְכֹּם – saffron
כַּרְפַּס – linen
בֻּסְתָּן – garden
אֲפַרְסֵק – peach is short for Persian apple

זוז – zuz
שַׁרְווּל – sleeve
אַרְדִּיכָל – architect
פַּרְבָּר – suburb
פִּתְגָם – epigram, a saying
סַפְסָר – speculator
גָּוֶן – color, we say מְגֻוָּן – colored and כְּגוֹן – as
זַן – kind, species
הַרְפַּתְקָא – adventure, generally harrowing

These titles are Persian, אֲחַשְׁדַּרְפָּן – satrap. If you slice off the first two letters, א doesn't count much and ח isn't found in English—and use your knowledge of interchangeable letters, you will see that " satrap " goes back directly to אֲחַשְׁדַּרְפָּן.

גִּזְבָּר – treasurer—a nun fell out between the ג and ז. The first part of the word is really גנז treasure and בָּר the last syllable is equivalent to " bear ". גִּזְבָּר simply means the bearer of the treasure.

GREEK WORDS IN HEBREW

The borrowing from Greek was extensive. There happened to be, also, a number of startling physical similarities, of course, accidental, with native Hebrew words. Thus:

From Greek:

כְּרוּב – cabbage; כְּרוּב – angel, tho, is a native Hebrew word. These two words are, of course, entirely unconnected. Similarly קַלֵּס to praise is Greek " kalos " which is used as an exclamation " Good ": the native Hebrew word קֶלֶס which means to mock or scorn is not to be connected with the borrowed קֶלֶס to praise.

Many of the Greek words in Hebrew are exactly like the English words that come from the same Greek words.

סַנְדָּל – sandal
בָּסִיס – base
מִסְתּוֹרִין – mystery
הִמְנוֹן – hymn
פַּסְיוֹן – pheasant
פִּיּוּט – poetry

קֻבִּיּוֹת קֻבִיָּה—dice sounds like the English word cubes which is used humorously for dice. נִמּוּס law. In Hebrew, it is used for good manners. Compare the English word autonomy which means ruling yourself.

אֻכְלוּסִיָּה – population.

תִּיק – bag, portfolio. Compare the English word the ticking of a pillow or a mattress.

אֲוִיר – air. The weak " w " sound dropped out in English. Hebrew built from this word אֲוִירוֹן airplane and מְאַוְרֵר ventilator.

אַמְבָּט – bath tub (English dropped the first syllable).

גִּלֵּף – carve. Hieroglyphics—sacred writings—" glyph " or its related form " graph " is frequently used in English words.

אוֹקְיָנוּס – ocean.

These words offer special little problems:

1. הֶדְיוֹט – plain, simple person. What English word comes from the same Greek word?
2. פִּזְמוֹן – a religious song. The " p " is silent in English.
3. דְּפוּס – in Hebrew the word means " print ". Two of

the letters of דִּפּוּס interchanged in the English form of the word.

4. בֻּרְסִי – a leather worker. What common container is made of leather?
5. כַּרְטִיס – a ticket. There are several English words from this word.
6. סְפוֹג – something that absorbs. A " nun " has fallen out of the Hebrew word.
7. פֻּמְבִּי – public. Two words in English come from the Greek word.
8. קַבַּרְנִיט – Hebrew " head of a ship ", " a leader ". What extremely common English word comes from this Greek word? A hint—the ק interchanges with a ג or hard g sound.

9. פֻּלְמוּס – a war
10. פְּלַסְתֵּר – fraudulent
11. הֶגְמוֹן – ruler

What are the parallel English words?

These words have English parallels but you just couldn't guess them because the meanings have changed too radically or the English words are not familiar to you.

דֻּגְמָה – example, but in English " dogma " an example of faith.

אַכְסַנְיָה – an inn—a place for strangers. " Xenophobia " is an important word to know. It means hatred of a stranger, which means also hatred of all minorities.

טֶכֶס – also spelt טֶקֶס means arrangment; טַכְסִיסָן is a strategist. These last two words are equivalent to the English word " tactics ". In English a " taxi "-dermist—a taxidermist arranges the skin (derma means skin).

טַקְסָן – is a master of ceremonies.

פְּסַנְתֵּר – piano is from Greek " psalteron ". Compare the word " psalter ".

דּוֹרוֹן – a gift. Theo*dore* means gift of God as does *Doro*thy.

קָטֵיגוֹר – prosecuting attorney. This word is clipped or rather shortened in the common idiom קְרָא תַּגָר which means: " call the prosecutor ".

נַנָּס – a dwarf. English has the word, " nanus "-dwarf.

בַּלָּן – bath attendant. Balnology is a branch of medical theraputics—the therapy of baths.

קֻפָּה – a box, container. From it we have the words chicken coop, a cup and coffin.

אִצְטְלָה – a stole—a robe worn by clergy; also a sort of long scarf worn by women.

Useful words from the Greek with no common English parallels:

פָּרַף – pin
פְּרוֹזְדוֹר – corridor
אֲלַכְסוֹן – diagonal
סַנְהֶדְרִין – Sanhedrin
פַּרְצוּף – face, countenance
פִּיּוּס – conciliation
סַנֵּיגוֹר – defender (in a court of law)
מֻקְיוֹן – clown
פִּנְקָס – a notebook
פָּנָס – lantern

FROM THE LATIN

There aren't nearly as many Latin words in Hebrew as there are in Greek. Israel was much nearer to Greece. Although Rome was in control of Israel for many centuries, the Greek cultural influence lingered on more than the Roman.

HEBREW BORROWS WORDS

Greek culture was so powerful a force that it overwhelmed its Roman conquerors and made their culture largely Greek.

Here are some of the Latin words used in Hebrew:

סִגְנוֹן – in Hebrew means style. Can you suggest several English words from this Latin word?

קֻנְטְרָס – in Hebrew it means a pamphlet, originally it was the Latin word " commentarus " (commentary) and referred to the commentary of רַשִׁ״י. The " m " of commentarus became a " nun " in Hebrew.

קֻפְסָה – a box. What English word with diminuative ending comes from this Latin word?

כְּלוּנְסָאוֹת – stilts. The parallel English word is " column ".

Some other Latin words are:

לִגְיוֹן – a legion
וִילוֹן – a curtain (English velum and velar)
דִּסְקוּס – a discus
סַפְסָל – a bench
פַּמַלְיָא – a family
טַבְלָה – a tablet
קֻלְמוּס – a pen
נַקְנִיק – a frankfurter
גַּרְדֹּם – execution block. Gradus, steps going up " grade "
לִבְלָר – a secretary, writer. The Latin word is " libelus ". Libel is a little book.
סֻלְיָה – sole
מִיל – mile. " Mil " means a thousand. A mile is a thousand steps
נוֹטְרִיקוֹן – abbreviation—think of making " notes "
פִּגְיוֹן – dagger—related to the word " pugnacious "

קַפֶּנְדַּרְיָא – short cut—think of compendium
קָרוֹן – a car—sounds like the English word and means the same
מוֹנִיטִין – fame. It is the Latin word " monetos "—money, currency

The well known idiom יָצָא לוֹ מוֹנִיטִין means " he became famous ".

פַּטְרוֹן – patron
טִירוֹן – tyro, a novice
טְרַקְלִין – a parlor

The Hebrew word בּוּל, postage stamp, is from the Latin bulla, seal. It is an extremely interesting word that came in by a roundabout road. From Latin it went to Turkish—from Turkish to Arabic, from which Israeli Hebrew borrowed it some generations ago.

Latin bulla originally meant a bubble, a blob. It was applied to blobs of wax or lead affixed to documents which received the impress of a seal; then to the seal itself, then to the sealed document, and finally the word came to mean a document in general.

This word pronounced in later Latin "bill" was applied to documents of many kinds—bills passed by Parliament, documents listing money owed, the Papal decrees called bulls etc. Who would dream that the Hebrew בּוּל stamp is the first cousin to the gas bill that you pay monthly, both going back to the same grandfather Latin bulla, a blob of wax.

ARABIC

There were two periods in which Hebrew actively borrowed from Arabic—in medieval times and in the last seventy years in modern Israel. In medieval days

Hebrew culture was greatly influenced by Arabic culture—particularly in philosophy, grammar, and medicine. The terms that Hebrew borrowed then were largely philosophic and abstract.

Some of them are:

עִלָּה – cause	קֹטֶב – pole
טֶבַע – nature	גֶּשֶׁם – body
אֹפֶק – horizon	גַּשְׁמִי – material

In modern times Hebrew in Israel has borrowed from Arabic many words, particularly for common everyday things, words for plants and vegetables, products of Israel. These were formerly lacking in Hebrew. Some of these modern borrowings, mostly introduced by Eliezer ben Yehuda, from the Arabic are:

זֻבְדָּה – cream	לַחַן – melody
גַּרְבַּיִם – socks	אָדִיב – polite
מִשְׁמֵשׁ – apricot	הִגֵּר – migrate
גְּלִידָה – ice cream	רִשְׁמִי – official
מוֹז – banana	לִטֵּף – pet
צַבָּר – cactus	נֶמֶשׁ – freckle
קַטָּר – locomotive	קְטִיפָה – velvet
תַּאֲרִיךְ – date	אַבְזֵם – buckle
דִּגְדֵּג – tickle	בֹּרֶג – screw

צְמִיג – a tire

Hebrew provides the roots of many words borrowed in a particular form from Arabic; thus מַחְסָן – a warehouse or store, is borrowed from modern Arabic, but the root חֹסֶן meaning " store " is found in the Bible.

מִטְבָּח – a kitchen is borrowed from Arabic, but טבח is an old Hebrew root. Apparently both the slaughtering and the cooking of the animal were done in the same area.

קַטָּר locomotive is obviously from the same Hebrew root as קְטֹרֶת – incense.

Often Hebrew would not borrow the Arabic word but would literally translate the Arabic into Hebrew. These are called translation loans. תְּנוּעָה is the Hebrew word for vowel. It comes from the root נוע move. It is the Hebrew word for vowel because the Arabic word for " vowel " comes from the Arabic word " to move ".

The Arabs would use the word for the root of a tree to indicate the root of a word. So the Hebrew took the word שֹׁרֶשׁ and used it to indicate the root of the word. The word in Arabic for introduction to a book comes from the Arabic word for " come " so Hebrew uses מָבוֹא for introduction.

MODERN EUROPEAN LANGUAGES

The generations of the Haskalah and of the national renaissance were deeply and profoundly influenced by the modern European culture. It was they who brought into Hebrew from the Russian, German, French, and to a lesser extent from the English the large number of cultural terms that are the common heritage of modern Europe. They are the international words that are used and known the world over.

It would not have been too difficult to create pure Hebrew words for all the elements of modern life. The Hebrew root with its vast array of verb and noun patterns offers an inexhaustable store from which to build. These international words stay on and serve as a sort of bond, binding Hebrew to world culture. There are quite a number of these words and here are some of the most frequently used.

טֶלֶפוֹן – telephone
רַדְיוֹ – radio
טֶלֶוִיזְיָה – television
סְפּוֹרְט – sport
אוּנִיבֶרְסִיטָה – university
פְּרוֹבְּלֶמָה – problem
אֲקָדֶמְיָּה – academy
אִרְגּוּן – organization
אוֹטוֹבּוּס – autobus
הִסְטוֹרְיָּה – history

HEBREW WORDS USED IN ENGLISH

Hebrew is one of the great languages in the world, one of its oldest and most beautiful. It has had a strong and continual influence on other world languages. Many Hebrew words have entered the English language. For some reason or other, very few even among those who know Hebrew well are aware of these words, except of course the most obvious and well-known ones such as sabbath, amen, and hallelujah. Yet there are quite a number of Hebrew words in English and almost everyone of them has a certain history and charm of its own.

Hebrew has many sister languages such as Arabic, Phoenecian, Syriac, Assyrian etc. The relationships of Hebrew with her sister languages are extremely close. The common every day, ordinary words, with slight changes, are usually the same; the grammatical structure is very similar. Phoenecian and Hebrew are practically identical; there is less difference between them than between English spoken in New York and in the South.

Now frequently, a word will come into English from a sister language, but this word may be a perfectly common and well-known Hebrew word. The word "abbot" meaning head of a monastery comes into English from Syriac but everyone will immediately recognize the Hebrew word abba. The word "emir", commander comes from the Arabic but we recognize the common Hebrew word אָמַר to say, to tell, to command.

These are a number of fairiy regular phonetic changes you must watch out for when tracing Hebrew words that have gone over to English.

Here are some:

Hebrew י becomes English "j"
יְהוּדָה becomes Judah
יַרְדֵּן becomes Jordan
Hebrew שׂ becomes English "s"
Thus שַׁבָּת becomes Sabbath
יְרוּשָׁלַיִם becomes Jerusalem
Hebrew ת becomes English "th"
Thus שַׁבָּת becomes Sabbath
בֵּית לֶחֶם becomes Bethlehem

Naturally words would come into English from incidents and events in the Bible. In English we have the expression " to raise cain " from Cain.

In all the days that man has lived on this earth, in all societies no matter how primitive, the taking of the life of a human being has been a serious and weighty matter; something never done lightly or except for serious cause. It is natural, therefore, that the first recorded murder in the history of the world should have made a profound impression upon the imagination of all mankind.

The name of Cain the first murderer has come to stand for violence, disorder, and dissension. And so TO RAISE CAIN has become a common phrase of our language.

BABEL

After the days of the great flood men on earth began to build a tower so high that they would be safe against any other flood. This despite the promise of the rainbow, the promise of the Lord God that He would never again send the flood waters over the whole earth.

This act, bold, arrogant, insolent, displeased God who sent among them a confusion of tongues. One morning they woke up and found that they were all speaking different languages. This took place in the land and city of Babylon and thus we have the English word " babel " meaning a mixture, a confusion of languages.

The Hebrew name בָּבֶל is from " babilu " gate of God. " Bab " means gate from the Hebrew word בָּא come into.

SACK

In the beautiful and wistful story of Joseph and his brothers there runs the theme of the sacks of wheat that the brothers carried to the famine stricken land of Israel.

The Phoenecians manufactured the coarse cloth which was called " sack " and exported it to many countries.

The word " sack " exists in many other forms in English.

sac – a medical term;

sachet – a little bag of perfume;

satchel – from the Latin. It was originally " sacc-ellus " and means a " little sack ".

We have the verb " *to sack* ". The soldiers " sack " the city. They put all the spoils and booty in sacks.

MANNA

In the desert where the children of Israel wandered for forty years, they ate a mysterious food that dropped down from the heavens. The first time they saw it they exclaimed, " מַן הוּא (Man-hoo) "—" What is it? " And so it was called " *manna* " and has come to mean any food showered upon us without our toil and sweat.

CANE - קָנֶה

Along the banks of the Nile River and the Jordan River there grew reeds, tall, slender and willowy. They were long and straight, usually with a hole through the center. The reeds were a striking feature of the landscape. The Hebrew for " reed " was קָנֶה.

The word " kaneh " reed passed on to Greek and Latin and from these two, to most of the languages of the west. Each language developed new uses for the word. English hospitably received almost all of them. Now we have a whole collection of words that go back to קָנֶה.

cane – the stick we use when we go for a stroll, also, sugar *cane*.

canister – a basket originally made of reeds.

cannon – after all it was a gigantic sort of reed long, round, with a hole in the center blowing out death and destruction. From it we have cannonade.

Latin used " canna " as a pipe. From the Latin uses of the word we have canal and channel.

AMEN

The word " Amen " is one of the most unusual and fascinating words in all human speech. It has a strange distinction. It has entered more languages—perhaps over 1,000—than any other single word in human speech.

How did it come about that this simple Hebrew word " Amen " has spread to practically every land and is used by almost all mankind? It is a somewhat long and charming story.

In Alexandria, Egypt around 250 B.C.E. there lived a large and flourishing Jewish community of over a half-million Greek-speaking Jews. The main synagogue of Alexandria was so gigantic that a man with a flag stood on a platform waving to indicate to the congregation when to make the response as the cantor chanted.

Alexandria was a great port city like New York today. It was among the Greek-speaking Jews there, that there was first felt a need for a translation of the Bible. There is a tradition that Ptolemy Philadelphus, king of Egypt, wanted a copy of the Hebrew Bible in Greek for his great library and that he requested that the translation be made. Seventy-two scholars worked for seventy days, hence the name " Septuagint ". Incidentally, this was the very first translation ever made of any book from one language to another.

There were many difficult problems. How could one express the intensely monotheistic, highly ethical culture of the Jews in a completely different language? How could one find in Greek a word that could express or contain the meaning of the Hebrew word " shabbat ". The Greek language had nothing remotely resembling the idea of " a day of rest and spiritual relaxation for all "—and this meant all men, women, children, slaves and even the animals. Where really in the great wide world, in any other human group, was there a day like this?

The translators came quickly upon the problem of translating the Hebrew word "Amen ". This word, a first cousin of the word אֱמֶת truth has the meaning, " May this prayer come true ". There was certainly no one Greek word carrying the meaning of the Hebrew word " Amen ". In order to express it adequately in Greek they would have had to use the whole above sentence.

Now the word " amen " occurs, as you can well imagine, quite frequently in the Bible. It was used regularly in the Bible as the closing for all prayers. It would be very clumsy indeed if this whole sentence would have to be used over and over again.

And so the translators hit upon a novel and simple expedient. They turned אָמֵן into a Greek word " amen " and made it part of the Greek language with the meaning of the original Hebrew word.

A tradition was thus established to keep the Hebrew word " amen ". When the Bible was translated into Latin they made " amen " a Latin word. This went on and on. The Bible has now been translated into over 1,000 languages and every one of them has accepted the Hebrew אָמֵן as their very own.

SOME OTHER HEBREW WORDS IN ENGLISH

אָלֶף בֵּית – alphabet. Many people do not realize that the English word alphabet is the familiar alef bet.

גִּימֶל – from גָּמָל is pronounced camel in English.

יוֹד – yod. It is from the Hebrew word for " hand ", represented by a little stroke of the pen. The " yod " is the tiniest letter in the alphabet and its small size has always made a profound impression upon all who learned to write.

The Greeks pronounce " yod " iota and this Greek name for the Hebrew letter " yod " became a word signifying " a tiny little bit ". We speak of " every single iota ".

The Roman pronounced the letter " yod " as " jot ".

גָּמָל

CAMEL

שַׂק

SACK

קָנֶה

REED, CANE GAVE RISE TO CANNON

יַעֲקֹב

JOCKEY FROM

ENGLISH BORROWS WORDS FROM HEBREW

(Remember that we pointed out above that Hebrew י became English " J "). Jot as a noun means also " a tiny little bit ". It is very much more familiar as a verb. " Jot " this down means to write it only in essential details, in as brief and compact a fashion as possible.

שַׁבָּת - *Sabbath.* The Romans ridiculed the Jews who spent one day in seven in complete idleness. Yet the Sabbath is one of the incalculably great blessings the Jews brought to this world. What would life be like with men working as they used to do—day after day all through the year; except of course for the rich; they did not work at all.

The Sabbath was the one great democratic institution that said that all, equally, must have rest from the strain and nervous tension of life, at least one day in seven. The Christian rest on Sunday, the Mohammedan rest on Friday, the general observance of at least one day of rest for all workers all over the civilized world flows directly from the Jewish Sabbath.

מָשִׁיחַ - Messiah. The verb מָשַׁח means " to annoint ". All kings were annointed as a consecration, a solemn appointment to their office; always by the use of oil poured on the head.

The word Messiah is specifically applied to a ruler who will come some day and redeem Israel, and usher in the days of universal peace.

יוֹבֵל - *Jubilee.* The fiftieth year coming after seven cycles of seven years marked a general release of all slaves and a return of all lands to their original owners. It was a year of great rejoicing, marked incidentally by the blowing of the ram's horn. יוֹבֵל means " ram's horn ".

Jubilee is used in English in the sense of a notable anniversary. Strictly speaking it should be used for the fiftieth anniversary. We also have the noun " jubilation ", and the adjective " jubilant ".

קַבָּלָה - Cabbala—is a general name for the mystical lore and thought of the Jewish people. The root קִבֵּל " receive " and the word Cabbala simply means " tradition "—that which is received from the generations that have gone before.

More specifically, Cabbala refers to the mystic teaching concerning God and the universe. It was supposed to have come down as a revelation to a privileged few from the remote past, and it was preserved only by a select few.

Some of the most exquisite prayers in our prayer book were written by *Cabbalists*.

The word " *cabal* " comes from the word cabbala—it means a small group united for some secret, mysterious and often sinister purpose.

WORDS FROM NAMES OF PERSONS

The parents bent lovingly over the newly born infant and they breathed a wish, a hope, a prayer for their child; that he would grow up to be tall and splendid, that God would be gracious to him and give him long years of life. And these wishes and hopes and prayers became names, the ancient and beautiful Hebrew names that have come down to us across the thousands of years and spread all over the world.

The old Hebrew names have an authentic charm and dignity and they reflect the deep religious feelings of the Hebrews and their passionate belief in the one God who is the ruler of the universe.

It is not too generally known that all names have meanings. A boy whose name was שְׁלֹמֹה carried with him a hope of peace in his life time; חַיִּים that his years would be long on this earth; יְהוֹנָתָן a prayer of thanks for this gift that God gave; and .דָּוִד a word telling of the love they bore their child.

תָּמָר was a date palm, tall and slender, giving shade and food, a blessing to all and so Tamar was a popular girl's name; חַנָּה is from חֵן charm, grace; שָׂרָה is a princess and so on.

What is certainly very little known is that many Hebrew names have given rise to English words—some of them very common and every day words. The average student does not have the faintest notion in the world that these words are Hebrew in their ultimate origin. Let us start with the name יַעֲקֹב.

JACOB יַעֲקֹב

The pet form of Jacob is " Jack " or " Jacky ". In Scotland this was pronounced " Jockey " and they called the man who rode the horses " hey *Jockey* " and this became the regular word for the generally short, wiry, athletic man who rides the horses in the races. This also became a verb. We speak of "*jockeying* for position ".

Jacket. The French pronunciation of Jacob is Jacques. The English word " jacket " comes from French " jacquette " which is a diminutive of the common French peasant name " Jacques ". Jacques is used to refer to a Frenchman in general. The jacquette was a garment worn by the French soldiers and peasants.

Jack in English is used in place of the word man, or to indicate a male. A *jack* of all trades is simply a man of all trades, a lumber jack is a man working at lumber; a *jack* rabbit or a jackass indicates the male of these species.

JOHANAN יוֹחָנָן

Johanan means " may God be gracious ". In English it is shortened to John.

In Holland it was written, JAN, pronounced " YANN ". The English called the Dutch settlers along the Hudson River " YANNKIS " which quickly became *Yankees*. The name spread all over the north. The southerners began calling all northerners Yankees; now it is a general nick-name for all Americans. *Uncle Sam* as a name for the American government comes from the Hebrew name שְׁמוּאֵל or Samuel.

THOMAS is another name that is of pure Hebrew origin. תְּאוֹם in Hebrew is a twin and *Tom* like *Jack* is used to indicate the male of the species. Thus we have " *tom Turkey* " or " tom cat ", the male and tougher variety of these interesting animals. A " tomboy " is a girl who acts like a boy.

חַנָּה – Hannah or Anna. There is no ח in English, so Hebrew words beginning with ח may simply drop it. חַנָּה is from חֵן meaning charm or grace. Just as Jack or Tom is used to indicate male, so Anna was used to indicate female. We have a " billy goat " meaning a male goat and we have " *AN ANNE GOAT* " meaning a female goat. In the most natural and inevitable fashion possible " an Anne goat " became a nanny goat.

WORDS FROM PLACE NAMES

English has a perfectly enormous number of words coming from the names of places usually, of course, because a certain product was made in this place and exported from there.

MILLINERY is from Milan; CHAMPAGNE from the city of Champagne; CALICO from Calcutta etc.

There are a number of English words coming from the names of places in and about Israel.

Gauze—was manufactured in the city of " Gaza ".

Scallions—there were great onion fields in the city of Ashkelon. They grew there that special small variety that has come to be known as scallions (remember that Hebrew " sh " becomes English S).

DAMASK—a fabric manufactured in Damascus.

ASPHALT—an ancient name for the Dead Sea was " Yam Shafelet " from the Hebrew word שָׁפֵל shafel meaning " low ". The surface of the Dead Sea is 1300 feet below sea level. The waters go down still another 1,300 feet making the bottom of the Dead Sea the lowest point in the land surface of the earth.

Along the shores of the " Yam Shafelet " was a tough, sticky, substance useful in road building. The Greek who dug it out called it " asphaltos ". The Greek language has no " sh " sound. This becomes the English word " asphalt ".

This small but interesting group, which passed not only into English but often into many other languages, these words, a few out of many, will certainly make it clear that Hebrew has contributed her share to the great world languages.

ANSWERS TO QUESTIONS

HEBREW BORROWED WORDS

Guessing the English form of Persian words borrowed by Hebrew.

1. Two common English words that come from the same word as does the Hebrew word דָּת are " data " that which is given or set down and " date "—at a given time.
2. The English word coming from the Persian word פַּרְדֵּס is " paradise ".

Guessing the English words coming from Greek words that are commonly used in Hebrew.

1. The English word derived from the same Greek word that הֶדְיוֹט comes from is " idiot ".
2. The English word coming from פִּזְמוֹן a religious song is " psalm ".
3. The English coming from דְּפוּס is " type ".
4. Common English words from בֶּרְסִי are " purse " and " purser " of the ship. Reimburse is to pay back. Bourse means stock market in France.
5. The English words from כַּרְטִיס are " card " and " chart ". Cartoons were so called because they were drawn on cards.
6. The English word coming from the Greek word סְפוֹג is a " sponge ". Hebrew has made a verb out of this noun סָפַג " absorbed ".
7. The two English words coming from the Greek word פֶּמְבִּי are first of all " pomp " and oddly enough " pump " the shoes worn on ceremonial occasions.
8. The English word coming from קַבַּרְנִיט is governor.

9. The English word coming from the Greek word פְּלֶמוֹס war is the adjective and the noun " polemic ".
10. The English word from the Greek פְּלַסְתֵּר fraudulent is " false ".
11. The English word coming from the Greek הֶגְמוֹן is " hegemony ".

Guessing the English words coming from Latin words commonly used in Hebrew.

1. Some English words from the Latin word סִגְנוֹן are " signature ", signal, sign, etc.
2. The English word coming from the Latin word קֻפְסָה a box is " capsule ".

QUESTIONS ON "HEBREW BORROWS WORDS"

1. What are some of the very few words that Hebrew borrowed from the Egyptian?
2. How was Assyrian rediscovered after about 2000 years had passed?
3. Give some examples of difficult Hebrew words whose explanation became clear and simple because of our knowledge of Assyrian.
4. What two chief changes must you watch out for as you go from Assyrian to Hebrew?
5. Name five common Hebrew words from Assyrian.
6. Why are the Sumerian words a little stranger than other borrowings?
7. How does Aramaic serve Hebrew?
8. What three great empires rules over Israel successively?
9. Give three Hebrew words from Persian that sound like and have a similar meaning to the words in English.
10. Why are כְּרוּב, angel, cabbage and קִלֵּס, mock, praise unconnectable?
11. Give three Hebrew words from Greek that sound like and have a similar meaning to words in English.
12. What are some useful Hebrew words from the Greek with no common English parallel?
13. What are three Hebrew words from Latin?
14. During what two periods did Hebrew borrow from Arabic? Give two examples from each period.

Can you match these columns?

1. הֵיכָל — פַּרְעֹה	1. ultimately from Sumerian
2. medieval borrowings from Arabic	2. קַבַּרְנִיט
3. נַחְתּוֹם — תַּרְנְגוֹל	3. Latin word giving rise to sign, signature, etc.
4. jockey, cannon	4. has in it the word דּוֹרוֹן gift borrowed from Greek
5. סְגְנוֹן	5. idiot—in Hebrew though, a simple fellow
6. כְּרוּב - cabbage	6. English words from Hebrew
7. two Hebrew words from Sanskrit	7. modern borrowings from Arabic
8. governor	8. now a pamphlet—originally referred to Rashi's commentary on the Talmud
9. Theodore	9. accidentally similar to Hebrew word for angel
10. two Hebrew words from Egyptian	10. " big house " in Egyptian and Sumerian
11. הֶדְיוֹט	11. cognate with a capsule—small box
12. דָּת — פַּרְדֵּס	12. אָחוּ — יְאוֹר
13. קֻפְסָה	13. עָלָה — טֶבַע
14. קֻנְטְרָס	14. Persian words in Hebrew
15. גֶּרֶב — בֶּרֶז	15. פִּלְפֵּל נֵרְדְּ

Chapter XV

Tables Have Legs and People Feel Blue

How odd is it, when one comes to think of it, that tables should have legs and people feel blue. How is it possible for a color to be loud or a question hard? Can colors be noisy?

All this brings us to one of the most pervasive, the most fruitful and subtle ways of word building. It is generally called figurative use of words and simply means that the original meaning of the word is shifted or extended to mean also something else, somewhat vaguely related. It is a process of word building, to which we are so accustomed and it is so much a part of our thinking and our speech that we hardly ever stop to analyze what we are saying and yet, by this simple trick, we have actually doubled and sometimes tripled our vocabulary.

How is this done or rather, how did it come about? There seems to be little doubt that every word in the beginning expressed or told of something that could be handled, felt, seen, heard or smelled. Every root expressed a primitive physical act of primitive man.

As years went by, ancient man felt the need for additional words. He wanted words to express ideas that were not physical at all, that could not be comprehended by the five senses. He wanted to pass moral judgements, he wanted to speak of religious ideals. He wanted to make intellectual distinctions. He wanted to describe emotional states. He needed, and needed badly, many words.

The human mind, then as now, was fairly lazy. Instead of creating or inventing new words for these non-physical concepts, ancient man would simply use one of his old stock of physical words. An important reason for his borrowing an old word rather than inventing a new word was that he could always chose from his limited stock of physical words one that would suggest, directly or indirectly, vaguely or specifically, what he wanted to say. Strange to say his limited stock of physical words hardly ever failed him. He could practically always find there what he wanted.

Did he want to say that one member of the tribe was outstanding, was important, had made significant contributions to the welfare of all? There swiftly came to his mind the adjective " big or great ". And so when we say today, " He is a big man or a great man " the reference is hardly ever to physical size.

Did ancient man want to say of a person that he was honest, that he dealt fairly with his fellow man? There was something about a straight line that suggested honesty and trustworthiness. So " straight " came to mean, in addition to physically straight, honest or upright.

Something unpleasant happened to him, humiliation, defeat, insult. He struggled, vainly at first, for a word to express what he felt. There came to his mind the taste of a bitter thing; and so " bitter " came to describe the feeling of frustration and defeat.

This borrowing was not only for the purpose of expressing

intellectual or moral or intangible ideas; the process was also frequently used to indicate new physical things that were somewhat related in appearance or function to the borrowed word. When tables were first made, a word was needed for the four posts that held it up. These posts bore a certain resemblance to the legs that hold up and propel men. The resemblance, vague though it was, did exist and so now tables have legs. Even a mountain has a foot.

PHYSICAL WORDS USED FOR MORAL CONCEPTS

Words for straight יָשָׁר, מִישׁוֹר have come to mean honest, upright; and conversely, words for crooked מְעֻוָּת, מְעֻקָּל came to mean dishonest, deceitful. Words for clean, clear, such as נָקִי, זַךְ, טְהָר יָדַיִם, חַף have all come to mean innocent, morally pure. Conversely, words for dirty, filthy, such as זֻהֲמָה, חֶלְאָה have all come to mean moral uncleanliness.

פָּרוּץ – burst forth, has come to mean immoral. It tells of one who has gone beyond the accepted rules of society.

חָטָא which now means to sin, originally simply meant to miss the mark.

עֲבֵרָה – transgression, and derived from it the verb עָבַר, transgress, both come from עָבַר which means to cross over, to go beyond the laws of the group.

אָסַר – physically tie up, and הִתִּיר physically loosen, have very naturally come to mean respectively, forbid and permit.

PHYSICAL WORDS USED FOR INTELLECTUAL CONCEPTS

Words which mean sharp, keen, have come to mean intellectually sharp, keen, alert. So we have חָרִיף keen which comes from the root to cut, or dig into. חָרוּץ diligent also comes from a root meaning to dig into.

בֵּאֵר – explain, is in all likelihood related to the word בּוֹר pit, and originally meant " to go deeply into ".

חַד – sharp, is now used for one who is intellectually keen.

נִתַּח – to cut, is the Hebrew for " he analyzed ".

הִטִּיף – to cause to flow (from נטף drop) also means " he preached ".

פִּלְפֵּל – is the sharp spice, " pepper ". פִּלְפּוּל is the word used for keen, involved discussions of complicated legal points.

עַמְקָן – a profound person, comes from עָמֹק deep.

פָּשׁוּט – means simple. פְּשָׁט means the simple meaning of the text. All come from the root פָּשַׁט spread out plainly before one's eyes.

פֵּרֵשׁ – to explain, also originally meant to spread out. The opposite of פָּשׁוּט simple, is מְסֻבָּךְ complicated, which comes from סְבַךְ a thicket.

פִּקֵּחַ – open eyed, has come to mean clear, intelligent.

סְיָג – a fence, has come to mean additional regulations to avoid the possibility of breaking a very important law. The word גָּדֵר a fence has given rise to הִגְדִּיר which means to define.

PHYSICAL WORDS USED FOR EMOTIONAL CONCEPTS

חֵמָה – anger, is easily derived from the root חַם warm; similarly הִתְלַהֵב becomes enthusiastic, naturally comes from לֶהָבָה a flame.

זָדוֹן – arrogance, comes from זוד to boil up.

עֶבְרָה – anger, is from עָבַר to cross over, to go beyond. Here the going beyond is emotional. Above, in the word

הַבָּחוּר
גָּדוֹל

THE BOY
IS BIG

EINSTEIN איינשטיין
IS GREAT אִישׁ גָּדוֹל

THE MAN
IS BOUND
IN CHAINS

הָאִישׁ אָסוּר
בַּזִּיקִים

SMOKING
FORBIDDEN

PHYSICAL WORDS ARE USED FIGURATIVELY

עֲבֵרָה sin, it had the meaning of crossing over or going beyond the norm morally.

קֹצֶר רוּחַ means impatience. When a person grows impatient, his breath comes short. And conversely אֹרֶךְ רוּחַ, which really means long of breath, has come to mean patience.

A haughty person is a גַּבְהָן from גָּבוֹהַּ high. סָבַל be patient is from סָבַל to carry a burden, so סַבְלָן becomes a patient person.

A FEW OTHER INTERESTING WORDS

חוּג – a circle—now means one's social or intellectual group.

לָחַץ – to press or squeeze has naturally to mean oppressed.

תָּלוּי – hanging down from has come to mean depending upon (the English " depend " literally means hanging from ").

דֶּרֶךְ — road, way has come to mean way of life, manner or custom.

מַדְרִיךְ – is a counsellor or guide.

נִסְמָךְ – to lean on physically has come to mean rely on.

שַׁלְשֶׁלֶת – a chain is now figuratively used as is the English word chain, to indicate a succession of events that follow closely upon or are dependent on one another.

צַמֶּרֶת – tree top is now used to indicate the top ranking officials of an organization.

All these examples given here of Hebrew words used figuratively are a very minute portion of the enormous number of words that are so used. A good sized volume could be written about just this one way in which Hebrew words have grown in usefulness. The examples given above are for the purpose of making you realize that the figurative use of words serves as an extremely important method of word building.

HEBREW AND ENGLISH DEVELOP THE SAME FIGURATIVE USES

Here is another point of unusual interest. You must have noticed the startling similarities between Hebrew and English in the figurative use of words. When Hebrew borrows a physical word for use in some other way we note strangely enough that English does precisely the same thing.

If יָשָׁר the Hebrew word for straight has come to mean honest, so too has the English word straight also come to mean honest.

The Hebrew word מַר bitter tasting has come to mean unpleasant, and similarly the English word bitter came to be used figuratively for unpleasant.

תָּפַשׂ in Hebrew means to grasp physically and also means to comprehend, to understand, to grasp mentally. The English word grasp meaning physically to get hold of, means to understand or comprehend.

These examples can be multiplied indefinitely. They show first of all that the human mind works in essentially the same way all over the world, whether in ancient Israel or modern England. The same physical experience will bring up the same mental, moral, or emotional reactions.

There are many resemblances between Hebrew and English. The relationship is very close and can be accounted for in this way. We must remember that the English Bible is a quite literal, word for word, translation of the Hebrew. The translators of the Hebrew Bible into English believed that all the words of the Bible were divinely inspired. They did not want to tamper with any words or change them in the slightest. Therefore all biblical Hebrew figurative uses of words have passed into English.

Hebrew has frequently borrowed figurative uses of words from modern European languages. In ancient Hebrew שְׁאֵלָה was actually a question asked, in modern Hebrew it is also a problem. נְקֻדָּה used to mean an actual dot or spot, now it is figuratively used to mean a point in a discussion. זֶרֶם in ancient Hebrew is an actual stream of water, now it is figuratively used for a stream of influence. תְּנוּעָה originally a physical movement now means a movement in the sense of a cause or an historical process. All these are simply modern adaptations taken by the Hebrew from European culture.

QUESTIONS ON CHAPTER FIFTEEN

1. With what type of words was ancient man at first content?
2. What kind of new words did he begin to need?
3. Why did the old stock of physical words suffice?
4. Give two examples of the early figurative use of Hebrew words.
5. Give two words used figuratively for intellectual concepts.
6. Give two physical words used figuratively for emotional concepts.
7. Give two physical words used figuratively for moral concepts.
8. What accounts for the fact that when a Hebrew used a word figuratively, English usually does so in the same way? Give three examples.

Chapter XVI

How Two Letters Become Three

ROOTS WERE PROBABLY, ORIGINALLY TWO LETTERED

We now come to something that we have been keeping a deep and dark secret. Please prepare yourself for a great surprise.

All that we have said about the tri-consonantality of the Hebrew root is true. But all the time we were talking about the root as it appeared in historical times; in the Hebrew of the literature that has been handed down to us since the invention of writing.

Actually, of course, Hebrew did not begin in this way. It is hardly possible that the Hebrew language began with this enormously regular tri-consonantal system, that all Hebrew words were born with three bright and shining letters. Scholars are fairly convinced that back of these three lettered roots lie old primitive two-lettered syllables. These two-lettered syllables represent some simple primitive action or thing. It does seem quite clear that there existed a bi-literal or two-letter base for many, if not most, of our three lettered roots. However, this can never be proven absolutely in all finality because the original Semitic language is lost beyond all recovery.

What seemed to have happened is this. The language of

the primitive Semites, ancestors of the Hebrews, began with a few two-lettered words, each of which carried a large and rather general, often vague, meaning. Early life was simple, full of fear and hunger. A limited number of words of one syllable, helped out with plenty of gestures, was all that was then needed.

But when they settled in one spot and planted seed to harvest grain, life became for them a more complicated affair. Civilization began to develop, and with it came what were even in those early days civilization's highly complex arts. They needed, and needed desperately more and more words to express this greater complexity of their life.

TWO LETTERED ROOTS BECOME THREE LETTERED

The small number of two-lettered syllables began to be highly inadequate. In order to obtain additional words they would add a third letter to the primitive two-lettered root, by this means creating new words. This new word would generally have a sharper, more specialized sense than the primitive root. We are not sure exactly how this process was carried on, because it took place so very long ago in prehistoric times.

All this sounds like mere words; let us now get down to examples and to making ourselves very clear.

A simple illustration of the transformation from two to three-lettered roots is to be found in the group of words that have גז as the first two letters. All of this group had the fundamental meaning of cutting with, of course, different shades of meaning. It is easy to see clearly how they are related, and in all likelihood, they were developed from the primitive two-lettered root, גז.

Here is the list:

גוז cut

גָּזַר cut, also—with metathesis גָּרַז the root of גַּרְזֶן axe

גָּזַע cut

גָּזַז to shear (sheep)

גָּזָה cut

גָּזָם – a locust, one who eats the produce and thus effectively cuts it from the field.

גָּזַל – rob, to violently tear something away from somebody.

Each of the words in turn gave rise to many other words. For example from גָּזַר cut we have מַגְזֵרָה an ax, גְּזֵרָה a decree. From גָּזַע we have גֶּזַע the stock of a tree; what's left after all the branches have been cut off. From גָּזַז shear, we have גִּזָּה sheared wool. גָּזָה is the root of גָּזִית which means " hewn stones ". From גָּזַל we have גְּזֵלָה – robbery.

Do not be surprised if so many of these comparatively few two-lettered roots mean to cut, to split, to slit, or slice. AFTER ALL, EVERYTHING THAT PRIMITIVE MAN DID IN THE WAY OF MAKING A LIVING FOR HIMSELF AND HIS FAMILY IN SOME WAY OR OTHER INVOLVED A CUTTING ACTION, whether it was wounding animals, felling trees, digging into the earth to plow or to find water, fighting his enemies, or dividing the prey that he brought home. The word " cut " in the Kaufman " English-Hebrew Dictionary " has over a hundred Hebrew translations, and actually there are even more.

In the example given above of words coming from גז the additional third letter in each case came at the end of

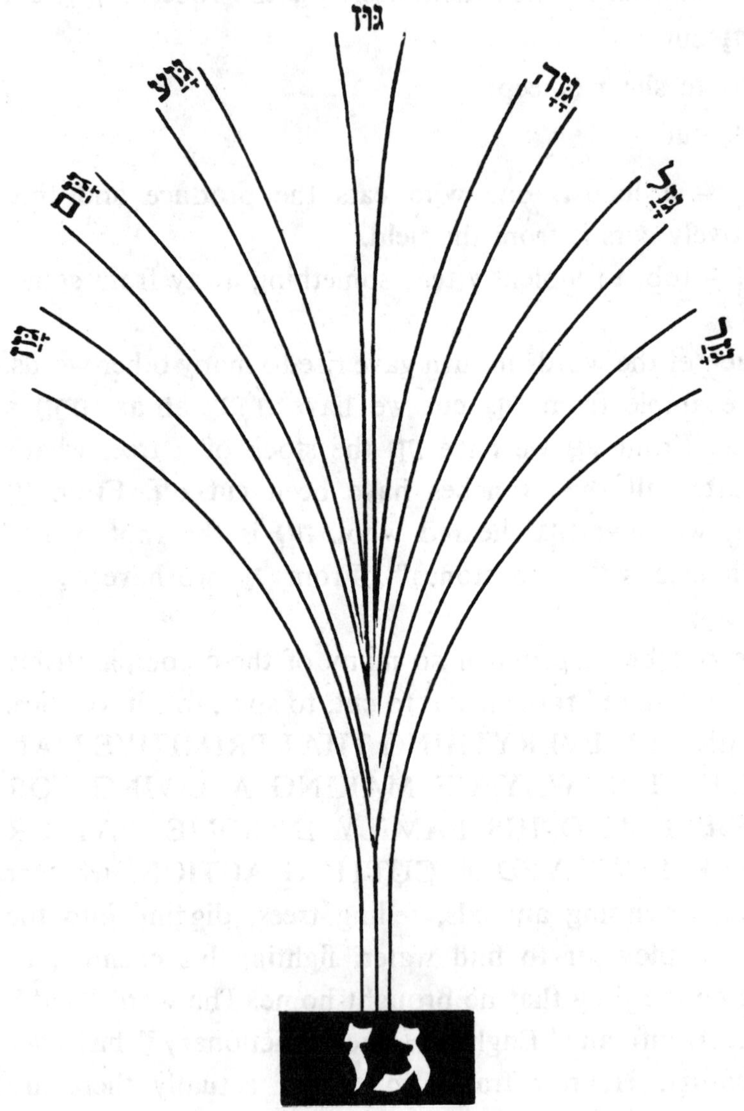

TWO LETTERED ROOTS BECOME THREE

the word. However, life will not be as simple as that in the examples chosen from now on. The third or additional letter may come anywhere, at the beginning, middle or at the end of these two-lettered primitive roots.

Look at the family of roots coming from the syllable חשׁ which means " to feel ", and notice the wide variety of shades of meaning all flowing from the primitive meaning.

We have:

חוּשׁ – feel
חָשַׁשׁ – apprehended
חָשַׁב – think
חָשַׁד – suspect
חָשַׁק – to strongly desire
רָחַשׁ – be astir with, feel

Now that you have the idea, let's see how you can work on your own.

1. The syllable בד is " to be alone, to be cut off, to be away from the group or the main body ". Can you guess some of the words coming from בד.

Or try a similar problem this time in reverse order. That is, I'll give you a family of words all of which come from one two-lettered syllable, שג, and you will try to work out the meaning of the syllable. The root must carry a broad meaning that will adequately cover all the words that are derived from it.

From שג we get the roots:

שָׁגָה or שגא to make a mistake. שְׁגִיאָה is a mistake.
שָׁגַג to commit a sin unwittingly.
שׁגע the root of מְשֻׁגָּע mad, from it we have שִׁגָּעוֹן madness, and הִשְׁתַּגֵּעַ to act like a madman.
שׁוּג the root of מְשׁוּגָה a mistake.

2. Now what is the meaning of the syllable שׂג?

The two lettered root גל means round. It has given rise to the following roots:

עָגַל – be round
גָּלַל – roll
גִּלְגֵּל – roll

This is a very interesting root-family of verbs and there are a large number of words that are derived from the גל roots.

From עגל we have:

עָגֹל – round	מַעְגָּל – a circle
עָגוּל – a circle	עֲגִילִים – earings
עֲגָלָה – a wagon	מַעְגֵּלָה – mangle iron

בַּעַל עֲגָלָה – a wagon driver or owner

From גָּלַל we have:

מְגִלָּה – a scroll. All books or volumes in ancient days came in rolls. The English word volume also means something that is rolled.

גַּל – pile, wave	גָּלִיל – district, circuit
גֻּלְגֹּלֶת – skull	גַּלְגַּל – wheel

גִּלְגּוּל – rolling, migration of souls

Now that you have developed a little skill we will let you try a whole series by yourself.

3. The root גב means to be prominent, high, foremost. Can you work out five common three-lettered roots coming from גב?

4. The root קט sounds just like the English word " cut " and means to cut. Can you give four three-lettered roots coming from קט?

5. The root חק means to carve or to engrave, cut into. Can you give three three-lettered roots coming from it?

עֲגָלָה

WAGON

עִגּוּל

CIRCLE

מְגִלָּה

SCROLL

גַּלִּים

WAVES

ג ל

ROUND

6. The word דח is to push, to strike at. Can you discover four common three-lettered roots coming from it?

7. The word חם, warm, is used in Hebrew to indicate all kinds of warmth; of the body, the warmth of friendship, of physical love, etc. Can you work out five roots having חם in them?

You are probably exhausted by now so we will let you rest and look at these three families.

קץ – CUT, GAVE RISE TO

קָצַץ cut, from it we have קֵץ end.

קָצָה cut, from it we have קָצִין captain, judge.

The word cut is figuratively used for deciding.

הִקְצָה – scrape off; מֻקְצֶה – set apart—forbidden for handling on Sabbath.

קַצָּב butcher; תַּקְצִיב is a budget.

קָצַע cut into; מִקְצוֹעַ – a profession—is what one is cut out for. מַקְצוּעָה is a carpenter's plane.

קָצַר – harvest—from it קָצֵר short; i.e. cut off.

חר – *dig*, is a prolific root. It gave rise to:

חוֹר – a hole	מַחְתֶּרֶת – tunnel, the underground
חָרַשׁ – a plough	חָרַז – pierce
חָרַט, חָרַת – engrave	חֲרוּזִים – strings of beads; figuratively line of poetry or rhymes
חֶרֶב – sword	
חָפַר – dig	
חֲפִירָה – excavation	נָחַר – bore
חָתַר – dig, row	נְחִירַיִם – nostrils

חָרוּץ – gold, diligent

Be careful—there is another חר root with the other ח meaning " free, noble ". From it we have " חֵרוּת freedom ", " חוֹר nobleman ".

כל *is to contain, have the capacity for, take in.* There is quite a collection of words containing this root.

כָּלַל – include, contain	נֵכֶל – craft, from it
יָכֹל – be able	כִּילַי – crafty, knavish person
שָׂכַל – catch on, be prudent	כְּלִי – vessel, implement
שֵׂכֶל – intelligence, prudence	כָּל – all, whole
כַּלָּה – bride, probably held for one man	כָּלִיל – entirely, whole
	מִכְלוֹל – perfection
נוֹכֵל – crafty, one who takes in people	הִשְׂכִּיל – have insight
	אָכַל – partake, eat

כֶּלֶא – prison

LETTERS INTERCHANGE IN BI-LITERAL ROOTS

Here, too, as is true all over in Hebrew, letters interchange and we therefore get entire families of two lettered roots. Thus:

צר = סר = זר – all mean "*to go around*", to encompass, to compress. Each of these three has given rise to a goodly family of its own. Thus from צר we have:

צוּר – bind up.

צָרַר – bind. From it צְרוֹר a bundle.

חָצֵר – a courtyard—that which encircles.

עָצַר – to restrain, hold back, retain. From it we have מַעְצוֹר restraint or hinderance, also מַעְצֵר is a brake. i.e. what restrains.

אָצַר – to lay up, store up, treasure up. From it we have אוֹצָר – storehouse, treasury.

Thus from סר we have סוּר to go around.

סֹהַר – prison, this is something which confines you, encompasses you.

אָסַר – tie up, bind, imprison, from here we have אָסִיר prisoner, also אָסוּר means prohibited, forbidden.

סָחַר – go around, travel about. From it we have סוֹחֵר a merchant, one who goes about with his wares—also סְחוֹרָה merchandise, מִסְחָר a business.

סְחַרְחַר – means whirling around, becoming dizzy.

From זר we have אָזַר to girdle, bind up. From it we have אֵזוֹר a girdle. By metathesis אָרַז to tie a package.

חָזַר – go around, repeat

We have כר = קר *dig*

From כר we get אִכָּר – a farmer, he was primarily in ancient times the digger.

חוֹכֵר – tenant farmer
כֶּרֶם – vineyard, from it we have כַּרְמֶל garden land
כָּרַת – cut off. From it we have כְּרִיתוּת divorce.
כָּרָה – dig, from it we have מִכְרֶה a mine
מְכוֹרָה – origin

From קר *dig*, we get

נָקַר – pierce
מָקוֹר – well, source, origin
מַקּוֹר – beak
קְעָרָה – a plate, something dug out
קֶרֶן – a horn, probably something dug or hollowed out
קָרַץ - pinch off, nip off, cut dough
עָקַר – pluck or root up

Another very famous and prolific family is the פל = פר – *to be separate*, *distinct*, *to be cut out*.

From פל we have:

פָּלַח – cleave, from it we have פֶּלַח a slice.

פָּלַג – split, divide, from it we have פֶּלֶג a channel, an artificial canal, both meaning a cleft in the earth; פְּלוּגָה

FARMER - אִכָּר
CUT - כָּרַת
PLUCK UP - עָקַר
DIVORCE כְּרִיתוּת
PLATE - קְעָרָה
VINEYARD - כֶּרֶם
PIERCE - נָקַר
DIG - כָּרָה
WELL - מָקוֹר
A MINE - מִכְרָה

קר = כר

DIG

division also a party, in the sense of a division or a group of men; מִפְלָגָה – political party.

פלה – be separated, distinct. The הִפְעִיל which has the form הִפְלָה means discriminate.

פֶּלֶא – a wonder, something that is separated from the ordinary. We have from it נִפְלָא wonderful.

Also פְּלָאִי – wonderful and mysterious.

פְּלִישָׁה – invasion

From פר we have:

- פֶּרֶץ – a break
- פָּרוּץ – means an immoral person, one who has broken the moral code
- פָּרַק – is to tear apart, tear away
- נִפְרַד – divided, separated
- הִפְרִיד – made a division
- פָּרָה – bear fruit, to be fruitful. The idea seems to be that the fruit bursts forth. Similarly, we have:
- פָּרַח – bud, sprout, shoot. From it we have:
- פֶּרַח – flower, also
- פָּרַח – means to break out with reference to leprosy and like eruptions
- פָּרַס – break in two, divide. From it we have:
- פְּרוּסַת לֶחֶם – a piece of bread
- פָּרַשׁ – made distinct, declare, separate oneself. The most famous verse in which this occurs is אַל תִּפְרֹשׁ מִן הַצִּבּוּר—Don't separate yourself from the community.

There are even more members of this פר family. I am afraid your head is spinning already, so I will stop here.

A tiny family, that is, comparatively speaking, is בל = מל – *dry, wither.*

From it we have:

נָבֵל – wither and fall, fade, languish. From it we have נְבֵלָה – a corpse. Also the word תֵּבֵל dry land comes from בל.

תֵּבֵל – does not mean the whole world or the earth in general. It really means only the dry land; therefore it frequently appears in contra-distinction to יַמִּים seas.

אָבַל – wither. This word is commonly used figuratively for mourn, lament. However, there are many passages in the Bible that speak particularly of the earth as being dry or withered.

בָּלָה – waste away, become old, worn out.

By interchange we have מָלַל wither, languish.

אָמַל – languish, be weak. From it we have the adjective אֻמְלָל feeble, unfortunate.

Another family is נג = נכ = נק all mean *to strike at*, to beat. Suppose you work for a change and give four common roots having נג as the first syllable all of which have the general sense of " striking at ".

Now continue and give three common roots with נק as the first syllable all of which have the general sense of striking at. If you are not able—see p. 315.

There is only one נכ root—it is נכה which is the root of הִכָּה strike.

Another family with pretty much the same general meaning is דך = דק also to strike at, beat, crush.

The root דך is a famous example of a two-lettered root that has many three-lettered forms all meaning pretty much the same. We have:

דָּכָא – crush
דָּכָה – crush
דּוּךְ – pound, beat

דָּכַךְ – is the root of דַּךְ crushed, oppressed

דִּכְדֵּךְ – crush

הָדַךְ – cast, tread down

The other form of this two-lettered root is דק and from it we have דָּקַק crush, pulverize. From it we have דַּק thin, דָּפַק beat, knock.

דָּקַר – pierce

שׂךְ = סךְ = סג = שׂג – *interwine, interweave.*

From סךְ we have:

סוּךְ – hedge, fence or shut in. The hedges were interwoven of branches or weeds. From it we have מְסוּכָה a hedge.

סְבַךְ – thicket, network, web. סִבֵּךְ means to tangle up or complicate matters.

סְבָכָה – network.

סִכְסֵךְ – entangle, ensnare. From it we have סִכְסוּךְ a conflict of opinion or quarrel.

שְׂמִיכָה – (entangle), (the root is here written with a שׂ) a blanket, an interwoven thing.

מָסָךְ – curtain, also interwoven.

שְׂבָךְ – network of boughs—שְׂבָכָה window lattice.

From סג = שׂג we have:

סוּג – fence about, also שׂוּג.

סְיָג – fence.

שָׂרַג – be intertwined. From it we have שָׂרִיג twig—from the idea of interlacing.

We will end up with a small but pleasant family.

אב = או – *desire, love, long for.*

From אב we have:

אָהַב – love

אָבָה – to desire, be willing, from it we have אֶבְיוֹן – to be in want, needy, poor. The idea is fairly widespread that the poor always want things because they have not got them.

תָּאַב – desire, from it we have תַּאֲבָה longing.

יָאַב – desire, long for.

From או we have אָוָה desire. From it we have the nouns אַוָּה desire, usually in the combination אַוַּת נֶפֶשׁ desire and תַּאֲוָה desire. תַּאֲוָה is usually used to denote " lust, appetite, covetousness ", that is, desire in a somewhat bad sense.

Some roots have probably arisen out of double suggestion; that is, not one but two different two-lettered roots have contributed to their formation.

Are you able to guess what two different two-lettered roots could have given rise to the following words?

נִחַם – comfort
חָקַר – investigate
קָצַר – harvest
דָּקַר – pierce

ANSWERS TO " TWO LETTERS BECOME THREE "

1. The syllable בד – to be alone, to be cut off, to be away from the group, gave rise to the following roots and words:

   בָּדָד – alone
   לְבַדּוֹ – by himself
   אָבַד – lost
   בָּדַל – the root of נִבְדַּל was separated, הִבְדִּיל made a separation, הַבְדָּלָה separation, the Saturday night ceremony marking the end of Sabbath is called הַבְדָּלָה; בְּדִיל tin, alloy—originally meant that which is separated from the precious metal.

2. The meaning of the syllable שׂג is “ to go wrong ”.
3. From the root גב to be prominent, high, foremost we have:
   גָּבוֹהַּ – high
   גִּבְעָה – hill
   גִּבּוֹר – strong man. From it we have גֶּבֶר a man, גְּבֶרֶת madam or miss. גְּבוּרָה heroism, and many other words.
   גְּבוּל – boundary—originally an earth wall serving as a boundary.
   גִּבֵּב גָּבַב – heap up, pile up
   גִּבֵּן – hunchback—the back rises high
4. Some three-lettered roots coming from קט cut are:
   קָטַע – cut, from it קִטֵּעַ person with limb missing
   קָטַף – pluck off or pluck out—from it we have קָטִיף orange harvest
   קָטָן – short, small, really means cut off
   קָטַל – kill, i.e., cut down
5. From the root חק meaning carve or engrave, we have:
   חָקַק – cut in, inscribe, and since laws are carved on stone it also came to mean “ decree ”. From חָקַק we have חֹק statute, also חֻקָּה an enactment. חִקָּה cut in, carved. From the meaning it has of “ carving ”, “ representing ” we get the common Hebrew word חִקָּה imitate.
   חָקַר – search out, explore, examine thoroughly
6. The root דח meaning to push, to strike at, has given rise to the following roots and word:
   דָּחָה – push. From it we have דְּחִיָּה delay, נִדְחָה postponed
   דָּחַף – push someone, drive
   דָּחַק – thrust, oppress
   נָדַח – impell, thrust away. In the nifal נִדַּח – was banished

7. The root חם warm

חָמֵם – be warm

חֹם – heat, חַם hot, חַמָּה sun

מְחַמֵּם – radiator

יחם – to be hot. From it we have חֵמָה rage

רַחֵם – have compassion, love; from it we have words such as רַחֲמִים compassion, רַחֲמָנוּת mercy, etc.

נִחֵם – to be sorry—to console

חָמַד – to desire

8. From the root נג

נָגַע – to touch, to strike

נִגֵּן – to play an instrument (touching or striking it)

נִגֵּד – to lash, to flog

נָגַף – to strike, to injure

from the root נק

נָקַר – to bore, pierce

נִקֵּף – to strike, strike off

נָקַב – to pierce, to bore

QUESTIONS ON CHAPTER XVI

1. Of what fact are scholars fairly convinced with reference to the letters of the Hebrew root?
2. What happened to the primitive root גז when the Hebrews needed words for different shades of the idea of cutting?
3. What are four three-lettered roots that come from the root חשׁ all of which have something to do with the concept of " feeling "?
4. What are eight Hebrew words that have in them the primitive root גל?
5. Give five different three-lettered roots having חר in them.
6. Give three different three-lettered roots having קץ in them.
7. Give five different three-lettered roots having כל in them.
8. Give one of each of צר = סר = זר family and show how each is related to the idea " of going around, encircling ".
9. Give three examples each of the כר — קר family.
10. Give three different three-lettered Hebrew roots having פר in them.

Can you match these two columns?

1. most present three-letter roots	1. שָׁגָה שָׁגַג שגע
2. bi-lateral כּר	2. gave rise to גָּזַז, גָּזַע, גָּזַר
3. חָשַׁק, חָשַׁשׁ, חָשַׁד	3. push, strike
4. round	4. may be from נוּחַ and חַם
5. דָּחַק, דָּחָה, דָּחַף	5. אָסַר, צָרַר, אָזַר
6. warmth	6. גַּל — עֲגָלָה — מְגִלָּה
7. go wrong	7. חֵמָה — רֵחֵם — חָמַד
8. go around	8. כָּרַת - cut, כָּרָה - dig
9. גז - cut	9. arose from חַשׁ - feel
10. נִחֵם	10. had two-letter base

Chapter XVII

All Sorts of Odds and Ends

COMBINATIONS

Combinations—that is, a word made up of two other words—were practically non-existent in ancient Hebrew. Such is the widely accepted belief. Almost the only examples we have from Biblical Hebrew are בְּלִיַּעַל of no worth, and בְּלִימָה nothingness.

This generally accepted statement is open to challenge. After all, in actuality many combinations do exist, but in a slightly veiled form. A word like תִּשְׁמֹר is really a combination and consists of, or rather is, a short, clipped way of saying אַתָּה שְׁמֹר, you watch. So נִשְׁמֹר is really אֲנַחְנוּ שְׁמֹר. The reflexive prefix הִתְ is quite definitely a remnant of the personal pronoun אַתָּה. הִתְרַחַצְתָּ would then be equivalent to אַתָּה רְחַץ אַתָּה, you wash you. The נ of the נִפְעַל is similarly a fragment of the personal pronoun אֲנַחְנוּ. Similarly לוּלֵא is לוּ לֹא, if not, and מַדּוּעַ – why, is מַה יָּדוּעַ what is known?

Mishnaic Hebrew began a fairly widespread use of combinations and modern Hebrew has developed this method of word building quite extensively. Here are some examples, mostly modern:

אַלְחוּט – wireless (no wires)
אַלְמָוֶת – immortality (no death)

דַחְפּוֹר – bulldozer (דָחַף, push – חָפַר, dig)
קוֹלְנוֹעַ – sound movies (sound-moves)
רַמְקוֹל – megaphone (high-voice)
גַּזְרְקַשׁ – machine for cutting grass (cut-hay)
עֲקוּמַף – crooked nose
חַיְדַק – bacteria (thin-living things)
כִּסְנוֹעַ – rocking chair (כִּסֵא – נוֹעַ)
אַבְחֹמֶר – protoplasm (אָב father – חֹמֶר matter)
עַדְכַּן – up to date
תַּרְנְהוֹד – turkey (תַּרְנְגֹל rooster, הֹדוּ India. It was believed that the turkey came from India)
קַטְנוֹעַ – scooter (קָטָן small, נוֹעַ move. A very popular method of transportation in Israel)
בִּנְאוּם – internationalization (בֵּין among, אֻם nation)
חַדְצְדָדִי – one-sided
חַדְגּוֹנִי – monotonous (one – hue or color)
בֻּבַּתְרוֹן – puppet theatre (בֻּבָּה – doll, puppet)

WORDS WITH דוּ

דוּ is adopted from the Greek word meaning two (compare duo, duet, dialogue).

Can you work out the meaning of:

1. דוּשְׁנָתִי	4. דוּקְרָב
2. דוּקִיּוּם	5. דוּשִׂיחַ
3. דוּחַי	6. דוּיָדִי

WORDS WITH אוֹר

אוֹר light is a popular combination word.

Can you get the meaning of:

1. זַרְקוֹר	3. מִגְדַּלּוֹר
2. מַדְאוֹר	4. עֲמָמוֹר

WORDS WITH מַד

מַד measure or meter (meter means measure), is a very important concept in all scientific work and study. All modern technological processes require the most exact measurements for successful operation. A large number of words combine with מַד. Try and create the following group of instrument names. All use מַד as the first element in the combination.

1. An instrument for measuring temperature, particularly the heat, i.e. a thermometer.
2. An instrument for measuring the weight or heaviness of the atmosphere, i.e. a barometer.
3. An instrument for measuring angles, i.e. a protractor.
4. An instrument for measuring pressure, i.e. a pressure gauge.
5. An instrument for measuring thickness, i.e. calipers—a thickness gauge.
6. An instrument for measuring road distance, i.e. an odometer.
7. An instrument for measuring the strength of a current, (זֶרֶם is a stream or current), i.e. an ammeter.
8. An instrument for measuring the time you park. (חָנָה is to camp or park somewhere).
9. An instrument for measuring the velocity of wind, i.e. an anemometer.
10. A timer.
11. An instrument for measuring the trembling of the earth, an earthquake, i.e. a seismograph.

    Of course there are the three familiar meters for the three utilities found in most homes.

12. A gas meter.
13. A water meter.
14. An electric meter.

WORDS FROM NAMES

English has a great many words that come from names of persons or places. A sandwich takes its name from the Earl of Sandwich, a busy, card-playing nobleman who created this peculiar thing; herculean means having the strength of the Greek god Hercules; bloomers were invented by a Mrs. Bloomer, etc.

From geographical places come names such as the following:

muslin takes its name from Mosul;
cordovan is named from Cordova;
turquoise comes from Turkey, etc.

Hebrew has only a few such words. כְּנַעֲנִי means a merchant, the word coming from the name of the land כְּנַעַן. In the days of old it was the Hebrews who were the farmers, and the native Canaanites who were the merchants. דַּמֶּשֶׁק —the word is found in Amos, seems to be the name of a fabric (as is damask in English). When the Children of Israel stood at the Red Sea and the Egyptian Army was in hot pursuit they were commanded to march forward. One of the princes, נַחְשׁוֹן בֶּן עַמִּינָדָב set an example of courage by leaping into the sea. Not until then were the waters parted. So in modern Israel they call the commando נַחְשׁוֹן. Hebrew has borrowed back the English word gauze calling it גָּזָה. Gauze is from the city of Gaza.

סִינַי after Mt. Sinai, now refers to any great scholar, who is filled with knowledge of Torah. בֹּעַז comes from

בֹּעַז in the Book of Ruth who seems mostly to have been a supervisor of the farmwork. Now in modern Israel, a בֹּעַז is a farmer on whose property others do the actual labor, while he is the general overseer.

There is an interesting Greek name that has become a common Hebrew word. The Greek philosopher, Epicurus, seemed to deny that there was a purpose in life and believed that pleasure was the chief end of our existence.

To the Hebrew this constituted a denial of God, and so the word אֲפִּיקוֹרְיס came to stand for non-believer.

WORDS FROM ABBREVIATIONS

Parchment was very expensive. Ink, too, was fairly costly and there wasn't too much time for study. Therefore the ancient Hebrews developed a great many abbreviations. This system of writing phrases and sentences by using just the first letter they called נוֹטְרִיקוֹן.

נוֹטְרִיקוֹן is a Greek-Latin word, the same word that gave us in English, notary and notes. Thus, for example: א״א would mean אַבְרָהָם אָבִינוּ; ג״פ would mean שָׁלֹשׁ פְּעָמִים — the ג equalling three.

There are really enormous numbers of these abbreviations, particularly in Rabbinic literature—at least about 10,000. Sometimes one abbreviation would have several meanings. Thus, א״א could mean: אִי אֶפְשָׁר, אֵין אוֹמְרִים, אַבְרָהָם אָבִינוּ.

Now some of these abbreviations were used so frequently and were pronounced so often in the abbreviated form that they began to be regarded and used as words in their own right. Lately, the Hebrew Academy has created some abbreviation words.

תַּנַ״ךְ – is an abbreviation of תּוֹרָה נְבִיאִים כְּתוּבִים. It is the regular Hebrew word for Bible.

שַׁ״ס – is an abbreviation of שִׁשָּׁה סְדָרִים. The phrase refers to the six orders of the Mishnah; but when we use the word שַׁ״ס now we mean the Talmud.

שַׁ״ץ – is an abbreviation of שְׁלִיחַ צִבּוּר – an emissary of the congregation, and refers to the cantor.

נַ״ט – is an abbreviation of נוֹתֵן טַעַם and is used for a flavoring.

חֲזַ״ל – is an abbreviation of חֲכָמֵינוּ זִכְרוֹנָם לִבְרָכָה our sages—their memory for a blessing.

עַכּוּ״ם – is an abbreviation of עוֹבֵד כּוֹכָבִים וּמַזָּלוֹת worshippers of stars and constellations—generally meaning idolaters.

יַ״שׁ – is an abbreviation of יַיִן שָׂרָף burning wine, i.e., whiskey.

Some of the modern words, which are made up of abbreviations, are:

סַכּוּ״ם – flatware—it is an abbreviation of סַכִּין כַּף וּמַזְלֵג.

תַּ״ז – orange—it is an abbreviation of תַּפּוּחַ זָהָב, more usually it is תַּפּוּ״ז.

מוֹ״ל – publisher—it is an abbreviation of מוֹצִיא לְאוֹר —one who brings forth to light.

דוּ״חַ – a reckoning—it is an abbreviation of דִּין וְחֶשְׁבּוֹן.

תַּ״ת – stands for Talmud Torah —תַּלְמוּד תּוֹרָה.

רַמַטְכָּ״ל – head of the general staff—רֹאשׁ מַטֶּה כְּלָלִי.

HEBREW BORROWS BACK WORDS FROM THE YIDDISH

The great and triumphant role that Yiddish has played and is playing in the life of the Jewish people is well known. For many centuries, for untold millions of Jews—in fact for the majority of Jews in the world—Yiddish was " mama lashon ", the language which their mother spoke to them and which they used all the years of their lives. Hebrew words that were borrowed by Yiddish had an independent life and development of their own inside the Yiddish language. This development sometimes carried the word far from its original meaning in Hebrew. The majority of speakers of Hebrew in Israel today, have Yiddish as their mother tongue. They carried many Yiddish words over to their spoken Hebrew. And so it happened that Hebrew would be frequently borrowing back a word in its newly developed Yiddish sense.

Here are just a few examples of these very interesting words:

1. מְצִיאָה – In Hebrew, of course, it means just " finding ". In Yiddish, it developed the sense of " a bargain ", and Hebrew has borrowed back this use of the word.
2. עֶרֶב – In the sense of the beginning of. In Hebrew we now say עֶרֶב הַמִּלְחָמָה, meaning the period immediately preceding the war.
3. מַזָּל – In the Rabbinic sources it meant " constellation, star ", and had, of course, implicit in it the idea of fortune. In Yiddish it broke apart entirely from the idea of a star and meant

purely and simply " luck ", which is its quite universal use today.

4. פָּרִ׳ץ – From the Hebrew word " פָּרֹץ, to break forth, to burst forth from the bounds of moral restraint ". The word was used in Yiddish to indicate a " nobleman."

5. חִיוּנָה – livelihood.

6. מְשֻׁלָּח – An emissary sent out to collect funds for the Yeshivot.

7. עִפּוּשׁ – In Hebrew, any rotten thing in general. In Yiddish, it has the specific sense of a pestilence.

8. גְּבִיר, נָגִיד, קָצִין – are three Hebrew words borrowed by Yiddish and used in the sense of a rich man. These words have been picked up by spoken Hebrew.

9. תַּכְשִׁיט – In old Hebrew meant an ornament. In Yiddish, used satirically for one who is not so well mannered, fine or gentlemanly.

The following two words were used in Yiddish as an abbreviation for a complete expression.

1. בְּרִית – In the sense of a בְּרִית מִילָה the covenant of circumcision. We generally use the one word בְּרִית to stand for the whole thought. This comes from the Yiddish.

2. פֵּאָה – In the sense of ear locks worn by the very religious. It is an abbreviation of the expression פְּאַת רֹאשׁ, corner of the head. פֵּאָה in the old Hebrew sources simply means a corner.

There are many expressions that were created in Yiddish and are now part of our Hebrew vocabulary.

1. חֲצִי חִנָּם – It has no real meaning in Hebrew. If we try to understand the words it is " half of nothing ", but is a Yiddish expression meaning very cheap.
2. לְמַעַן הַשֵּׁם – for God's sake.
3. רָשָׁע מְרֻשָּׁע – extremely wicked.
4. מַגָּע וּמַשָּׂא – contact.
5. בַּר מִינָן – a corpse. It literally means " not on us."
6. בַּר מִצְוָה – designating the party in celebration of the religious ritual.

An extremely common formation in Hebrew is a combination of בַּעַל meaning " owner, one who has " with some other word. Many of these combinations using בַּעַל were first created in Yiddish, and later entered Hebrew. Here are some of these:

1. בַּעַל תְּפִלָּה – one able to chant the prayers, not quite with the ability of a cantor.
2. בַּעַל שִׂמְחָה – one celebrating a happy occasion.
3. בַּעַל פָּסוּק – one who knows the Bible.
4. בַּעַל גַּאֲוָה – a proud person.
5. בַּעַל בִּטָּחוֹן – a person who has faith.
6. בַּעַל דָּבָר – Satan.
7. בַּעַל מִדּוֹת – one having good qualities.
8. בַּעַל דֵּעָה – one who has an opinion.

Many abstract nounsending in וּת were first created in Yiddish.

חַזָּנוּת – the art of a cantor.
מְלַמְּדוּת – the art of a teacher.
מַגִּידוּת – the art of a preacher.
קַצָּבוּת – the vocation of a butcher.
עַם הָאַרְצוּת – ignorance.

Many words in the פַּעְלָן pattern similarly were first created in Yiddish and then passed on to Hebrew. Some of these are:

יַקְרָן – a merchant who charges too much.
בַּדְחָן – a jester, a master of ceremonies at the old Jewish weddings.
חַלְפָן – money changer.
יַדְעָן – a person who knows a lot.
קַבְּרָן – a grave-digger.
בַּטְלָן – In Hebrew used to mean simply an idle person. In Yiddish it came to be used as an impractical person which is its present use.
עַקְשָׁן – a stubborn person; first used in that sense in Yiddish.

NEW WINE FROM OLD VESSELS

There are many words in the Bible, the meanings of which are not too sharp or not too clear or not too certain. A word whose meaning is vague is fairly useless. A sharp, insistent need of the new growing Hebrew language is for a sharp, clear meaning for each word. An ancient Hebrew word from the sources is of no value; it is just an idle curiosity unless it has a clear, specific meaning.

Certainly one of the very useful things that the Hebrew

Academy has done is to assign a definite meaning to these ancient, and, until our day, neglected words. Here, then, are just a few examples of this interesting linguistic development.

מֶשֶׁק – from the story of Abraham, now in extremely common use for a farm and all its equipment and livestock.

מוּסָךְ – seems to mean a covered structure of some sort —now " garage ".

מֵזַח – pier.

טְוָח – range—from כִּמְטַחֲוֵי קֶשֶׁת in the Bible (the distance of a bow shot).

זָן – variety.

מוֹקֵשׁ – used to mean an obstacle in general, is now used for a mine—that is the kind that blows up on the battle field.

מֵיכָל – a tank—that is a container for gasoline, etc.

עוּגָב – some sort of musical instrument—now an organ.

פְּסַנְתֵּר – also a musical instrument—now piano.

חַשְׁמַל – electricity.

מְפַעְנֵחַ – deciphers. Joseph was called in the Bible צָפְנַת פַּעְנֵחַ, and the Midrash says מְפַעְנֵחַ means one who reveals secrets.

יָזַם – initiate.

מְחַטֵּא – A privitative piel of חָטָא with a meaning to cleanse. It has the specific sense of disinfect.

SOME UNUSUAL WAYS OF WORD CREATION

Words were sometimes made by imitating the sounds of foreign words, when such an imitation also made sense in Hebrew. Thus the word " protocol ", which means " all the regulations governing some institution ", was rendered in Hebrew פְּרוֹטוֹקוֹל, literally meaning " all the details ". Cholera was called in Hebrew חֳלִירַע, literally " the bad sickness ". Cutlet, a cut which comes from the side of an animal, is כָּתְלִית in Hebrew, as though it comes from כֹּתֶל, wall. מַסֵּכָה, is the word now used for mask. The old Hebrew word מַסֵּכָה means molten image.

Plurals of words sometimes became words in their own right, words sometimes different in sense from the original singular. Thus knife, סַכִּין, seems to have been originally the plural of the word סִכָּה, a pin; קָצִין, now a thorn, was originally the plural of the word קוֹץ, thorn; אוֹבוֹת, spirits, is probably a dialect form of the plural word אָבוֹת, fathers. דּוֹרֵשׁ אֶל הָאוֹבוֹת would be the person who would call up the spirits of the ancestors.

Sometimes we have what is called a ghost word, that is a word that arises out of an error made in writing or printing; a word that never had any original meaning in speech. An example is אֶפַע which means " nothing ", and was simply a mis-reading of the word אֶפֶס—the ס and the ע looked very much alike in the ancient Hebrew script.

THE DEFINITE ARTICLE ה IS INCORRECTLY ADDED AND SUBSTRACTED

The definite article " an " is often incorrectly divided in English, thus creating new words. A napron has become an apron (napron, by the way, goes back to Latin "mapa" which in turn goes back to the Hebrew מַפָּה, a cloth); a nadder has become an adder, a small poisonous snake; a narang has become an orange. Conversely an anny· goat has become a nanny goat, an eke name has become a nickname. The word eke means additional.

Something like this has happened in Hebrew. The definite article ה has been incorrectly added to and made part of words to which it does not belong.

הַלְוָיָה is a funeral, but the word should be לְוָיָה from לַוֵּה, escort. The verb הַלְוֵה, which would give rise to הַלְוָיָה, means lending. It has nothing to do with escorting. In Yiddish the word is still correctly לְוָיָה.

דוֹר הַהַפְלָגָה – The generation of the division of mankind into different groups. This happened after the speech of men had been confused, when they were building the Tower of Babel. This word should be פַּלְגָה from פַּלֵּג, divide. הִפְלִיג, which would give rise to the noun הַפְלָגָה, has nothing to do with division.

We have an example of the very opposite. The word רְאָיָה means proof. It seems that the word must have originally been הַרְאָיָה. The hifil of רָאָה namely caused something to be seen, to show, to prove is הֶרְאָה. The ה was misunderstood as a definite article and neatly sliced off. Possibly, though, it may merely have been clumsy to say הַהַרְאָיָה, the proof, and the Hebrew sensibly dropped one ה.

PLURALS OF NOUNS

Hebrew has a number of very irregular plurals of nouns. They arise, generally speaking, in a very simple way. Ancient Hebrew frequently had two words, often only slightly different for the same thing. But frequently the plural of only one of these words survived in common use.

Thus אִישׁ means man; the plural is אֲנָשִׁים; but the word is really the plural of quite another word אֱנוֹשׁ, also meaning man. עִיר city—plural עָרִים. Unquestionably, Hebrew had a word עָר which also meant city; עָרִים is really the plural of עָר. In the same way, יוֹם - day, יָמִים - days; רֹאשׁ - head, רָאשִׁים - heads, with a kammatz gadol, pronounced " ah " in Israel. The plural רָאשִׁים is from a different word רַאשׁ also meaning head.

בַּיִת house, plural בָּתִּים from בַּת, another word for house. The word בַּת, daughter, used to have a נ and was בַּנְת. The frequently occuring expression in the Bible בַּת צִיּוֹן probably means " house of Zion ".

Sometimes the trouble arises because a נ drops out. אִשָּׁה, plural נָשִׁים. Originally the word was אִנְשָׁה. בַּת, originally בַּנְת or בִּנְת, plural בָּנוֹת.

Words in the singular sometimes develop two different meanings each of which is differentiated in the plural.

כַּף – palm, spoon. Plural: כַּפַּיִם palms, כַּפּוֹת spoons.

יָד – hand. Plural: יָדַיִם, hands – יָדוֹת, artificial hands, namely, the arms of a throne.

עַיִן – eye, well. Plural: עֵינַיִם eyes, עֲיָנוֹת fountains.

קֶרֶן – horn, horns of the altar. Plural: קַרְנַיִם horns. קְרָנוֹת horns of the altar.

אוֹת – sign, letter of the alphabet. Plural: אוֹתוֹת signs, אוֹתִיּוֹת letters of the alphabet.

IN DAYS OF OLD MANY WORDS WERE PRONOUNCED DIFFERENTLY

If you were to have walked about London in the 1600's, in the days of William Shakespeare, there is no doubt in the world that you would have had considerable difficulty in understanding the speech of the people about you. If you were to move further backward to the 1200's, the days of Chaucer, your comprehension would be extremely limited. Chaucer's works are read today with the help of a dictionary.

If this is true of English, in a span of only seven or eight hundred years, please do not be startled if you are told that three, four or five thousand years ago quite a number of Hebrew words were pronounced differently. Startled is, of course, not the word. We want you to understand clearly why there are sometimes sharp differences between a word as a word by itself and when it is used with my, yours, his, etc.

יֶלֶד is a child. Good. But my child is יַלְדִּי, so also דֶּרֶךְ becomes דַּרְכִּי. Something emerges very clearly. The old Hebrew word for child was יַלְד and not יֶלֶד.

סֵפֶר is book. סִפְרִי is my book. The old Hebrew word for book was something like סִפְר. So דֶּגֶל is flag; my flag is דִּגְלִי. Again the old Hebrew was דִּגְל and not דֶּגֶל.

In the same way now that you have the idea, work out the old Hebrew forms of בַּיִת, עַיִן, and אֹזֶן.

Now that we have gotten so far it should not be difficult for you to analyse words like שִׂמְחָתִי, my joy or תּוֹרָתִי, my Torah. In ancient days, the last syllable of all nouns now ending in ָה used to be ַת; thus the word שִׂמְחָה used to be שִׂמְחַת. This goes for all words now ending in ָה.

It is interesting to note that the old form of a noun frequently appears in the סְמִיכוּת or construct state. We say בֵּית הַסֵּפֶר and בֵּית, of course, is the old Hebrew word for house. We say עֵין הַיֶּלֶד, the eye of the child, and עֵין is the old way of pronouncing עַיִן. We say שִׂמְחַת יוֹם טוֹב, the joy of the holiday, and שִׂמְחַת, the construct form, is the way this word was pronounced thousands of years ago.

Sometimes the last letter of an ancient word dropped off, but reappears in the forms with the possessive my, yours, his, etc. Look at the word for your father, his father, etc. It is אָבִיךָ, אָבִיו, אָבִינוּ. It is fairly obvious that the ancient

Hebrew word for father was אָבִי and not as at present אָב. The same goes for the word אָח, brother.

Some prepositions that have apparently plural forms go back to the presence of the י.

עָלַי, on me, עָלֶיךָ on you. This is the singular with plural-looking forms. The plural-looking forms are due to the fact that the old Hebrew word for " on " was not עַל, it was עֲלַי. Similarly אֶל used to be אֱלֵי.

A FEW WORDS ABOUT THE HEBREW VOWELS

Way, way back, at the beginning of the book, we wrote about the Hebrew alphabet and the strange, dramatic and interesting fact that it was invented without letters for the vowel sounds.

The essential and basic meaning of a word in Hebrew depends only on the consonants. Any word from קדש must have something to do with holy; from כתב with writing; from ראה with seeing, and so on. They were able largely to get along without vowel letters.

Nevertheless, very, very early in the history of Hebrew writing certain letters were used as vowels to help out in reading. There were four letters so used. They were ה, א, י, ו and were called by the odd name mater lectiones, in Hebrew אִמּוֹת הַקְּרִיאָה; mothers, i.e. guides to reading. There are many vowel sounds and these four letters were only a partial help because each one could indicate more than one vowel sound.

The י could indicate ee, ay or eh.
The ו could indicate oo or aw.
The א could indicate ah, eh or aw.
The ה could indicate ah, eh or ay.

In the 600's, in the city of Tiberias, there was perfected a series of symbols for the Hebrew vowels. These are the well-known vowel signs that we now use. They were gradually introduced into the Hebrew writings.

It has long, for many centuries, traditionally been held that five of the vowels are long—meaning as far as the word means anything—that they are to be pronounced or held for a long time, and that five of them are short.

The five long vowels are supposed to be:

1. ָ qamatz gadol—the long ah sound.
2. וֹ a long aw sound.
3. וּ a long oo sound.
4. ֵ an ay sound.
5. ִי a long ee.

Corresponding to these, there are supposed to be five short vowels.

1. ַ a short ah sound.
2. ָ qamatz qatan—a short aw sound.
3. ֻ a short oo sound.
4. ֶ sound of eh.
5. ִ without a yod—a short ee sound.

I'm sorry to say that this traditional theory of the five long vowels and the five short vowels is simply not true. It has no basis whatsoever in the realities of Hebrew pronounciation. It never was the intention of the creators of the vowel system to distinguish between the vowels as regards their quantity.

A qamatz gadol is supposed to be a long ah, a patah a short ah. Samuel David Luzzato, one of the most famous Hebrew scholars of the 19th century, an Italian, wrote very simply, " All my life I grew up among Sephardic Jews, many of them distinguished scholars and rabbis. I have never heard once anyone distinguish between the ah sound of a qamatz gadol and a patah."

There is similarly no distinction between a holem and qamatz qatan. Nor is there, similarly, any difference between shuruk וּ and qubbitz ֻ. Some try to pronounce words like תֻּפֵּי דֻּבֵּי with a short oo like in the word " book "; it is an artificial distinction and has no basis in reality. In the old, old days of the אִמּוֹת הַקְּרִיאָה, i.e. the use of אהוי, as guides in reading a ו indicated oo and aw. The inventors of the vowel system wouldn't dream of tampering with the letters of the Bible text—so with a simple dot on the top or in the middle they indicated whether it was aw or oo. For the specific sound of oo where there was no letter ו —and there were large numbers of words in the Bible that had an oo sound not indicated by a ו —they created the symbol ֻ. There was no intention whatsoever on their part of distinguishing different quantities of the sound oo, namely, one long and one short.

We now come to the next pair, hiriq gadol and hiriq qatan. The hiriq does have two pronounciations, a long and short one. The hiriq is pronounced long namely as an ee sound in an open syllable; it is pronounced short namely as ih in a closed syllable.

What is an open syllable?

It is a syllable that ends with a vowel, that does not end with a consonant. In the word דּוֹדִי, both syllables are open. The first is דּוֹ ending with a וֹ; the second is דִי also ending with a vowel.

What is a closed syllable?

It is a syllable that is closed by a consonant. In the word מִזְמוֹר, both syllables are closed; that is they both end with a consonant. The syllable מִז ends with the consonant ז; the syllable מוֹר ends with the consonant ר.

When a hiriq occurs in open syllables like in the word שִׁירִי, it is pronounced ee; when it occurs in a closed syllable like מִזְמוֹר or יִגְמֹר it is pronounced ih. In words like דִּבֵּר and לִבּוֹ where the first syllable is supposed to be closed because of a dagesh in the second letter, it, the syllable, is universally regarded, certainly in the consciousness of readers and speakers of Hebrew, as being open and the hiriq is pronounced as ee.

What is true and valid in the traditional distinction between long and short vowels? About the only thing we can say is:

1. The so-called long vowels are usually found in open syllables; for example, אֵלֶּה, דוֹדִי, קוּמִי, כָּתַב. If they are accented they may be in closed syllables namely תַּלְבֵּשְׁנָה, שִׁיר, קָם.

2. The so-called short vowels are usually found in closed syllables; for example, יִצְחָק, דֶּבִּי, יַלְדִּי, חָדְשִׁי, and the second syllable of בֶּגֶד. A short vowel can be found in an open syllable if it is accented as for example in the first syllable of words like בֶּגֶד, יֶלֶד, נַעַר, etc.

There are enormous numbers of departures from this general rule. There are a great number of short vowels in open syllables that are not accented. For example, the vowel of the first syllable of such words as יֵאָסֵף, יַעֲשֶׂה, נַחֲלַת, מְחוּט, מַהֵר, פִּחֵד, רִחֵם and רָחֲמָה is short.

All these syllables are thus open, unaccented and short, in violation of the generally accepted rule.

The vowels ‥ and ֶ are simply two different sounds; ‥ is equal to ay, and ֶ is equal to eh. The best scholars and authorities in Israel wish to maintain this distinction.

THE VOWELS SHORTEN

You surely must have noticed that in English when the accent moves forward from a syllable, the vowel of that syllable shrinks, shrivels, dies away to practically nothing. So the word cigar becomes cigarette—the ah of cigar equivalent to a qamətz sound in Hebrew becomes an ih equal to a sheva in Hebrew. Similarly, in English, exclaim becomes exclamation; explain becomes explanation. The ay sound of exclaim is roughly equivalent to a Hebrew צֵירֶה. It became an ih equivalent to a Hebrew sheva, when the main beat of the word shifted from the syllable with the long ay sound.

The very same sort of thing happens so continually in Hebrew, that you ought to be clearly aware of what is taking place. In Hebrew, when the first syllable has a ָ, that ָ will shrink, shrivel, and disappear, becoming just a sheva any time the accent shifts far away from that syllable.

Thus גָּדוֹל becomes גְּדוֹלָה, and גְּדוֹלִים; קָטָן becomes קְטַנָּה and קְטַנִּים.

סָגַרְנוּ becomes סְגַרְתֶּם, when the accent shifts to the תֶּם.

Similarly, the צֵירֶה becomes a sheva.

מֵבִין becomes מְבִינָה and מְבִינִים; מֵבִיא becomes מְבִיאָה and מְבִיאִים.

ANSWERS TO QUESTIONS

Combination

WORDS WITH דו

1. two a year—semi-annual	דּוּשְׁנָתִי
2. co-existence	דּוּקִיּוּם
3. amphibious—(living in both land and water)	דּוּחַי
4. duel (battle—two)	דּוּקְרָב
5. dialogue (two people speaking)	דּוּשִׂיחַ
6. ambidextrous (using both hands)	דּוּיָדִי

WORDS WITH אוֹר

1. throwing light (projector)	זַרְקוֹר
2. photometer (an instrument for measuring light)	מַדְאוֹר
3. lighthouse	מִגְדַּלּוֹר
4. light dimmer	עֲמָמוֹר

WORDS WITH מַד

1. thermometer	מַדְחֹם	8. parking meter	מַדְחָן
2. barometer	מַדְכֹּבֶד	9. anemometer	מַדְרוּחַ
3. protractor	מַדְזָוִית	10. a timer	מַדְזְמַן
4. pressure gauge	מַדְלַחַץ	11. seismograph	מַדְרַעַד
5. calipers	מַדְעֹבִי	12. gas meter	מַדְגַּז
6. odometer	מַדֶּרֶךְ	13. water meter	מַדְמַיִם
7. ammeter	מַדְזֶרֶם	14. electric meter	מַדְחַשְׁמַל

QUESTIONS ON CHAPTER SEVENTEEN

1. What are two ancient examples of combination words?
2. What are three modern examples of combination words?
3. What are some English words coming from names of persons or places?
4. What are some Hebrew words coming from names of persons or places?
5. What are some Hebrew names of places that have become English words?
6. What is meant by נוֹטְרִיקוֹן?
7. What are two ancient abbreviations that are used as words; two modern?
8. What are three words back-borrowed from Yiddish in a slightly different sense?
9. What are some בַּעַל combinations that arose first in Yiddish; some words ending in וּת?
10. What are three Hebrew words from the Bible whose meanings were vague, that are now used in a sharp, clear sense?
11. What two words were made by imitating the sound of the word in the foreign language, the imitation making sense in Hebrew?
12. What are two Hebrew words to which a ה has been incorrectly attached?
13. How do you account for אֲנָשִׁים as the plural of אִישׁ; עָרִים as the plural of עִיר?

14. How do you account for יַלְדֵי arising from יֶלֶד; סִפְרִי from סֵפֶר; שִׂמְחָתִי from שִׂמְחָה; אָבִינוּ from אָב?

15. What are the אִמּוֹת הַקְּרִיאָה?

16. What are the five so-called long vowels, and the five so-called short vowels?

17. What is the actual difference in pronunciation between קָמַץ גָּדוֹל and פַּתַּח; between קָמַץ קָטָן and חוֹלֶם; between שׁוּרֶק and קִבּוּץ?

18. Where are the so-called long vowels usually found; the so-called short vowels?

Can you match these two columns?

1. מִזְמוֹר, יִגְמֹר	1. words from abbreviations
2. דוּ, אוֹר, מַד	2. all the syllables are open
3. אהוי	3. אַלְמוּת, קוֹלְנוֹעַ
4. These words come from names of persons and places	4. shouldn't have a first letter ה
5. חַשְׁמַל – electricity, מֶשֶׁק – farm	5. these are frequently used to form combination words
6. בָּתִּים is really from בַּת	6. חֲלִירַע – cholera, מַסֵּכָה – mask
7. חַזַ״ל, תַּנַ״ךְ, שַׁ״ס	7. the אִמּוֹת הַקְּרִיאָה
8. made by imitating the sound of the foreign word	8. formerly were pronounced יַלְד and סִפְר
9. הַפְלָגָה – division, הַלְוָיָה – funeral	9. בַּת־צִיּוֹן is really house of Zion
10. two combination words	10. כְּנַעֲנִי, גָּזָה, נַחְשׁוֹן
11. סֵפֶר, יֶלֶד	11. these words were given a sharp, clear meaning only in recent years
12. דּוֹדִי, בּוֹאִי	12. all the syllables are closed